Humour in Contemporary France

Controversy, Consensus, and Contradictions

Studies in Modern and Contemporary France   3

Studies in Modern and Contemporary France

Series Editors

Professor Gill Allwood, Nottingham Trent University
Professor Denis M. Provencher, University of Arizona
Professor Martin O'Shaughnessy, Nottingham Trent University

The Studies in Modern and Contemporary France book series is a new collaboration between the Association for the Study of Modern and Contemporary France (ASMCF) and Liverpool University Press (LUP). Submissions are encouraged focusing on French politics, history, society, media and culture. The series will serve as an important focus for all those whose engagement with France is not restricted to the more classically literary, and can be seen as a long-form companion to the Association's journal, *Modern and Contemporary France,* and to *Contemporary French Civilization*, published by Liverpool University Press.

Humour in Contemporary France

Controversy, Consensus, and Contradictions

JONATHAN ERVINE

Liverpool University Press

First published 2019 by
Liverpool University Press
4 Cambridge Street
Liverpool
L69 7ZU

British Library Cataloguing-in-Publication data
A British Library CIP record is available

ISBN 978-1-78962-051-1 cased

Typeset by Carnegie Book Production, Lancaster
Printed and bound by CPI Group (UK) Ltd, Croydon CR0 4YY

Contents

Acknowledgements

Since the French classes of Mr Grove and Mr Jessop during my school days at Madras College in St Andrews, humour is something that I have associated with learning French and studying French society. They deserve great thanks for the considerable wit and inspiration that ultimately led to me studying French at university and writing this book. During my time as a student at the University of Leeds, studying a final year module entitled 'Comedy from neo-romanticism to the absurd' was one of the first times when I started to think in more detail about the power and meaning of humour in a French context, and that owes much to the frequently entertaining classes of Jim Dolamore.

As a student and subsequently as a lecturer, I am very grateful to have met many people with whom I have had the opportunity to converse about humour in France. On several occasions, conferences organized by the Association for the Study of Modern and Contemporary France (ASMCF) and the French Media Research Group (FMRG) have provided a fantastically welcoming and supportive environment in which to discuss such matters. I would like to thank Patrice Bouche for helping me to obtain several issues of *Charlie Hebdo* that I discuss in this book, and extend my gratitude to Olivier Mazuy for first introducing me to the *Jamel Comedy Club*.

Soon after starting as a lecturer in French at Bangor University, I took advantage of an opportunity to interview the American comedy trio Allah Made Me Funny while working on a book chapter about Islam, music, and new media for a volume edited by Kamal Salhi. The discussion I had with Azhar Usman, Preacher Moss and Mohammed Amer was extremely thought provoking, and I am grateful to them for agreeing to meet me and saying much that inspired me to pursue my exploration of humour further. It has been a real privilege to have been able to interview several French comedians and actors while conducting the research that has resulted in the publication of this book, and I would like to thank Hassan Zahi, Zangro, Dédo, and Noom Diawara for agreeing to meet me.

I am profoundly grateful to Liverpool University Press for the opportunity to write this book and their support whilst working on the manuscript. Particular thanks are due to Anthony Cond and Chloé Johnson, as well as two anonymous reviewers who provided very constructive and helpful feedback on the initial draft, and also the copy editor for their meticulous work. I should add that all translations unless stated are my own, and I take full responsibility for them.

It is while working at Bangor University that I have done the work that has led to this book being published, and I am extremely thankful to numerous colleagues in Modern Languages whose presence and collegiality has been such a positive feature of my working life. I should also thank the many students who have endured my attempts to work jokes into French classes in a manner that probably illustrates why I became a lecturer rather than a comedian.

Finally, I would like to thank my family for all their support and encouragement, as well as bringing much humour to my life on a regular basis. My parents tell me that one of my childhood ambitions was to write a joke book, so this publication has clearly stemmed from an enduring interest in humour. My wife Viv once said that she married me despite my sense of humour rather than because of it, and my friends would doubtlessly say that she deserves much credit for listening to me tell many jokes of variable quality. It thus seems fitting to dedicate this book to Viv as well as our sons Tomos and Harri, who were both born while I was researching humour in France. All three bring much laughter and joy to my life on a daily basis, and this is something for which I am tremendously thankful.

Introduction

Humour: a serious issue
in contemporary France

The fatal attack on the offices of *Charlie Hebdo* in January 2015 provoked considerable debate in France about humour and freedom of expression, as well as topics such as humour and offensiveness, and the limits of humour. However, surprisingly little had previously been written about humour and national identity in a specifically French context. Within Anglophone studies of humour around the world, such as Christie Davies's iconic work *The Mirth of Nations*, references to humour in France generally concern ways in which the French have a tendency to tell jokes that mock the supposed stupidity of their Belgian and Swiss neighbours or the stinginess of inhabitants of the Auvergne region.[1] However, such jokes are often relatively banal as they generally involve the mocking of neighbouring countries with whom France has not had a particularly antagonistic history. In the case of the Auvergnats's perceived meanness, a stereotypical behavioural trait is being mocked but not the extent to which the regions' inhabitants are truly French.

When we examine humour within the context of the ethnic, racial, or religious diversity of French society, it can potentially be much less innocent if it involves stereotypes that reinforce hegemonic power relations. Although it can provide a means of challenging, or re-appropriating stereotypes, negotiating a way through issues surrounding immigration, diversity, and the legacies of colonialism can

---

1 Christie Davies, *The Mirth of Nations* (New Brunswick and London: Transaction Publishers, 2011), p. 9.

be a fraught process. Discussions of humour in France, as with so many other aspects of French society, are influenced by France's political culture, and the vocabulary utilized in such debates is often dictated by France's republican ideology. Within this context, for example, the concept of multiculturalism is seen as un-French due to being incompatible with Republican ideals of universality and the single and indivisible nation.[2] However, recent decades have seen a questioning of the extent to which France really is a single and indivisible nation that is as egalitarian as it aspires to be. This has coincided with attempts by French governments to increasingly define national identity, and censure those who mock figures such as the President.[3] Furthermore, these developments have occurred against the backdrop of increasingly intense debates about immigration and integration in a post 9/11 context.[4] In addition to being a period where France has sought to manage community relations in a tense context, this time has also been one marked by discussion of socio-political humour in France, and in particular what is and is not considered taboo. Despite politicians' attempts to impose a fixed notion of national identity, it has been argued that the performance of many contemporary French comedians has created 'des rires qui reconfigurent le terrain de la francité' ['forms of laughter that reconfigure the domain of Frenchness'].[5] In other words, humour has taken on increased significance within the context of exploring national identity in France.

Some comedians have sought to argue that the act of laughing itself constitutes a symbol of tolerance and integration. Michel Boujenah has argued – somewhat simplistically – that 'si on peut rire ensemble, on peut vivre ensemble' ['if we can laugh together, we can live together'].[6] However, it is important to acknowledge that humour has the potential to divide as well as unite. As Jimmy Carr and Lucy Greeves argue, 'a

2   Jeremy Jennings, 'Citizenship, Republicanism and Multiculturalism in Contemporary France', *British Journal of Political Science*, 30.4 (2000), p. 589.
3   See: Jeanne Favret-Saada, 'On y croit toujours plus qu'on ne croit: sur le manuel vaudou d'un président', *L'Homme*, 190 (2009), pp. 7-25.
4   See: Vincent Geisser, *La Nouvelle islamophobie* (Paris: La Découverte), pp. 9-11.
5   Maxime Cervulle, Sébastien M. Barat, Julien Mustin and Nelly Quemener, 'Du rire aux armes', *Poli: politique de l'image*, 2 (March 2010), p. 8.
6   In: Michel Bellenger, *Rire et faire rire: pourquoi l'humour change la vie* (Paris: ESF Éditeurs, 2008), p. 11.

joke thrown into a tense political situation can just as easily create chaos as promote understanding'.[7] This dual potential of humour to unite and divide, or provoke as well as reduce tension, will be central to this book's exploration of humour and identity in France. Certain controversies are already well known when it comes to humour and multiculturalism in France, notably allegations of anti-Semitism that have been levelled at the stand-up comedian Dieudonné M'Bala M'Bala. Furthermore, the decision of the satirical newspaper *Charlie Hebdo*'s to publish cartoons depicting the prophet Muhammad generated debate in many different branches of the media, and in many different countries. Within this context, analysing precisely how and why Dieudonné and *Charlie Hebdo* caused controversy remains important, as does assessing how and when comedy can promote tolerance and understanding.

Humour has long played a role in how different groups in society are represented or seek to represent themselves. Indeed, perceived foreignness or difference is the basis of many jokes.[8] Jimmy Carr and Lucy Greeves have argued that 'without foreigners and foreignness, there would be far fewer jokes' and that it is common 'to pick a regional, social or ethnic group to stereotype in our jokes, as a kind of shorthand for an undesirable comedy trait'.[9] The question of who tells such jokes, and about whom, raises many significant issues that concern power relations, as will be explored in the ensuing chapters. However, focusing on foreigners and other minorities primarily as subjects of jokes runs the risk of ignoring how these groups have used jokes themselves, often as a means of seeking to deal with complicated questions of identity. As Michael Billig suggests, the variety of different ways in which this occurs demonstrates that 'humour is a matter of moral, political and aesthetic debate'.[10] Leon Rappoport argues that humour's potential to provide light relief helps to explain why it is 'particularly important for minorities who have traditionally suffered from prejudice and discrimination'. He pursues this argument by stating that the ways

---

7   Jimmy Carr and Lucy Greeves, *The Naked Jape: Uncovering the Hidden World of Jokes* (London: Penguin, 2007), p. 219.
8   See: Davies, *The Mirth of Nations*, pp. 1–16.
9   Carr and Greeves, *The Naked Jape*, p. 208.
10   Michael Billig, 'Violent Racist Jokes', in Sharon Lockyer and Michael Pickering (eds), *Beyond a Joke: The Limits of Humour* (Basingstoke: Palgrave Macmillan, 2009), p. 30.

in which minorities in the United States of America have used humour illustrates their evolving social status and presence.[11] This is a notion that he further develops by referring to Laurence Mintz's analysis of the evolution of Jewish humour, and by arguing that this process is also applicable to how Black Americans have used humour. Mintz has described four key stages: being the subject of jokes, internalizing these jokes to create 'self-critical humour', providing a form of humour more akin to 'realism' and then mocking those who used to create jokes that made Jews a subject of ridicule.[12]

When exploring ways in which different groups in French society use humour, a crucial question concerns whether or not their approach constitutes an example of *humour communautaire*. *Communautaire* is an adjective that is often used in French to describe something that is perceived to lack the universalist ethos of French Republicanism due to being overly focused on a single group or community. France's Republican model of citizenship is based on people having rights as individual citizens rather than as members of groups defined by criteria such as race, ethnicity, gender, sexuality, or religion. In theory, the French nation is single and indivisible. A focus on group identities that cuts across the important national/non-national distinction that is a key factor in determining access to citizenship is thus perceived as a threat to national unity. Within such a context, *communautarisme* equates to a refusal to integrate and a refusal to adopt important French values. Several analysts have argued that *humour communautaire* and *humoristes communautaires* are becoming increasingly present within contemporary stand-up comedy in France.[13] When evaluating the veracity of such assertions, it is important to consider both the focus of comedians' material and its intended audience. A focus on one's own community need not necessarily imply introspection; when discussing how indigenous and minority communities around the world use the internet, Kyra Landzelius distinguishes between what she terms 'in-reach' and 'outreach'. 'In-reach' involves people interacting with members of their own community whilst 'outreach' describes

11   Michel Rappoport, *Punchlines: The Case for Racial, Gender and Ethnic Humor* (Westport, CT: Praeger, 2005), pp. 30, 65–6.
12   Rappoport, *Punchlines*, pp. 99–100.
13   See: Olivier Mongin, *De quoi rions-nous? Notre société et ses comiques* (Paris: Plon, 2006), p. 29; Bellenger, *Rire et faire rire*, p. 58.

the process whereby a minority population seeks to present itself to the majority population.[14] This distinction is highly pertinent when assessing intended audiences of jokes and how comedians seek to engage audiences. Within this context, questions of power relations often arise. Carr and Greeves argue that 'jokes have this wonderful potential to create moments of social informality, a sort of levelling-out of the teller's and hearer's sometimes very unequal roles'.[15] Jean-Marc Moura similarly argues that humour can be a means for minority groups to negate attempts to deprive them of power.[16] However, this process of striking back involves exercising a largely symbolic form of power, and the ways in which people do so are worthy of study due to wider issues that they raise about social and cultural hierarchies.

Bergson, Freud, and the philosophy of humour

Within studies of humour, Henri Bergson's *Le Rire* and Sigmund Freud's *The Joke and Its Relation to the Unconscious* constitute frequent reference points. Although they were highly respected figures in their respective fields of philosophy and psychoanalysis, some important questions have been raised about their work on humour. Before considering these criticisms, it is worth examining how Bergson and Freud approached the subject of humour.

Henri Bergson originally wrote the articles that were to become part of his book *Le Rire* in 1899 in order to explore how comic events provoked laughter. According to Bergson, the coming together of people in groups was a pre-requisite for laughter to emerge from comic situations. In *Le Rire*, he argued that 'on ne goûterait pas le comique si l'on se sentait isolé' ['one would not savour what is comic if one felt isolated'] and 'notre rire est toujours le rire d'un groupe' ['our laughter is always the laughter of a group'].[17] Although the American

---

14 Kyra Landzelius, *Native on the Net: Indigenous and Diasporic Peoples in the Virtual Age* (Oxford: Routledge, 2006), p. 11.

15 Carr and Greeves, *The Naked Jape*, p. 31.

16 Jean-Marc Moura, *Le sens littéraire de l'humour* (Paris: Presses universitaires de France, 2010), pp. 40–1.

17 Henri Bergson, *Le Rire* (Paris: Presses Universitaires de France, 1940), pp. 4–5.

philosopher and academic Ted Cohen argues that people can and do laugh when alone, he has described the process of laughter in his 1999 work *Jokes: Philosophical Thoughts on Laughing Matters* using terms that recall those of Bergson:

> When we laugh at the same thing, that is a very special occasion. It is already noteworthy that we laugh at all, at anything, and that we laugh all alone. That we do it together is the realization of a desperate hope. It is the hope that we are enough like one another to sense one another, to be able to live together.[18]

This extension of Bergsonian logic shows how the act of laughter, and conditions that facilitate its emergence, are closely connected to the ways in which people in a given society interact with each other. Cohen's words are reminiscent of Bergson's arguments in *Le Rire* that 'le rire doit répondre à certaines exigences de la vie en commun' and that 'le rire doit avoir une signification sociale'.[19]

In addition to discussing dynamics and conditions that facilitate the production of laughter, Bergson devoted much of *Le Rire* to describing and classifying types of jokes that are liable to produce laughter. A key element of Bergson's analysis of laughter focused on the concept of 'du mécanique plaqué sur du vivant' ['the mechanical encrusted upon the living'], the idea that a living being acting in a highly mechanical manner can often be a source of laughter. For Bergson, this principle explained vaudeville and puppet shows, and also why laughter can be a response to people who are unaware of the presence of others.[20]

In some respects, Bergson's general principles about the social function of laughter, and the importance of groups coming together to laugh, remain highly pertinent to studies of humour such as the one being conducted here. Nevertheless, there are also significant criticisms of Bergson's theories that need to be considered in order to fully assess their continued relevance. Given Simon Critchley's contention that 'Bergson's account of laughter really comes alive when one thinks of silent cinema',[21] it is worth asking to what extent it

18   Ted Cohen, *Jokes: Philosophical Thoughts on Joking Matters* (Chicago: Chicago University Press, 1999), p. 29.
19   Bergson, *Le Rire*, p. 6.
20   Bergson, *Le Rire*, pp. 29, 44, 102–3, 111.
21   Simon Critchley, *On Humour* (Abingdon: Routledge, 2002), p. 56.

remains relevant to the contemporary stand-up comedy, sketch-based comedy, and cartoons that will be analysed in this book. Michael Billig has provided a wider and potentially more damaging criticism of Bergson by arguing that 'he was not a specialist in "laughter studies" who happened to write an innovative book on his chosen speciality' but rather 'a great philosopher who happened to write on humour'.[22] Given this book's focus on humour and identity, and the ways in which humour can promote tolerance as well as provoke controversy, there are other more specific problems with Bergson's approach that it is necessary to address. A notable example stems from Bergson's apparent failure to have acknowledged this dual potential of humour. Billig argues that Bergson believed that 'humour, far from being intrinsically warm-hearted and positive, has a cold cruelty at its core'.[23] When he considers questions of racial diversity in *Le Rire*, Bergson provides what now appears to be an un-nuanced and very dated perspective by explaining how and why people laugh at a *nègre* [negro].[24] For Bergson, a *nègre* is a potentially comic figure as 'un visage noir serait [...] pour notre imagination un visage barbouillé d'encre ou de suie' ['a black face could be (...) for our imagination a face smeared with ink or soot'].[25] In the century that has elapsed since Bergson wrote *Le Rire*, France (like many other countries) has become more used to the presence of black people in many different walks of life and thus Bergson's notion that the concept of alterity intrinsically turns a black person into a comic character appears misplaced. However, the legacy of such dated and potentially offensive notions has provided a context that informs the work of black comedians, both in France and elsewhere. Race, status, and humour were key themes in Roschdy Zem's 2016 film *Chocolat*, which tells the story of a black clown named Raphaël Padilla who performed under the stage name Chocolat. Padilla was descended from Cuban slaves and became famous in France in the late nineteenth and early twentieth century as part of a double act alongside the white British clown George Foottit. Zem's film was inspired by a book by

---

22   Michael Billig, *Laughter and Ridicule: Towards a Social Critique of Humour* (London: Sage, 2005), p. 111.
23   Billig, *Laughter and Ridicule*, p. 125.
24   The use of the term *nègre* to describe a black person is in itself somewhat dated and potentially offensive.
25   Bergson, *Le Rire*, p. 31.

French historian Gérard Noiriel entitled *Chocolat, clown nègre : l'histoire oubliée du premier artiste noir de la scène française* [*Chocolat, the negro clown: the forgotten story of the French stage's first black artist*].[26] Following the success of this film, theatre critic Judith Sibony made an hour-long television documentary about race and humour entitled *Chocolat: histoire de rire* [*Chocolat: a history of laughter*] that explores the history of black comedians in France from the time of *Chocolat* to the present day.

Sigmund Freud, a contemporary of Bergson, initially published *The Joke and its Relation to the Unconscious* in 1905 and drew upon his earlier work on dreams. Freud attributed much greater importance to the study of his jokes than many other early twentieth-century intellectuals, and sought to make this very point at the start of *The Joke and its Relation to the Unconscious*.[27] In this work, Freud endorsed elements of Bergson's theories by arguing that 'the exposure of psychic automatism belongs to the technique of the comic'.[28] In other words, he provided a psychoanalytical version of the idea that 'du mécanique plaqué sur du vivant' ['the mechanical encrusted upon the living'] is a major source of humour. Many of the jokes that Freud cites in *The Joke and its Relation to the Unconscious* are pun-based witticisms; within such jokes, Freud argues that a form of 'displacement' occurs and that this 'openly put[s] some absurdity, some nonsense, some foolishness on view'.[29] He also indirectly alluded to his work on repressed desires by arguing that 'tendentious' jokes possess elements that mean that they create greater 'pleasure' than 'innocuous' jokes. Freud also stated that a key way that jokes function is by 'disburdening us from the compulsion of our intellectual education'. He also argued that jokes often work due to brevity that involves 'economizing on a psychical expenditure'.[30]

This latter principle of jokes provides a framework for understanding how pun-based witticisms procure pleasure or laughter, and Freud also discusses this in in the earlier parts of *The Joke and Its Relation to the Unconscious*.[31] Although this provides a potential means of

---

26   Gérard Noiriel, *Chocolat, clown nègre: l'histoire oubliée du premier artiste noir de la scène française* (Paris: Bayard, 2012).
27   See: Sigmund Freud, *The Joke and Its Relation to the Unconscious*, tr. Joyce Crick with introduction by John Carey (London: Penguin Classics, 2002), p. 3.
28   Freud, *The Joke*, p. 56.
29   Freud, *The Joke*, pp. 43, 47.
30   Freud, *The Joke*, pp. 93–4, 124.
31   See: Freud, *The Joke*, pp. 11–16.

contextualizing modern jokes that involve one-liners and pithy puns, the extent to which Freud focuses on this issue also limits his work's continued relevance to humour as a whole. In general terms, the contemporary relevance of Bergsonian theories has been questioned by contemporary psychologists who view Freud's work on the unconscious as having become less relevant.[32] In his introduction to the 2002 Penguin Classics edition of *The Joke and Its Relation to the Unconscious*, John Carey suggests that not many of the jokes cited by Freud are likely to be considered funny by those studying his work today.[33] The communications scholar Jerry Palmer has also questioned Freud's quest to analyse humour via a procedure derived from his theories on dreams given that dreams are defined by the 'role of sleep' and the way that it 'release[s] the mind from certain forms of conscious control'. He also adds that 'the presence of a listener [...] is essential to the joke structure [...] but [...] is clearly absent in the dream'.[34] In addition to the general concerns raised about Freud's work on humour, Carey has argued that Freud devoted insufficient attention to the potentially 'xenophobic ends' of some of the jokes he analysed.[35] This constitutes a highly significant failing and shows the potential problems that arise when seeking to use Freud and Bergson's theories as a reference point within studies of race and humour. Freud and Bergson are frequent reference points within the study of humour, but need to be situated within the context of the time in which they were written. Indeed, they have now become somewhat dated and appear somewhat inadequate tools to use when seeking to analyse diverse forms of contemporary humour in France and elsewhere. One could certainly argue that it is time to go in search of a new philosophy of humour that is more suited to the age in which we are now living. For this reason, it is important to consider more recent studies of jokes and humour have contributed to the analysis of humour and identity.

32   Peter McGraw and Joel Warner, *The Humor Code: a Global Search for What Makes Things Funny* (New York: Simon and Schuster, 2014), p. 7.
33   Freud, *The Joke*, p. xvii.
34   Jerry Palmer, *Taking Humour Seriously* (London: Routledge, 1994), p. 87.
35   See: Freud, *The Joke*, p. xiv.

Contemporary approaches to humour: moving beyond Freud and Bergson

In his seminal work *L'Ère du vide* [*The Age of the Void*], Gilles Lipovetsky argued that, by the late 1980s, humour was becoming ever more present within French culture and taking on new forms that lacked the satirical bite of earlier types of humour.[36] Such a characterization is in keeping with the way in which Lipovetsky sought to argue that the 1980s were a time when an ideological vacuum was developing as French society became increasingly individualistic and consumerist. Within this context, Lipovetsky argues that French comedy of the time lacked depth and was becoming somewhat frivolous:

> À la dénonciation railleuse corrélative d'une société fondée sur des valeurs reconnues s'est substitué un humour positif et désinvolte, un comique *teen-ager* à base de loufoquerie gratuite et sans prétention. […] L'humour de masse ne repose plus sur fond d'amertume ou de morosité: loin de se masquer un pessimisme et d'être la 'politesse de désespoir', l'humour contemporain se veut sans épaisseur et décrit un univers radieux.[37]

> [What has taken over from the mocking denunciation that is a consequence of a society founded on recognized values is a positive and casual humour, a teenage form of the comic that is madcap, gratuitous and unassuming. (…) Mass humour is no longer based on content that is bitter or morose: far from hiding pessimism and being the 'politeness of despair', contemporary humour aims to lack depth and describe a radiant universe.]

The association made between humour and youth culture is in many ways valid; 1984 saw the launch of the French cable television channel Canal Plus, and Canal swiftly became associated with youth-focused cultural output and helped to boost the careers of many French comedians. However, it is somewhat simplistic to argue that humour in 1980s France was necessarily depoliticized and utopian. To do so is to ignore the impact of a humourist such as Coluche in the first half of the 1980s; at the start of the decade he was already a household name

36   Gilles Lipovetsky, *L'Ère du vide* (Paris: Folio, 1989), pp. 196–7, 200.
37   Lipovetsky, *L'Ère du vide*, p. 200.

and indeed harboured ambitions of running for president in 1981.[38] Towards the end of the decade in 1988, Canal Plus launched its popular show *Les Guignols*, and sketches featuring latex puppets of leading personalities provided a daily satire of French political and cultural life.

During the post-millennium period with which this book concerns itself, French humour has frequently become anything but frivolous as it has engaged with issues to do with identity, inequality, diversity, and immigration. Many French humourists have during this period sought to pose serious questions about what it means to be French, and about the values on which French society is based during a time of social, economic, and political turbulence. These trends have emerged within a range of forms of humour, both ones that have a long association with France, and others which have developed more recently. Publications such as *Charlie Hebdo* have kept alive the tradition of French political satire in a written or illustrated form, often mocking those in power in an uncompromising or deliberately exaggerated manner. Andrew Stott has described satire as 'the most directly political of comic forms' and argued that it 'aims to denounce folly and vice and urge ethical and political reform through the subjection of ideas to humorous analysis'.[39] Although stand-up comedy does not have the same long-standing history in France as it does in the United States or the United Kingdom, it constitutes another form of humour that has played a role in commenting on and questioning French society in recent decades. It involves a comedian addressing an audience – at times entering into dialogue with them – and provides a means for the performer to put forward their vision of the world, and share experiences that are recounted as if true but are often somewhat exaggerated. By directly addressing spectators, stand-up comedy engages the audience in a different manner to sketch-based comedy. Stand-up comedy is more strongly based on the establishment of a rapport between the performer and audience, and at times makes the audience part of the joke, whereas sketch-based comedy involves greater distance between the performer and the audience. Nevertheless, sketch-based comedy does

---

38   Coluche announced his attention to stand in the 1981 presidential election on 30 October 1980 but withdrew on 16 March 1981, less than two months before François Mitterrand was elected President of the Republic.

39   Andrew Stott, *Comedy: The New Critical Idiom* (London: Routledge, 2005), p. 109.

to a certain extent share a degree of the informality associated with stand-up comedy. It has a longer history in France and has often been performed by groups in *café-théâtres*, often smaller and more informal venues than traditional theatres. Nevertheless, performers of this brand of comedy have often had greater theatrical training than stand-up comedians, and leading figures have performed in large theatres in major French cities.[40]

The existence of this range of types of humour poses a problem for the somewhat narrow focus of Bergson and Freud, as does the pair's failure to adequately discuss the political and sociological context in which humour exists. The fact that Bergson and Freud overlooked what are now highly significant issues in the studies of laughter and jokes is consistent with how Jerry Palmer has described the study of humour:

> Humour and comedy are studied in most human science or humanities disciplines: there is an anthropology of humour, a sociology and psychology of it, theorising it is basic to modern Freudianism, and to film and literary criticism its study is as central as the study of tragedy or realist narrative. In each of these fields there is an abundant literature on the subject [...]. Yet, as one reads the material, something very striking emerges: until roughly ten years ago, remarkably few of these specialists in their own disciplines bothered to read material deriving from any of the others.[41]

In the last two decades, a more interdisciplinary approach has emerged and this has been demonstrated by the range of different disciplines that are represented by academics who have contributed to collective volumes about humour, such as Sharon Lockyer and Michael Pickering's *Beyond a Joke: the Limits of Humour*. Within recent studies of laughter and jokes, much greater attention has been devoted to the context and power dynamics involved in the creation and telling of jokes. These issues are particularly pertinent to the study of humour and identity in France, and within this context there are several important matters need to be addressed. These include, for example, the way that joke

---

40   For more background on the humour of *le café-théâtre*, please see: Nelly Quemener, *Le Pouvoir de l'humour* (Paris: Armand Colin/INA, 2014), pp. 31-6.
41   Palmer, *Taking Humour Seriously*, p. 3.

tellers seek to present modern France and French people. This includes how positively or negatively they do so as well as the extent to which their visions are compatible with Republican ideology. In addition, contextual issues such as the social, racial, or ethnic background of the performer who is telling the joke, and the audience who is hearing it, are also important since these factors help to understand the objective and intended meanings of the material performed.[42] Given that many minority groups have been subjected to stereotyping, it is also necessary to consider if and how they engage with, or reference, existing stereotypes and to what ends.

Stereotypes are particularly important as they can provide revealing insights into power dynamics. Performances of comedy have the potential to both perpetuate and challenge stereotypes. The exploitation of recognizable stereotypes can enable a performer to engage an audience by acting out something of which they are already aware. As Andrew Stott points out, 'watching a parade of stereotypes […] affords the comfort of confirming an audience's stereotypes'.[43] Stereotypes are devices that are particularly suited to times of crisis, or societies that are not entirely at ease with themselves, as they allow the joke teller to 'overcome anxieties about [their] own shortcomings and reaffirm [their] own community identity'.[44] With diverse societies, a particular problem posed by stereotypes is that they do little to acknowledge or attempt to comprehend complicated and often hybrid identities. Instead, they possess a simplifying and dismissive element that involves 'une opération de réduction du sens toujours inscrite dans les rapports de pouvoir'.[45] In other words, they demonstrate that comedy is not always a subversive art form. This is particularly true of the many jokes in which groups are stereotyped in order to create 'a kind of shorthand for an undesirable character trait'.[46] Although some argue that those who tell jokes that involve clear racial stereotypes are not necessarily racist themselves, such jokes create a challenge if one is to 'rire des stéréotypes

---

42   See: Cohen, *Jokes*, pp. 85–6.
43   Stott, *Comedy*, p. 44.
44   Carr and Greeves, *The Naked Jape*, p. 210.
45   Eric Macé, 'Rions ensemble des stéréotypes: Anti-stéréotypes humoristiques d'Arabes et de musulmans dans les médiacultures', *Poli: politique de l'image*, 2 (March 2010), p. 18.
46   Carr and Greeves, *The Naked Jape*, p. 207.

sans que l'ironie ou le second degré ne soit pris pour du racisme ou de la stéréotypisation'.[47] This shows that stereotypes can at times be signs of a society that is ill at ease and also render audiences ill at ease.

Despite the aforementioned problematic aspects of stereotypes, it is also important to acknowledge that they can also provide important opportunities for comedians from groups that are stereotyped. As Mireille Rosello argues, those who are the subject of stereotypes can 'learn how to re-use stereotypes in striking and imaginative ways' or find a way to 'steal the negative image and put it to good use'.[48] This is consistent with Leon Rappoport's description of how Jewish and African-American comedians have engaged with stereotypes (see above), and we will see in this book that several French comedians have adopted a similar approach. The process of re-using a stereotype somewhat paradoxically involves simultaneously internalizing and rejecting the notions on which it is based, and Rosello contends that this is potentially problematic. She argues that the process of repeating the stereotype that one wishes to challenge 'involves a minimum, if unconscious, yet unavoidable element of allegiance'.[49] This further highlights the complexities of identity negotiation through the use of humour and is an important issue to consider when analysing humour and multiculturalism in contemporary France.

Comedy, controversy, cartoons, and consensuality

This book will examine four case studies that raise significant questions about multiculturalism and humour in France, facilitate comparisons between different forms of comedy, and lend themselves well to analysis of how different minority groups have been depicted. The time span with which we will concern ourselves is from 2002 to the present day, a period that was been characterized by the intensification of debates about diversity, integration and identity following the World Trade Center attacks of 11 September 2001 and Jean-Marie Le Pen coming second in the French presidential elections of the following year. It is

47   Macé, *Rions ensemble des stéréotypes*, p. 23.
48   Mireille Rosello, *Declining the Stereotype: Ethnicity and Representation in French Cultures* (Hanover, NH: University Press of New England, 1998), pp. 13, 71.
49   Rosello, *Declining the Stereotype*, p. 36.

a period that is also defined in political terms by the rise in profile of Nicolas Sarkozy. Sarkozy swiftly became recognized as a figure who was unafraid to court controversy when discussing immigration and integration after being initially appointed Interior Minister in 2002. This trend continued during his time as president from 2007–2012. During the Hollande presidency of 2012–2017, attacks on the offices of *Charlie Hebdo* provoked debates about humour and freedom of expression, as did attempts by government ministers to prevent the comedian Dieudonné from performing shows that they felt included anti-Semitic material. Although the period that we will examine in this book is punctuated by several high-profile flashpoints concerning humour and multiculturalism in France, it is important to note that there were also significant trends of a very different nature. For this reason, this book will group four case studies into two thematic pairs that will first involve assessing how humour can provoke controversy, before then analysing how humour can be used to promote tolerance and understanding.

The first chapter of this book will focus on *Charlie Hebdo*, a publication involved in the most dramatic and shocking event concerning humour to have taken place in France during the period of study. It will begin by assessing reactions to *Charlie Hebdo*'s publication of cartoons depicting the prophet Muhammad in 2006 and 2011. These events provoked questions about taboos and sensitivity to difference within the supposedly universalist French Republic. During these discussions, Republican ideology was evoked both by those who supported the publication of the controversial cartoons and those who condemned the actions of *Charlie Hebdo*. In considering the impact of the cartoons, it is important to acknowledge both the nature of reactions from inside and outside of France. Within France, there was a particular focus on freedom of expression within the context of secular society, as well as the balance between seeking to promote freedom of expression and ensuring harmonious inter-community relations in a diverse society. Following the 2015 attack on the *Charlie Hebdo* offices that left many of its leading cartoonists dead or seriously injured, a previously marginal publication suddenly came to symbolize a widely felt sense of grief and outrage in France and abroad. However, this chapter will analyse ways in which the supposedly consensual nature of declaring 'Je suis Charlie' ['I am Charlie'] in the aftermath of the attacks revealed several significant paradoxes or contradictions concerning attitudes to the publication and its unashamedly provocative brand of humour.

The second chapter will pursue the first chapter's study of humour, provocation, and offensiveness by analysing the stand-up comedian Dieudonné M'Bala M'Bala. It will concentrate in particular on his career trajectory since his appearance on a popular French television talk show in December 2003 that led to accusations of anti-Semitism and forms part of a radical transformation of his image. Dieudonné, as he is generally known, had in the 1990s built a reputation as a performer who often gently mocked prejudice, and as a left-wing anti-racism activist. However, he has more recently courted controversy due to performances and public declarations that have resulted in accusations of anti-Semitism and also due to his alleged links with figures associated with the far right. Dieudonné's performances, and reactions to them, provide a means of assessing how and why humour can be highly divisive as well as what is and is not considered taboo with both the media in France and French society in general.

The divisiveness of many of Dieudonné's recent one-man shows and public declarations is in stark contrast to the *raison d'être* of the *Jamel Comedy Club,* which is the subject of the third chapter. Founded in 2006 by the actor and comedian Jamel Debbouze, the club sought to provide increased exposure for aspiring French comedians, many of whom shared with Debbouze the fact that they were of foreign descent and/or grew up on the periphery of a large city. Several series of the *Jamel Comedy Club* have been televised by Canal Plus as part of an attempt to increase the cultural visibility of members of visible minorities in France following the suburban unrest of autumn 2005. This, and the way that many of the performers celebrate difference, demonstrates how humour and identity can be associated in positive ways that promote tolerance and unity. Nevertheless, the precise nature of how the comedians involved in the *Jamel Comedy Club* engage with stereotypes and represent members of certain lower profile minorities in France has sometimes been problematic.

Ways that humour can be used by members of minority groups lacking cultural visibility will also be analysed in the fourth chapter, which focuses on Islam and humour in France. The cultural visibility and influence of Muslims in France is of particular importance and sensitivity due to the country's secular traditions, and accusations that recent government-led debates about secularism in France have led to Muslims being unfairly scapegoated. The way in which debates about cartoons depicting the prophet Muhammad have sometimes been held up as a symbol of the supposed incompatibility between Islam and humour should not be allowed to obscure the presence in France of comedians who have over the last decade sought to use their Muslim roots as a source of humour. In 2008, a website entitled *À part ça tout va bien.com* started to produce humorous videos about Muslims in France that have appeared under the tag-line 'qui a dit que les musulmans n'avaient pas d'humour?' ['who said that Muslims had no sense of humour?']. These videos provide not just a counterpoint to the *Charlie Hebdo* controversy but also a starting point for a more detailed study of how Muslims are increasingly using humour as a form of self-(re)presentation in France. Mirroring certain aspects of the *Jamel Comedy Club*, it provides a further example of French comedians becoming increasingly influenced by North American approaches to humour and identity. This chapter will also explore ways in which French secularism has informed reactions to stand-up comedians in France who have sought to make their religion a defining part of their comedy material.

Overall, these four cases studies will provide significant insights into contemporary debates about national identity in France within the context of evolving attitudes towards questions of identity and integration. More specifically, it will also provide a key way of gauging French attitudes to humour, and especially where, when, and why certain types of socio-political jokes are considered unacceptable. This will shed much needed light on how social cohesion and humour interact with questions of local, national, and transnational identities in a variety of different contexts. Crucially, this book will demonstrate the importance of focusing on significant – and often political – aspects of contemporary French humour. It will assess both how humour has been discussed in the French and international media, and the role that various forms of media have played in shaping French humour. *Charlie Hebdo* exists within the French media landscape, and is a publication that has provoked considerable media debate concerning its brand of humour. Dieudonné's relationship with the French media has evolved as the nature of his comedy material has evolved, and he too has found himself at the centre of debates about provocative humour and the extent to which the media should engage with comedians whose work is accused of being inflammatory and/or discriminatory. The *Jamel Comedy Club* provides an example of predominantly youth-focused humour that fits in with the ethos of Canal Plus and the way in which the channel has helped to launch, or develop, the careers of many

French comedians. The French media landscape is evolving, and so is the way in which people engage with media, and the forms of media that they consume. It is within this context that the examination of online forms of humour, such as representations of Muslims within the web series *À part ça tout via bien*, is particularly relevant. The conclusion of this book will assess how attitudes to humour and identity in France have been affected by the January 2015 attacks on *Charlie Hebdo*, and also how they are likely to evolve at a time when the importance of the internet as a source of news and entertainment increases.

Chapter 1

Charlie Hebdo: from controversy to consensus?

Introduction

Given the amount of debate provoked in France and internationally by *Charlie Hebdo*'s decision in 2006 to print a series of cartoons depicting the Prophet Muhammad, and the relative recentness of the 2015 fatal attack on the offices of *Charlie Hebdo*, it appears appropriate for the opening chapter of this book to focus on the now iconic satirical publication. Exploring reactions to key events involving *Charlie Hebdo* from 2006 to 2015 provides a way to trace the evolution of debates about humour in France during a turbulent decade. During this period, public reactions to the attacks meant that, within a few years, *Charlie Hebdo* had gone from being a relatively marginal and often controversial publication to becoming the focus of much greater public consensus. As we will see, such a trajectory is highly paradoxical given the publication's roots and its own sense of what constitutes *l'esprit Charlie*. This chapter will examine several paradoxes that have formed part of debates about *Charlie Hebdo*, and these will include ways in which both those who have defended the publication and those who have opposed it have sought to justify their approach by appealing to French Republican values. As we will see, there have been several different interpretations of the implications of *laïcité* [French secularism], Republican universalism, and the freedom of expression.

    Charlie Hebdo is a largely satirical publication, and has a long tradition of mocking those in power via cartoons and articles. However, much of the focus of writings on *Charlie Hebdo* has tended to concentrate on its most well-known cartoons – especially those on its front cover – without adequately discussing the extent to which such cartoons have been accompanied by articles on related themes. This chapter will seek to address this failing by providing a more complete exploration of the types of content that one finds within the pages of the weekly publication. It is important to see *Charlie Hebdo* as more than just a contemporary example of the long-lasting tradition of French satire due to the specificity of its humour and the debates that this brand of humour have provoked. As mentioned in the introduction to this book, Andrew Stott has stated that satire is a type of humour that often 'aims to denounce folly and urge political reform through the subjection of ideas to humorous analysis'.[1] The perceived follies denounced by *Charlie Hebdo* are not always those of the ruling classes, which raises issues that will be explored here about how it chooses its targets. Furthermore, the publication on occasion denounces or mocks without necessarily seeking to provide a solution. Stott has argued that satire is 'generally understood according to its degree of viciousness'[2] and *Charlie Hebdo* has long been unafraid of provoking controversy and has taken pride in indulging in particularly vicious satire. Slogans such as 'bête et méchant' ['stupid and nasty'] and 'journal irresponsable' ['irresponsible newspaper'] regularly appear on its front cover, demonstrating a desire to celebrate an anarchic approach that is not always particularly sophisticated. This attitude is in many ways akin to that of a school pupil who celebrates receiving a bad school report and takes particular pride in the most strident criticism. An understanding of these principles has been surprisingly lacking in much of what has been written about *Charlie Hebdo* since the fatal attacks of January 2015 which resulted in the deaths of twelve people, including five of its leading cartoonists. Freedom of expression has regularly been the prime focus, but the specific brand of humour that characterizes *Charlie Hebdo* has generally been treated as a secondary issue. However, it is essential that the nature of *Charlie Hebdo*'s humour is properly analysed if one is to fully understand how and why it has depicted the Prophet Muhammad (and indeed many other religious and political figures) in an at times highly unflattering manner. Jane Weston Vauclair and David Vauclair have been particularly critical of the way in which they see certain people in the United Kingdom – including academics – as having sought to 'instrumentaliser *Charlie Hebdo* pour leur carrière ou leurs disputes

---

1   Stott, *Comedy*, p. 109.
2   Stott, *Comedy*, p. 153.

personnelles' ['exploit *Charlie Hebdo* to further their career or due to their personal agendas'].[3]

Responses to the January 2015 attacks on *Charlie Hebdo* have often sought to explore what lessons they can teach about wider topics such as the freedom of expression, tensions within contemporary French society and the threat of terrorism. It is particularly telling that one volume of essays written by a group of Norwegian-based academics following the attacks is entitled *The Event of Charlie Hebdo: Imaginaries of Freedom and Control*. The event discussed is the attack of January 2015 and the work makes little attempt to provide a detailed examination of *Charlie Hebdo*'s brand of humour. This is symptomatic of many writers and journalists' tendency to explore wider issues following the attacks rather than seek to gain a more detailed understanding of what *Charlie Hebdo* represents, and how this has evolved under the leadership of different editors over a period of several decades. As Weston Vauclair and Vauclair argue, discussions of the values on which *Charlie Hebdo* is based frequently lack sufficient nuance:

> 'L'esprit Charlie' est invoqué avec régularité, en dépit de son ambiguïté – s'agit-il de l'esprit du journal, et si oui duquel, celui de Cavana et Choron, de Val, de Charb, de Riss? Ou s'agit-il de l'esprit de la communauté nationale que certains perçurent lors des manifestations de janvier [2015], un brouillon de l'identité française?[4]

> ['The spirit of Charlie' is regularly evoked, despite its ambiguity – is it about the spirit of the publication, and if so which, that of Cavana and Choron, of Val, of Charb, or Riss? Or is it about the spirit of national unity that some perceived during the demonstrations of January (2015), a rough version of French identity?]

Due to the time period with which we are concerning ourselves here, it will primarily be the *Charlie Hebdo* of 2006–2015 that is of interest. This is a period during which several editors have sought to take the publication in different directions, and several have faced criticism for doing so.

---

3   Jane Weston Vauclair and David Vauclair, *De Charlie Hebdo à Charlie: enjeux, histoire, perspectives* (Paris: Eyrolles, 2016), p. 85.
4   Weston Vauclair and Vauclair, *De Charlie Hebdo à Charlie*, p. 11.

Due to the need for greater analysis of *Charlie Hebdo*'s ethos and brand of satire, this chapter will begin with a section entitled 'The humour of *Charlie Hebdo*' that will explore the meanings of key terms such as 'bête et méchant' and 'journal irresponsable'. This will then form the basis of further discussion of the publication's decision in 2006 to reprint cartoons of the Prophet Muhammad that had initially appeared in the Danish newspaper *Jyllands Posten*. The second main section of this chapter will also examine the court case brought against *Charlie Hebdo* in 2007 by several Muslim organizations in France and the ways in which both sides in the case sought to evoke France's Republican values in order to strengthen their case. Before considering the attacks of 2015 and their aftermath, the third main section of this chapter will analyse reactions to the firebombing of *Charlie Hebdo*'s offices in 2011. It will be argued that examination of public debates about *Charlie Hebdo*'s brand of humour at this time reveals some significant differences in tone compared to debates that took place in 2006 and 2007. The final main section of this chapter will consider the events of January 2015 and their aftermath, and in particular the ambiguity and paradoxes surrounding reactions to the attacks from both figures of authority and the wider public. The conclusion of this chapter will examine what the future holds for *Charlie Hebdo* and its brand of humour.

The humour of *Charlie Hebdo*

The lack of British or American equivalents of *Charlie Hebdo* has created difficulties for commentators in what the French term *le monde anglo-saxon* [the Anglo-Saxon world] when it has come to situating and explaining what *Charlie Hebdo* represents.[5] From a British perspective, it may seem tempting to compare *Charlie Hebdo* to *Private Eye* as both publications share a suspicion of those in power and frequently mock such figures. However, the shared focus on satire should not mask other significant differences. *Private Eye* is more closely associated with

5   For discussion of this term, which is generally used to refer to the United Kingdom and the United States of America, see: Emile Chabal, *The Divided Republic: Nation, State And Citizenship In Contemporary France* (Cambridge: Cambridge University Press, 2015), pp. 105–33.

investigative journalism than *Charlie Hebdo*. The sort of investigative journalism associated with *Private Eye* finds a more natural home in France in the more newspaper-like satirical weekly *Le Canard Enchaîné*.[6] Furthermore, cartoons play a much more prominent role in *Charlie Hebdo* than *Private Eye*. It is telling that whilst the front cover of *Charlie Hebdo* almost always features an illustrated depiction of a recent news event, *Private Eye*'s front cover almost always involves a photograph of figures who have been in the news and who are lampooned via the addition of speech bubbles that mock their actions. Crucially, the presence of many privately educated Oxbridge graduates among the founders and editors of *Private Eye* points towards an air of sophistication to which the unashamedly 'bête et méchant' *Charlie Hebdo* appears not to aspire.

Jane Weston describes this 'bête et méchant' approach as a form of 'humour [that has] favoured scatology, sexually explicit material and black humour in general' and Weston Vauclair and Vauclair describe *Charlie Hebdo*'s humour as symbolizing 'un mauvais goût revendiqué' ['self-declared bad taste'].[7]

The phrase 'bête et méchant' was initially associated with the satirical publication *Hara-Kiri* that was banned in 1969 following the publication of an edition that marked the news of Charles de Gaulle's death with the front page headline 'Bal tragique à Colombey: un mort' ['Tragic ball in Colombey: one death']. This choice of words showed a willingness to ignore what many would perceive as the boundaries of good taste by playing down the significance of Charles de Gaulle's death by referencing a nightclub fire that claimed the lives of 146 people eight days previously. The somewhat puerile approach that is evident within elements of *Charlie Hebdo*'s 'bête et méchant' humour means that it in fact shares certain attributes with the unashamedly vulgar British comic *Viz* rather than the more sophisticated *Private Eye*. However, it is important to note that *Viz* is generally much less political than *Charlie Hebdo*.

---

6 It is worth noting that investigative journalism in France is increasingly finding a home online at the website of *Médiapart*, a publication that does not seek to provide satire but often exposes hidden stories concerning the behaviour of those in power.

7 Jane Weston, '*Bête et méchant*: Politics, Editorial Cartoons and *Bande dessinée* in the French Satirical Newspaper *Charlie hebdo*', *European Comic Art* 2.1 (2009), p. 109; Weston Vauclair and Vauclair, *De Charlie Hebdo à Charlie*, p. 90.

Weston argues that Philippe Val's period as editor of *Charlie Hebdo* (1992–2009) was characterized by 'an increasingly serious, and less juvenile, satire'.[8] As the publication of cartoons depicting the Prophet Muhammad in 2006 – and on several other occasions – demonstrated, *Charlie Hebdo* under Val nevertheless remained unafraid of being perceived as provocative.[9] Indeed, number 712 of *Charlie Hebdo* published on 8 February 2006 and depicting the Prophet Muhammad on the front cover lamenting 'c'est dur d'être aimé par des cons', contained several other cartoons that showed that the publication was continuing to represent religious and political figures in a puerile or vulgar manner. Indeed, the last decade has seen *Charlie Hebdo* regularly mock religion in a manner that demonstrates that it is maintaining its tradition of anticlericalism.

2006 depictions of the prophet and ensuing court case

Charlie Hebdo's decision in 2006 to reprint cartoons of the Prophet Muhammad that had appeared in the Danish newspaper *Jyllands Posten* needs to be placed in both a French and international context when it comes to assessing both the initial motivations and reactions to the publication of these images. Furthermore, when one examines the arguments presented in the court case brought against *Charlie Hebdo* by French Muslim groups in 2007, one can learn much about competing uses of French Republican discourse to justify differing attitudes to humour and offensiveness. Indeed, much of the court case focused on the fact that Islam is far from the only religion that has been mocked in *Charlie Hebdo*.

The 8 February 2006 edition of *Charlie Hebdo* (number 712) provoked controversy not just due to its decision to reprint twelve cartoons that had appeared in *Jyllands Posten* in autumn 2005, but also due to several additional cartoons depicting the Prophet Muhammad that *Charlie Hebdo*'s cartoonists drew for the occasion. One of the most striking of these was a drawing by Cabu that adorned the front page; it featured the headline 'Mahomet débordé par les intégristes'

---

8   Weston, '*Bête et méchant*', p. 110.
9   See: Frédérique Roussel and Isabelle Hanne, '"Charlie", satire dans tous les sens', *Libération*, 7 January 2015, http://www.liberation.fr/ecrans/2015/01/07/charlie-satire-dans-tous-les-sens_1175870 [accessed 14 March 2017].

['Muhammad overcome by fundamentalists'] and a picture of the prophet with his head in his hands lamenting 'c'est dur d'être aimé par des cons' ['it's hard being loved by jerks']. Despite the presence of a heading that specifically mentioned fundamentalists, much of the ensuing controversy stemmed from the assumption that the 'cons' mentioned in the speech bubble were Muslims in general rather than Muslim fundamentalists. Philippe Val, editor of *Charlie Hebdo* at the time of the 'c'est dur d'être aimé par des cons' ['it's hard being loved by jerks'] cover, has stated that 'être opposé à l'islamisme, ce n'est pas être anti-arabe' ['being opposed to Islamism is not the same as being Anti-Arab'] and that 'ce que l'on critique, ce n'est jamais leur origine, c'est leurs idées' ['what we are criticizing is never their origins, it is their ideas'].[10] As we will discuss later, many of the arguments in the 2007 court case brought against *Charlie Hebdo* focused on the extent to which the cartoons that were the subject of the court case could be considered to refer to, or be offensive to, Muslims as a whole. Knut Rio has argued that the 'c'est dur d'être aimé par des cons' ['it's hard being loved by jerks'] front cover instantly changed the status and prominence of *Charlie Hebdo*:

> In 2006 *Charlie Hebdo* sold 500,000 copies of the famous issue with the cartoon of a weeping Muhammad stating 'C'est dur d'être aimé par des cons' (It's Hard Being Loved by Jerks). For a journal that normally sold copies in the tens of thousands, this was a step up to a different league of international publishing. From random nonsense and obscene mockery of politicians and celebrities, it suddenly touched on something of a whole other order: an indefinable terrain of massive popular interest, an intimation of danger, of stepping across a line. It seemed that this was what the masses longed for – the desecration of the one thing that the barbarians held especially sacred: Muhammad.[11]

Initially, the above comments appear to illustrate a degree of understanding of *Charlie Hebdo*'s 'bête et méchant' humour. Furthermore, they feature some largely valid points about the 'c'est dur d'être aimé

10   Weston Vauclair and Vauclair, *De Charlie Hebdo à Charlie*, p. 50.
11   Knut Rio, 'The *Barbariat* and Democratic Tolerance', in Alessandro Zagato (ed.), *The Event of Charlie Hebdo: Imaginaries of Freedom and Control* (New York/ Oxford: Berghahn, 2015), p. 18.

par des cons' front cover – and indeed edition – of *Charlie Hebdo* had on its sales figures. Nevertheless, Rio's comments also overstate the novelty of *Charlie Hebdo*'s depiction of the Prophet Muhammad. As was mentioned by lawyers defending *Charlie Hebdo* in the 2007 court case, the publication has a long history of mocking religious figures and it had in fact depicted the Prophet Muhammad on several occasions in the decade preceding 2006. The reference to the 'c'est dur d'être aimé par les cons' front cover 'touch[ing] on [...] an indefinable terrain of massive popular interest' also fails to acknowledge that mocking major news events via its front cover was a routine event for such a proudly impertinent satirical publication.

Before examining the reactions to this now famous edition of *Charlie Hebdo* in greater depth, it is important to first understand the context in which the original *Jyllands Posten* cartoons were published. The cartoons printed in the 30 September 2005 edition of the centre-right Danish newspaper appeared under the heading 'Muhammeds ansigt' (The Face of Muhammad). Jytte Klausen identifies this framing as a provocative act in itself as 'the choice of headline proclaimed the newspaper's intention to violate the Muslim taboo against the pictorial representation of Muhammad'.[12] However, it would be more accurate to refer to 'the *perceived* Muslim taboo against the pictorial representation of Muhammad'. As Klausen herself acknowledges elsewhere in the same book, Islamic art includes works that visually represent the Prophet Muhammad.[13] Furthermore, the historian François Boespflug argues that the Koran itself 'ne contient aucune condamnation formelle des images [du prophet]' ['does not contain any formal condemnation of images (of the prophet)'] and that it is merely in hadiths – handed down stories about the life of Muhammad that carry less weight that the text of the Koran – that one finds references to such a ban.[14] Despite the fact that the *Jyllands Posten* cartoons originated from an invitation

12   Jytte Klausen, *The Cartoons That Shook the World* (New Haven and London: Yale University Press, 2009), p. 14.
13   Klausen, *Cartoons*, p. 8. Klausen nevertheless suggests here that there is an important distinction to be made between 'the human prophet' and the 'divine', and suggests that it is merely that the latter whose representation is forbidden by the Koran. See also: Mohamed Sifaoui, *L'Affaire des caricatures: dessins et manipulations* (Paris: Éditions Privé, 2006), p. 54.
14   François Boespflug, *Caricaturer Dieu? Pouvoirs et dangers de l'image* (Paris: Bayard, 2012), p. 41.

to draw the Prophet Muhammad, the ethnologist Jeanne Favret-Saada observes that more than half of the twelve caricatures did not explicitly represent the Prophet Muhammad and that only four of the drawings can easily be termed caricatures of the Prophet Muhammad. Of these four images, Favret-Saada argues that three depict the subjugation of women and one associates – via what appears to be an image of the Prophet Muhammad with a bomb in his turban – Islam and terrorism.[15] However, there is a degree of ambiguity as to what this final and most controversial of the twelve drawings actually represents. Klausen has stated that this striking image was created in order to mock negative attitudes to Islam in Denmark and Kurt Westergaard – the cartoonist who drew the picture – has stated that he never intended his cartoon to be seen as a representation of the Prophet Muhammad but that he wanted to make a comment about 'des terroristes qui se servaient de l'islam et du Coran comme une façade' ['terrorists who were using Islam and the Koran as a façade'].[16] Such nuances were lost on many, not least those who protested against the cartoons many hundreds (or thousands) of miles away from where the drawings had been published. However, some Muslims in France also argued that an apparent depiction of the Prophet Muhammad with a bomb in his turban, by extension, represented Muslims as a whole as terrorists. This was an argument made by Fatiha Kaoues (journalist for the Muslim current affairs and cultural website Oumma.com) during a televised discussion of the cartoons that took place on 6 February 2006,[17] and also by Fouad Alaoui (secrétaire général de l'Union des Organisations Islamiques de France [general secretary of the Union of Islamic Organisations of France]) on French television the following week.[18]

However, there were many differing views within Europe about the decision of *Jyllands Posten* and *Charlie Hebdo* to print the cartoons. Favret-Saada has noted that a significant proportion of the political left in both Denmark and France was critical of *Jyllands Posten*'s decision to

---

15 Jeanne Favret-Saada, *Comment produire une crise mondiale avec douze petits dessins* (Paris: Les Prairies ordinaires, 2007), pp. 84–5.
16 Klausen, *Cartoons*, pp. 21–2; Weston Vauclair and Vauclair, *De Charlie Hebdo à Charlie*, p. 48.
17 'Peut-on rire de tout?', *Question d'actu*, LCI, 6 February 2006.
18 'Caricatures: choc des images ou des civilisations?', *Ripostes*, France 5, 12 February 2006.

print the original cartoons and that such an attitude was in stark contrast with the way that many on the left had so fervently defended Salman Rushdie at the time of the *Satanic Verses* controversy.[19] Furthermore, a survey by CSA/La Croix published in the newspaper *La Croix* on 10 February 2006 suggested that 54% of French people were opposed to the publication of the cartoons by *Charlie Hebdo*.[20] However, the Association du manifeste des libertés [Association for the Expression of Freedoms] argued in the 15 February 2006 edition of *Charlie Hebdo* that this apparent disapproval of the cartoons by a majority of the French public may have been due to their fear of the consequences of the cartoons' publication, which itself could be perceived as a sign of prejudice associating Muslims and violence.[21]

It is also important to remember that *Charlie Hebdo*'s publication of the cartoons on 8 February came a week after a group of nineteen European newspapers had collectively decided to publish some or all of the *Jyllands Posten* drawings in order to defend the freedom of the press. *France-Soir* was initially the only French newspaper to participate although it was later joined by *Le Monde* and *Libération*. However, *Charlie Hebdo*'s printing of the *Jyllands Posten* cartoons – along with several of their own – needs to be placed in a slightly different context to the decision taken by the European newspapers mentioned above. Following the printing of the cartoons, *France-Soir*'s owner Raymond Lakah sacked the newspaper's editor Jacques Lefranc. Philippe Val states that this was one of the prime reasons why *Charlie Hebdo* published the *Jyllands Posten* cartoons, and that by doing so *Charlie Hebdo* was making a comment about freedom of expression in France in addition to expressing its solidarity with *Jyllands Posten*.[22]

Much of the debate about *Charlie Hebdo*'s decision to reprint the drawings that appeared in *Jyllands Posten*, and add several of their own,

---

19   Favret-Saada, *Comment produire une crise mondiale*, p. 11. Philippe Val criticized the French left for their failure to make themselves more audible in debates about the caricatures in an editorial article entitled 'Ils sont grands parce que nous sommes à genoux', that appeared in the 8 March 2006 edition (no. 715) of *Charlie Hebdo*. See: Philippe Val, 'Le Choix de Chirac', *Charlie Hebdo*, 715, p. 2.

20   Boespflug, *Caricaturer Dieu?* p. 20.

21   Association du manifeste des libertés, 'Persévérance', *Charlie Hebdo*, no. 713, 22 February 2006, p. 2.

22   Weston Vauclair and Vauclair, *De Charlie Hebdo à Charlie*, p. 52.

has failed to discuss the texts that accompanied the images that were present in the 8 February 2006 edition. This does little to further understanding of *Charlie Hebdo*'s motivations for printing the drawings or its ethos. Much of Gérard Biard's article immediately inside the front cover of the 8 February 2006 edition focused on the international importance of freedom of speech in the face of threats posed by Islamic fundamentalism in the West; it also criticized radical Islamists who use terrorist violence against those they disagree with rather than 'répondre au crayon et à la plume' ['respond using the pencil and the pen']. The most prominent feature of the second page of this edition of *Charlie Hebdo* was a declaration entitled 'pour la liberté d'expression' ['in favour of freedom of expression'] that was written by Tewfik Allal of L'Association du Manifeste des libertés, a French organization of Muslims – both believers and non-practicing people who consider themselves culturally Muslim – that denounces Islamic fundamentalism. The twelve cartoons from *Jyllands Posten* appeared across the second and third pages, and an editorial by Philippe Val on the third page provided a historical and cultural context concerning Islam, depictions of the Prophet Muhammad, and freedom of expression. This editorial discussed differences between different groupings of Muslims, and notably the fact that Sunni Muslims are not permitted to depict the Prophet whereas Shiites do not adhere to such a belief.[23] In the same article, Val argued that the controversial image that appeared to depict Muhammad with a bomb in his turban was 'suffisament faible pour être interprété n'importe comment par n'importe qui' ['sufficiently weak for it to be interpreted in any way by any person'] and that he saw the image as representing 'la version de l'islam et du prophète qu'ils [les fondamentalistes] ne veulent pas voir représenter' ['the version of Islam and the prophet that they (the fundamentalists) do not want to see represented'].[24] The depiction of the Prophet Muhmmad that *Charlie Hebdo* added to the twelve drawings from *Jyllands Posten* on the second and third pages of their 8 February edition actually mocked the Danish people rather than Islam. The drawing by Wolinski showed a gleeful Prophet Muhammad holding a piece of paper on which the word 'caricatures' is visible, and exclaiming 'c'est bien la première fois que les

23 Philippe Val, 'Petit glossaire d'une semaine caricaturale', *Charlie Hebdo*, no. 712, 8 February 2006, p. 3.
24 Val, 'Petit glossaire d'une semaine caricaturale', p. 3.

Danois me font rire!' ['it's certainly the first time that the Danish have made me laugh!']. One of the most explicit justifications for *Charlie Hebdo*'s decision to reprint the *Jyllands Posten* cartoons was provided in an article by Caroline Fourest on the fourth page of the 8 February 2006 edition that ended with the following statement:

> La mondialisation de la haine et de la lâcheté a un revers. Non négligeable. Celui de mondialiser les solidarités. C'est pourquoi *Charlie*, comme d'autres journaux français et européens, a décidé de publier ces dessins. Par solidarité. Pour montrer que l'Europe n'est pas un espace où le respect des religions prime sur la liberté d'expression. Parce que la provocation et l'irrévérence sont des armes pour faire reculer l'intimidation de l'esprit critique dont se nourrit l'obscurantisme.[25]

> [The globalization of hatred and cowardice has another side to it. It is not insignificant. It is the globalization of solidarity. This is why *Charlie*, like other French and European newspapers, decided to publish these drawings. In solidarity. To show that Europe is not a space where respect for religions takes priority over freedom of expression. Because provocation and irreverence are weapons for reducing the mental intimidation on which obscurantism feeds.]

Much of Fourest's article places the cartoons within a specifically French context, and she insists upon the need to challenge criticism of their publication from figures such as France's then Chief Rabbi Joseph Sitruk and Mouloud Aounit of French anti-racist organization *Le Mouvement contre le racisme et pour l'amitié entre les peuples* (MRAP).

A more light-hearted reflection on religion, humour, and offence – which subsequent events have made appear somewhat prophetic – was provided on the centre pages of the 8 February 2006 edition of *Charlie Hebdo* by the illustrator Luz. A comic strip entitled 'Soyons syncrétiquement corrects' ['Let's be syncretically correct'] jokingly sets out to provide a guide to avoiding social faux-pas over dinner and begins with a man asking 'comment vivre normalement sans blesser la foi de nos contemporains?' ['How is it possible to live normally without offending

25 Caroline Fourest, 'Tout ce fouin pour douze dessins!', *Charlie Hebdo*, no. 712, 8 February 2006, p. 4.

the faith of our contemporaries?']. It ends with the conclusion 'ne jamais représenter dieu […], sinon le bordel' ['never depict God (…), if not it'll be chaos'] and the final frame shows firefighters attending to a house on fire from which the following speech bubbles are emerging: 'Seigneur, il pleut, c'est l'apocalypse! / C'est le visage du prophète! / Non celui de Yahvé! / C'est le Christ! / Ron Hubbard!' ['Lord, it is raining, it's the apocalypse! / It's the face of the prophet! / No, that of Yahve! / It's Christ! / Ron Hubbard!'].[26] This last image provides a vision of the fate that befell *Charlie Hebdo* when its offices in Paris were firebombed in November 2011 after the newspaper had announced that the Prophet Muhammad would be the editor-in-chief of its next edition, which is discussed in the next section of this chapter. The back page of the 8 February 2006 edition of *Charlie Hebdo* depicts a collection of alternatives to the front-cover drawing, and several of these could be interpreted as depicting the Prophet Muhammad. However, the prime objective of these drawings appears to be mocking what *Charlie Hebdo* see as excessive or illogical reactions to the publication of caricatures representing the Prophet Muhammad. This echoes a view expressed by Philippe Val in a televised discussion of the caricatures that took place on 6 February 2006 and during which he argued that 'on parle avec moins d'indignation du 11 septembre aujourd'hui que des caricatures' ['people today speak with less indignation about September 11 than the caricatures'].[27]

The thrust of the cartoons that were on the back cover of the 8 February 2006 edition was evident in the following week's edition of *Charlie Hebdo*, which pursued the criticism of those in France who had expressed their opposition to the publication of the *Jyllands Posten* cartoons. Jacques Chirac's use of the phrase 'provocation inutile' ['pointless provocation'] to describe *Charlie Hebdo*'s 8 February 2006 edition was used against him on the front cover of the 15 February 2006 edition (number 713). Riss's cover cartoon recreates a very innocent image that is one of the most recognizable and memorable from Antoine Saint-Exupéry's novel *Le Petit Prince*; in response to the little prince saying 'dessine-moi un mouton' ['draw me a sheep'] a visibly enraged Chirac retorts 'pas de provocation inutile' ['no pointless provocation'],

26 Luz, 'Soyons syncrétiquement corrects', *Charlie Hebdo*, no. 712, 8 February 2006, pp. 8–9.
27 'Peut-on rire de tout?', *Question d'actu*, LCI, 6 February 2006.

as a bemused figure wearing a turban pokes his head up from a crater on the planet on which the prince is standing. The cover also features a red box that mentions that, following the previous week's edition, '89% des messages qui nous sont parvenus sont des témoignages de soutien' ['89% of the messages we received were expressions of support'] and that 'parmi eux, de nombreux Juifs, Arabes et chrétiens [sont] d'accord sur un point: le choc de civilisations ne passera pas par eux' ['among them, numerous Jews, Arabs and Christians agree about one thing: the clash of civilizations will not be of their doing']. In other words, there is a clear attempt to present the previous week's edition of *Charlie Hebdo* as lacking the inflammatory potential attributed to it by its critics. This notion is further emphasized in an article by Philippe Val entitled 'les preuves de manipulation' ['the evidence of manipulation'] that appears just inside the front cover. Val notes that the Egyptian newspaper *Al Fajr* printed the *Jyllands Posten* cartoons a fortnight after their initial publication in Denmark and that this did not provoke a reaction. Immediately below this article, a cartoon by Cabu depicts Chirac as a radical Islamic preacher leaning out of a minaret labelled 'Elysée' and declaring 'halte aux provocations' ['stop provocative acts'].[28] In an editorial on the following page, Val argued that Chirac's denunciation of *Charlie Hebdo*'s supposed 'provocation' was motivated by his long history of doing business with Arab dictators and was unworthy of a President of the Republic.[29] *Charlie Hebdo*'s then editor sought to situate the publication's depiction of Islam within the context of its long history of mocking religion, and in particular extreme elements of religions, via the following declaration to French Muslims:

> Nous critiquons avec autant de liberté la religion chrétienne dans laquelle la majorité des Français ont été élevés. Que cette critique ne s'adresse pas exclusivement à l'islam, mais à toutes les religions quand leurs représentants manipulent des fidèles à des fins politiques.[30]
>
> [We criticize with equal freedom the Christian religion within which the majority of French people have been brought up. May

28 Philippe Val, 'Les preuves de la manipulation', *Charlie Hebdo*, no. 713, 15 February 2006, p. 2.
29 Philippe Val, 'Provocation', *Charlie Hebdo*, no. 713, 15 February 2006, p. 3.
30 Val, 'Provocation', p. 3.

this criticism not just apply to Islam, but all religions when their representatives manipulate their followers for political reasons.]

In a televised discussion about the cartoons controversy a few days earlier, Val had argued that criticism of religions, and the freedom to criticize religions, had led to the establishment of *laïcité* [French secularism], a key concept in France's Republican constitution.[31] In the court case brought against *Charlie Hebdo* by two French Muslim organizations that is discussed in the next section, we will see that the sort of argument cited above was to become a feature of the trial. The fact that Muslim figures and Islam were being criticized within *Charlie Hebdo* alongside those of other religions was a key argument used by the publication. Indeed, it claimed that this approach demonstrated that Islam was receiving precisely the same treatment as other faiths.

Caricatures in the courtroom: the 2007 case brought against *Charlie Hebdo*

In 2007, the Grande Mosquée de Paris [Grand Mosque of Paris] and l'Union des Organisations Islamiques de France (UOIF) [the Union of Islamic Organisations of France] sued *Charlie Hebdo* for 'injure à l'égard d'un groupe de personnes en raison de leur religion' and focused on three specific cartoons that were published in the 8 February 2006 edition. This showed that the plaintiffs sought to characterize certain cartoons published in *Charlie Hebdo*'s 8 February 2006 edition as an attack on Muslims as a whole rather than merely part of an attempt to mock Muslim extremism. The first of the three cartoons on which the case focused was the previously discussed image from *Jyllands Posten*, supposedly showing the Prophet Muhammad with a bomb in his turban. The second of these was also from *Jyllands Posten* and depicted what appear to be suicide bombers arriving in heaven to be told 'stop, we ran out of virgins'. The final image was Cabu's 'c'est dur d'être aimé par des cons' ['it's hard being loved by jerks'] drawing which had adorned the front cover of *Charlie Hebdo*.

At the time of the court case, there was discussion in the media of the fact that *France-Soir* – the first newspaper in France to have

---

31 'Caricatures: choc des images ou des civilisations?'.

reprinted the *Jyllands Posten* cartoons – was not being sued by the Grande Mosquée de Paris and the UOIF. Dalil Boubakeur, then recteur de la Grande Mosquée de Paris, explained that '*France Soir* était dans un rôle d'information, en rendant compte le premier de ces caricatures' ['*France Soir* was acting in a journalistic role, by being the first to report on these caricatures'].[32] This refusal to see a journalistic motivation for *Charlie Hebdo*'s printing of the *Jyllands Posten* images, and several drawings by their own cartoonists, appears to ignore *Charlie Hebdo*'s argument that their decision was driven by a desire to intervene in debates about freedom of expression. Furthermore, the prosecution's approach does not appear to have acknowledged the presence of several detailed articles about religion and freedom of expression in the 8 February 2006 edition of *Charlie Hebdo*, or the publication's participation in a debate about freedom of expression via texts as well as images. Boubakeur was highly cynical about *Charlie Hebdo*'s motivations for printing the cartoons, arguing that 'en les publiant après coup, dans un numéro spécial, retiré à plusieurs reprises, [il] a choisi d'être dans la provocation à caractère lucratif' ['by publishing them after the event, in a special edition that was reprinted several times, it chose to enter into a lucrative form of provocation'].[33]

From a strategic perspective, it was significant that the plaintiffs in the court case chose only to focus on a small number of the cartoons produced in *Charlie Hebdo*. One of their lawyers, Francis Szpiner, said that this demonstrated that 'nous acceptons que l'on puisse caricaturer le Prophète, mais nous n'acceptons pas leur caractère raciste' ['we accept that one can caricature the Prophet, but we do not accept their racist character'].[34] In other words, their case was not simply constructed in response to a perceived breach of a religious taboo. This latter approach would have been highly unlikely to succeed due to the way in which French laws on the freedom of expression treat religion:

32   Stéphanie Le Bars, 'Caricatures: les organisations musulmanes hésitent à lancer des poursuites systématiques', *Le Monde*, 7 February 2007, <http://abonnes. lemonde.fr/societe/article/2007/02/07/caricatures-les-organisations-musulmanes-hesitent-a-lancer-des-poursuites-systematiques_864552_3224.html?h=15> [accessed 16 March 2017].
33   Le Bars, 'Caricatures'.
34   Le Bars, 'Caricatures'.

la loi n'interdit pas de se moquer d'une religion – la France est laïque, la notion de blasphème n'existe pas en droit (à l'exception de l'Alsace-Moselle) – mais elle interdit en revanche d'appeler à la haine contre les croyants d'une religion ou de faire l'apologie de crimes contre l'humanité.[35]

[the law does not forbid the mocking of a religion; France being secular, the notion of blasphemy does not exist in law (except in Alsace-Moselle). However, France does nevertheless forbid the incitement of hatred against believers of a religion or seeking to excuse crimes against humanity.]

In other words, the Grande Mosquée de Paris and the UOIF appear to have deliberately sought to frame their basis for suing *Charlie Hebdo* within a context shaped by France's Republican political culture. As Max Silverman has noted in a more general context, such a strategy constitutes a crucial step when seeking to voice a grievance about inequality in France.[36] A year before the case against *Charlie Hebdo*, its journalist Caroline Fourest argued that French anti-racist organizations such as le MRAP – who had criticized the publication of the cartoons – were effectively 'en train de transformer l'antiracisme en lutte anti-blasphème' ['in the process of transforming anti-racism into an anti-blasphemy struggle'].[37]

The court case against *Charlie Hebdo* involved many French politicians appearing in court, or providing written statements, in defence of *Charlie Hebdo*. One of the most notable was a written statement that *Charlie Hebdo*'s defence team received from then presidential candidate Nicolas Sarkozy during the trial:

Que votre journal soit caricatural, outrancier et parfois déplacé est un fait incontestable. J'en ai été très souvent la cible privilégiée. Ce qui m'autorise à me faire l'interprète de ceux que l'on croque de façon irrévérencieuse mais qui l'acceptent au nom de la liberté de sourire de tout. Je puis tout à fait comprendre que certains dessins incriminés aient pu heurter les convictions de certains de

---

35   Weston Vauclair and Vauclair, *De Charlie Hebdo à Charlie*, p. 39.
36   Max Silverman, *Deconstructing the Nation: Immigration, Racism and Citizenship in Modern France* (London: Taylor and Francis, 1992), p. 119.
37   Caroline Fourest, 'Les confusions de l'antiracisme', *Charlie Hebdo*, no. 713, 15 February 2006, p. 7.

nos concitoyens musulmans. Le nier serait injuste à leur égard. Ce serait négliger l'authenticité spirituelle qui les anime. Pour autant, je préfère l'excès de caricature à l'absence de caricature. La force d'une société démocratique, comme d'ailleurs la force d'une religion aussi brillante que la religion musulmane, se juge à leur capacité à accepter la critique et l'impertinence, fussent-elles excessives.[38]

[That your publication is caricatural, outrageous and sometimes inappropriate is an undeniable fact. I have very often been its prime target. This allows me to make interpretations from the perspective of those who are depicted in an irreverent manner but who accept it in the name of laughing about everything. I can fully understand that certain incriminating drawings may have offended the convictions of some of our Muslim fellow citizens. To deny it would be unfair to them. It would be to disregard the spiritual authority which animates them. Nevertheless, I prefer the excess of caricature to the absence of caricature. The strength of a democratic society, and indeed the strength of a religion as great as the Muslim religion, is measured by its capacity to accept criticism and impertinence, even when it is excessive.]

Sarkozy's status as a figure regularly mocked by *Charlie Hebdo* made him an unlikely ally, and Weston argues that his reference to 'la liberté de sourire de tout' is close to an endorsement of the 'bête et méchant' approach.[39] Nevertheless, Weston – like others – tempers this by suggesting that Sarkozy's comments appeared to be partially motivated by political opportunism in the run-up to France's 2007 presidential election, a view also expressed by the prosecution lawyer Francis Szpiner during the trial.[40] In his ultimately successful presidential election campaign, Sarkozy sought to present himself as being noticeably different to the incumbent Jacques Chirac. Despite being members of the same centre-right party, Chirac and Sarkozy have had many

38   Quoted in Vauclair Weston and Vauclair, *De Charlie Hebdo à Charlie*, pp. 65–6.
39   Weston, 'Politics, Editorial Cartoons and Bande dessinnée in *Charlie Hebdo*', p. 126.
40   Weston, 'Politics': p. 126. Szpiner is shown making these comments in Daniel Leconte's 2008 documentary film *C'est dur d'être aimé par des cons*.

disagreements and Chirac's previous criticism of *Charlie Hebdo*'s alleged 'provocation' in printing the cartoons of the Prophet Muhammad provided Sarkozy with another opportunity to define himself in opposition to a person whose political office he craved.

When one looks more closely at debates about humour, Sarkozy's attitude towards being the target of ridicule is far from consistent. In 2008 he took legal action against the producers of a Nicolas Sarkozy voodoo doll in an act that demonstrated a lot less capacity to accept mockery than the statement he made in defence of *Charlie Hebdo* in 2007. Furthermore, the management theorist and academic Lionel Bellenger has argued that Chirac has often demonstrated much greater ability than Sarkozy to employ self-depreciating humour to defuse potentially tense situations.[41] However, Chirac's denunciation of *Charlie Hebdo* in 2006 also appears somewhat paradoxical given that he had previously telephoned Anders Fogh Rasmussen, the Danish Prime Minister, to express his solidarity with Denmark at the height of the controversy that stemmed from *Jyllands Posten*'s publication of the cartoons that would later be reprinted in *Charlie Hebdo*. However, it is worth considering that Chirac's criticism of *Charlie Hebdo*'s supposed provocation could be interpreted as a comment about the potential outcome of the publication of the cartoons rather than the motivations for printing them. Given that Chirac talked about the need to 'condamner [...] les provocations manifestes susceptibles d'attiser dangereusement les passions' ['condemn (...) obviously provocative acts liable to dangerously arouse passions'],[42] it seems that he was more concerned about the cartoons' impact on public order rather than merely the notion that their publication breached a taboo. In other words, his comments appear to be motivated by concerns for the French nation as a whole rather than ones that are uniquely relevant to members of a specific religion.

Despite Sarkozy's clear desire to support *Charlie Hebdo* via his statement to the court, his choice of words shows that he also set out to appease Muslims by evoking their 'authenticité spirituelle' ['spiritual authenticity'] and describing Islam as 'une religion si brillante' ['a religion so great']. As Interior Minister in 2003, Sarkozy had played an instrumental role in the creation of the Conseil français du culte

41 Bellenger, *Rire et faire rire*, p. 99.
42 Quoted in Favret-Saada, *Comment produire une crise mondiale*, p. 158.

musulman (CFCM) [French Council of the Muslim Faith], an umbrella organization that facilitated dialogue between the Muslim community in France and the French state.[43] Indeed, footage in Daniel Leconte's documentary *C'est dur d'être aimé par des cons* [*It's hard to be loved by jerks*] – of the day of the trial on which Sarkozy's statement in support of *Charlie Hebdo* was read out – suggests that some Muslim groups considered withdrawing from the CFCM due to Sarkozy's stance. In this film, Philippe Val argues that Dalil Boubakeur – then president of the CFCM and recteur of the Grande Mosquée de Paris – did not actually want the trial against *Charlie Hebdo* to take place as he is mainly a representative of 'musulman laïcs' ['secular Muslims'], who accept the principle of the separation between state and religion in France. However, we also see Abdallah Zekri of the CFCM's Observatoire sur l'islamophobie [Islamophobia Monitoring Group] argue that their court case was important due to what he saw as *Charlie Hebdo*'s attempt to portray all Muslims as 'cons' ['jerks'] and the Prophet Muhammad as a terrorist. In addition to the fact that such reasoning can easily be countered for reasons previously stated in this chapter, it could also be said that advancing this type of argument is potentially counterproductive. The French-Algerian journalist and writer Mohamed Sifaoui was critical of what he termed 'les représentants officiels de l'islam de France qui créent eux-mêmes l'amalgame entre idéologie islamiste et religion musulmane' ['the official representatives of Islam in France are themselves creating the amalgam between Islamist ideology and the Muslim religion'].[44] In other words, Sifaoui appeared to be effectively endorsing Mireille Rosello's argument that alluding to an existing stereotype – which she terms a 'meta-utterance' – can effectively give a degree of credence to the idea originally evoked via the stereotype.[45]

The history of *Charlie Hebdo*'s brand of anarchic and anti-establishment humour was a key issue during the 2007 court case. In court, its lawyer Richard Malka cited examples of *Charlie Hebdo* cartoons

43   Although the term 'Muslim community' is often used to collectively refer to Muslims in France, it is important to remember that there are various different groups within France's 'Muslim community' that are defined by types of belief and nationality/ethnicity. This has sometimes created divisions within the CFCM.

44   Sifaoui, *L'Affaire des caricatures*, p. 115.

45   Rosello, *Declining the Stereotype*, p. 36. See discussion of stereotypes on pp. 13–14 of the introduction to this book.

mocking Catholicism, Buddhism and Sikhism in order to ask what sort of 'égalité de traitement' ['equality of treatment'] the Grande Mosquée de Paris [Great Mosque of Paris] was seeking. He pursued this argument to suggest that the institution was not actually acting in a manner that was as consistent with Republican universalism as they were claiming, and that their demands were tantamount to requesting 'un régime de faveur' ['preferential treatment'].[46] The judge in the court case found *Charlie Hebdo* not guilty of breaching French anti-racism laws. In so doing, his verdict underlined that 'il ne faut pas confondre injure (condamnable) et blasphème (libre)' [one must not confuse slander (punishable by law) and blasphemy (permitted)'].[47] In other words, the judge effectively ruled that *Charlie Hebdo* had not insulted Muslims via the three cartoons that were the subject of the court case. His words imply that the cartoons could be potentially perceived as blasphemous, but that this was not in itself enough for them to be considered deliberately insulting towards Muslims as a whole. When this judgement was upheld on appeal in 2008, the judge announcing the verdict found that *Charlie Hebdo*'s decision to print the three cartoons that were singled out in the court case formed part of a legitimate journalistic endeavour.[48] The appeal judge thereby appeared to implicitly reject the plaintiffs' argument that the caricatures printed in *Charlie Hebdo* could not be treated in the same way as those that had appeared in a variety of European newspapers in February 2006. Indeed, Jane Weston suggests that the verdict of Jean-Claude Magendie actually went further than this as he 'situated the right to laugh within the broader accepted tradition of provocative satire in France'.[49] In other words, the provocative approach of *Charlie Hebdo* that had been criticized by Chirac was effectively branded as a perfectly acceptable symbol of long-held French values by the judge.

---

46   These arguments are cited in some detail in Daniel Leconte's documentary film *C'est dur d'être aimé par des cons* [*It's hard to be loved by jerks*].
47   Pascal Ory, *Ce que dit Charlie: treize leçons d'histoire* (Paris: Gallimard, 2016), p. 103.
48   Parts of his judgement are cited in the closing moments of Daniel Leconte's documentary *C'est dur d'être aimé par des cons* [*It's hard to be loved by jerks*], including the following words; 'les caricatures poursuivies, comme toutes celles qui figurant dans ce numéro [du 8 février 2006] de l'hebdomadaire, ont, par leur publication, participé au débat d'intérêt général sur la liberté d'expression'.
49   Weston, *'Bête et méchant'*, p. 126.

2011 firebombings of *Charlie Hebdo*'s offices

Although *Charlie Hebdo*'s right to mock religions such as Islam was endorsed by the 2007 court case discussed above, the events of early November 2011 demonstrated that the publication's decision to mock the Prophet Muhammad had also brought about potentially fatal consequences. Following an announcement that the Prophet Muhammad was to be the guest editor of a special edition, *Charlie Hebdo*'s offices were destroyed by a firebomb attack in the early hours of 2 November 2011, the very day that the edition in question was published. This was a much more rapid and violent response compared to when *Charlie Hebdo* depicted the Prophet Muhammad in 2006. Indeed, the 2011 attack took place before the edition in question (number 1011) had started to be sold.

It is also significant that the 2 November 2011 edition of *Charlie Hebdo* – supposedly guest edited by the Prophet Muhammad – was printed in a different context to the February 2006 edition that led to the court case discussed above. Whereas the February 2006 edition was part of a concerted attempt at a French and international level to raise questions about freedom of expression and show solidarity with *Jyllands Posten*, *Charlie Hebdo* was to a much greater extent acting on its own in November 2006. Indeed, its approach was more gratuitous and not backed up by quite as many serious articles that established a context for its strategy in the same way as the 'c'est dur d'être aimé par des cons' ['it's hard to be loved by jerks'] edition of February 2006 had done. The 2 November 2011 edition thus appears to provide a clearer example of the 'bête et méchant' spirit of *Charlie Hebdo*, which may in part have been a consequence of Philippe Val's departure and his replacement as editor by Charb.[50] The cover of edition 1011 of *Charlie Hebdo* featured

---

50   Following Philippe Val's departure to become director of radio station France Inter in 2011, it could be argued that he was technically replaced as editor of *Charlie Hebdo* by Charb and Riss due to the precise names of the posts concerned. Val had been 'directeur de la publication et de la rédaction' ['publication director and managing editor'] in February 2006, whilst in November 2011 Charb was 'directeur de la publication' ['publication director'] and Riss was 'directeur de la rédaction' ['managing editor']. Since the 5 January 2015 attacks that killed Charb and several of his colleagues, Riss has become the 'directeur de publication' ['publication director'] and 'directeur de la rédaction' ['managing editor']. Gérard Biard remains 'rédacteur en chef' ['editor-in-chief'],

a picture of the Prophet Muhammad exclaiming '100 coups de fouet si vous n'êtes pas morts de rire!' ['100 lashes if you are not dying of laughter!'] and the masthead featuring the words *Charlie Hebdo* was partially obscured by an overlaid version on a red background featuring the temporary title *Charia Hebdo*. The page immediately inside the front cover is entitled 'Charia madame' and is filled with a series of cartoons that provide fashion and lifestyle advice for female Muslims, many of which are characterized by very dark humour. One cartoon depicts what appears to be a woman buried by rocks painting her nails, and includes the slogan 'des ongles parfaits pour un coup de lapidation' ['perfect nails for a lapidation']. Another entitled 'mode spécial femmes battues' ['beaten women fashion special'] features advice on how women can adopt 'le style "racaille"' ['"chav" style'] in order to go about their daily life in a discreet manner after having been victims of violence. A mock competition encourages Muslim women to cut out their hymen and send it to 'Charia Madame, jeu concours, Tripoli, Libye' ['Charia Madame, competitions, Tripoli, Libya'] in order to potentially win a spa holiday in the Dead Sea.

The third page features an editorial attributed to Mohamed Rassoul Allah (literally, 'Muhammad messenger of God'), whose contact e-mail address is listed as 'leprophete@charliehebdo.fr'.[51] Much of the article discusses elections in Tunisia and it includes a picture of a pipe-smoking Prophet Muhammad and the phrase 'il n'y a de dieu que Dieu (sinon, c'est le bordel)' ['there is no God but God (otherwise it's chaos)']. Several of the ensuing pages include a picture of the Prophet and his comments on topics such as the *Parti socialiste* leadership elections, declarations by right-wing politician Christine Boutin, and the Israel-Palestine conflict. An article by regular *Charlie Hebdo* contributor and paramedic Patrick Pelloux discusses laïcité [French secularism] in French hospitals and, in particular, an incident in which a Muslim man tried to prevent his wife being treated by a male doctor.[52] Although certain articles – such as one by Zineb el Rhazoui entitled 'Le Guide Routard de la

a post he occupied at the time of the editions featuring the Prophet Muhammad in both February 2006 and November 2011.

51   Mohamed Rassoul Allah, 'L'Édito de Mahomet', *Charlie Hebdo*, no. 1011, 2 November 2011, p. 3.

52   Patrick Pelloux, 'En route vers le moyen âge!', *Charlie Hebdo*, no. 1011 2 November 2011, p. 7.

Charia' ['The Rough Guide to Charia'] – focus on the influence of Sharia law in predominantly Muslim countries of North Africa and the Middle East, there is also a thread running through this edition of *Charlie Hebdo* that is critical of conservative Catholicism in France.[53] The aforementioned cartoon, in which the Prophet Muhammad mocks Christine Boutin, includes the slogan 'on critique l'islam, mais chez les cathos, c'est pas mieux: regardez la gueule de Boutin, c'est une charia à elle toute seule' ['Islam is criticized but with Catholics things aren't any better: look at the face of Boutin, it's a form of Charia in itself']. Christine Boutin is a staunchly conservative centre-right politician who in 2009 left the post of Ministre du Logement et de la Ville [Minister for Accommodation and Cities] in order to found the *Parti chrétien-démocrate* [Christian Democratic Party]. She has talked about the importance of Catholic values and has been a critic of civil partnerships and gay marriage, and French satirists regularly portray her as being not just being an outspoken conservative but also being somewhat nonsensical. Given the importance of the separation between the state and religion established by French laïcité [French secularism], it is somewhat paradoxical for a government minister to form a party that publicly seeks to use Christian values as a basis for policy making. Next to the cartoon that mocks Christine Boutin is an article by Jean-Yves Camus that is critical of conservative Catholics in France. In the article, entitled 'Cathos et musulmans intégristes main dans la main' ['Catholic and Muslim fundamentalists, hand in hand'], he is critical of French Catholics who protested against a supposedly blasphemous play by Romeo Castellucci that was taking place in Paris.[54]

One of the most significant elements that emerged during public discussions of *Charlie Hebdo* following the firebombing of their offices in November 2011 was an apparent softening in attitudes towards the publication from leading representatives of French Muslims. Their interventions in public debates, especially in current affairs discussion shows on French television and radio, struck a somewhat different note compared to their appearances at the time of the court case brought against *Charlie Hebdo* in 2007. Indeed, the events of November 2011 did

---

53   Zineb El Rhazoui, 'Le Guide Routard de la Charia', *Charlie Hebdo*, no. 1011, 2 November 2011, p. 11.
54   Jean-Yves Camus, 'Cathos et musulmans intégristes main dans la main', *Charlie Hebdo*, no. 1011, 2 November 2011, p. 6.

not see *Charlie Hebdo* and French Muslim groups compete with each other to claim that their stance was the one that more truly reflected French Republican values. Indeed, Mohammed Moussaoui (head of the CFCM) stated that the *Charia Hebdo* edition 'wasn't of the same order' as the 8 February 2006 edition of *Charlie Hebdo* in terms of how it depicted the Prophet Muhammad and that he felt that the earlier edition had been 'a lot more violent'.[55] Similarly, the CFCM's deputy president Chems-Eddine Hafiz said in a radio discussion shortly after the 2011 attack on the *Charlie Hebdo* offices that he did not see the 2 November 2011 edition of *Charlie Hebdo* as being controversial.[56] During the same discussion, he also pointed out that the *Charia Hebdo* edition of *Charlie Hebdo* focused mainly on elections in Libya and Tunisia, and that it only became relevant to French Muslims after the *Charlie Hebdo* offices in Paris were destroyed in the firebomb attack. Later on, Hafiz argued that caricaturing the Prophet Muhammad was not a problem in itself and indeed not mentioned in the Koran. In a nuanced discussion of the issue, he argued that people were free to caricature the Prophet Muhammad but that it was something that he, as a Muslim, would not do as it was incompatible with principles that had formed the basis of his 'tradition' and 'éducation' as a Muslim. Although Hafiz argued that there was 'un climat d'Islamophobie' in France, he did suggest that it was inflamed by *Charlie Hebdo*. Furthermore, he engaged in a warm handshake with *Charlie Hebdo* cartoonist Luz, the other main guest in the discussion.

The spirit of reconciliation displayed by Luz and Chems-Eddine Hafiz on French television appeared to be visually represented in the front cover of the 9 November 2011 edition of *Charlie Hebdo*, the first to be published after the firebomb attack. The cover showed an imam and a *Charlie Hebdo* journalist passionately kissing in a manner that is reminiscent of the embrace shared by Leonid Brezhnev and Erich Honecker at celebrations to mark the thirtieth anniversary of the creation of the German Democratic Republic in 1979.[57] The

55   Angélique Chrisafis, 'French Magazine Offices Petrol-Bombed After It Prints Muhammad Cartoon', *The Guardian*, 2 November 2011, https://www.theguardian.com/world/2011/nov/02/french-magazine-bomb-muhammad-cartoon [accessed 27 March 2017].

56   Comments were made as part of an item entitled 'Le face à face: islam, Charlie a-t-il forcé le trait?' that was broadcast on France 5's programme *Médias, le magazine* on 6 November 2011.

57   A painting of this moment by Dmitri Vrubel can be found on the East Side

9 November 2011 edition of *Charlie Hebdo* sought to justify more explicitly the publication of the cartoons in the previous week's *Charia Hebdo* edition. In a defiant article entitled 'Même pas mal' ['Didn't even hurt'], Charb argued that being non-Muslims means that 'nous avons le droit de représenter Mahomet, de manger du porc et de rigoler de tout et de n'importe quoi' ['we have the right to depict Muhammad, to eat pork and to laugh about anything and everything'] before also observing 'nous ne sommes pas non plus chrétiens, ni juifs, ni bouddhistes' ['we are also not Christians, nor Jews, nor Buddhists']. Charb also empathized with French Muslims as he argued that they were 'les premières victimes' ['the first victims'] of the attack as 'il faut attendre à ce que cette agression soit instrumentalisée par l'extrême droite pour jeter le discrédit sur tous les musulmans' ['one must expect this attack to be exploited by the far right to discredit all Muslims'].[58]

There are many reasons why the 7 January 2015 attack on *Charlie Hebdo* was very different to the firebombing of 2011, and these are not limited to the scale of injuries and loss of life. Whereas the 2011 attacks appear to have been a direct and rapid response to a decision by *Charlie Hebdo* to have an edition in which the Prophet Muhammad is portrayed as the 'guest editor', the 7 January 2015 attack does not appear to have been a response to a specific edition of the publication. Rather, it appears to have been a consequence of *Charlie Hebdo* – and some of its journalists such as Charb – having been the subject of a fatwa following the 'C'est dur d'être aimé par des cons' edition of 2006. In the years between 2011 and 2015, *Charlie Hebdo* remained unafraid of depicting the Prophet Muhammad, and in 2013 published a special edition in book format that provided an illustrated story of *La Vie de Mahomet* [*The Life of Muhammad*].[59] Following violent events in Egypt, the front cover of the 10 July 2013 edition of *Charlie Hebdo* (number 1099) showed bullets being fired at a bearded Muslim in traditional dress who is seeking to hold up a Koran to protect himself. The headline on the cover that accompanied the cartoon was 'Le Coran c'est de la merde, ça n'arrête pas les balles' ['The Koran is shit, it doesn't stop bullets'].

Gallery, an almost mile-long section of the Berlin Wall that remains preserved and is adorned by pictures and words that celebrate freedom.

58   Charb, 'Même pas mal', *Charlie Hebdo*, no. 1012, 9 November 2011, p. 3.
59   Charb and Zineb, *La Vie de Mahomet* (Paris: Les Échappés, 2013).

The 2015 attacks against *Charlie Hebdo*

The shock and horror felt by many people in France and around the world following the January 2015 attacks on *Charlie Hebdo* that left twelve people dead generated much discussion of what the publication represented. However, the focus on the consequences of the attacks – the loss of life, numbers of people injured, subsequent attacks in the following days – was not mirrored by an intense focus on what *Charlie Hebdo* represented as a publication prior to the fatal events of January 2015. Freedom of expression, social tensions within France, and the threat of terrorism were much more widely discussed than the brand of humour that characterizes *Charlie Hebdo*. In other words, the ultimately fatal consequences of *Charlie Hebdo*'s depictions of the Prophet Muhammad received a lot more attention than the ethos and type of humour that provides the context for its portrayal of the Prophet Muhammad, and indeed many other religious or political figures. Jane Weston Vauclair and David Vauclair's *De Charlie Hebdo à #Charlie: enjeux, histoires, perspectives* [*From Charlie Hebdo to #Charlie: issues, stories, perspectives*] stands out as a rare example of a book about *Charlie Hebdo* – published shortly after the 2015 attacks – that provides detailed analysis of its humour and history in addition to seeking to examine the significance and symbolism of the shootings and their aftermath. The vast majority of the other works published about *Charlie Hebdo* at this time – including many academic articles[60] – focused on freedom of expression rather than humour and take January 2015 as a starting point for exploring wider issues about French society. They often do so without seeking to understand or assess the content, values, and humour of *Charlie Hebdo*. A prime example of one such publication is the collective volume *The Event of Charlie Hebdo: Imaginaries of Freedom and Control*, edited by Alessandro Zagato, containing articles by a group of Norway-based researchers. The reference to 'the event of *Charlie Hebdo*' in the title is quite revealing and indeed symptomatic of how *Charlie Hebdo* appears to have become, for many, shorthand for the fatal shootings that occurred at their offices on 7 January 2015 rather than a publication whose history and key editions need to be analysed in greater depth. In other words, the shootings of January 2015 are often

---

60   See, for example, those that featured in edition 26.3 of the journal *French Cultural Studies* that was published in 2016.

a starting point for looking outwards towards wider issues rather than inwards to analyse the history and evolution of *Charlie Hebdo* since its inception. The articles in Zagato's volume primarily focus on broad debates about political theory and philosophy, seemingly seeking to make the relevance of *Charlie Hebdo* clear to those working outside of fields such as French studies, media studies or sociology, and indeed people who may not be familiar with France. Edward M. Iacobucci and Stephen J. Toope adopt a similar approach in their edited volume *After the Paris Attacks: Responses in Canada, Europe, and Around the Globe.*[61] In his introduction to *After Charlie Hebdo: Terror, Racism and Free Speech*, Gavan Titley explains that the edited volume's intention is to focus on the attacks as a 'political and communicative event' and distinguishes between *Charlie Hebdo* (the publication itself) and 'Charlie Hebdo' (the 2015 attacks on the offices of the publication, and what they have come to symbolize).[62]

In *Ce que dit Charlie: treize leçons d'histoire* [*What Charlie represents: thirteen history lessons*], Pascal Ory explores reactions to the events of January 2015 from a historical perspective, and also examines what the aftermath of the attacks shows about French society and its core values. There are also many works that have sought to analyse the meanings behind the #JeSuisCharlie hashtag that was widely used on social media following the fatal attacks of 7 January 2015. Some works have used #JeSuisCharlie in order to pay tribute to the victims of the attacks, and these include books featuring brief reflections and short essays by a diverse range of collaborators and published as early as February 2015.[63] In addition, other works have sought to explore the nuances of competing uses of #JeSuisCharlie, and indeed why some might not want to declare #JeSuisCharlie. Prime examples include Michel Duvivier's *Je suis Charlie…?* [*I am Charlie…?*] and Michel Collon's *Je suis ou je ne suis pas Charlie?* [*I am or I am not Charlie?*]. Furthermore, there

---

61   Edward M. Iacobucci and Stephen J. Toope (eds), *After the Paris Attacks: Responses in Canada, Europe and Around the Globe* (Toronto/Buffalo/London: University of Toronto Press, 2015).
62   Gavan Titley, 'Becoming Symbolic: from *Charlie Hebdo* to 'Charlie Hebdo', in Gavin Titley, Des Freedman, Gholam Khiabany and Aurélien Mondon (eds), *After Charlie Hebdo: Terror, Racism and Free Speech* (London: Zed Books, 2017), p. 2.
63   Examples include the collectively produced titles *Je suis Charlie: liberté, j'écris tes mots* and *Nous sommes Charlie: 60 écrivains pour la liberté d'expression*.

are works that have sought to challenge the supposed universality and consensuality of the #JeSuisCharlie sentiment and argue that behind it lies much more ambiguity than may first appear. The sociologist Emmanuel Todd's *Qui est Charlie? Sociologie d'une crise religieuse [Who is Charlie? The sociology of a religious crisis]* adopts this approach, and indeed provoked much debate – and a degree of criticism – following its publication.[64] Works such as the collective publication *Je suis Charlie, ainsi suit-il... [I am Charlie, so it follows that...]* have also set out reasons to challenge sentiments underpinning the #JeSuisCharlie sentiment.

The #JeSuisCharlie sentiment is difficulty to analyse due to the tension in the paradox between its status as a hashtag used many millions of times on social media following the attacks, and the fact that *Charlie Hebdo* had a weekly print run of approximately 60,000 copies prior to the January 2015 attacks. In other words, the vast majority of those who used the hashtag #JeSuisCharlie during the early months of 2015 were not regular readers of the publication. As Michel Duvivier observes, a great many of those who took to the streets at the national demonstration of 11 January 2015 had taken little interest in the publication prior to the attacks of 7 January 2015.[65] Teasing out the meaning, or meanings, of #JeSuisCharlie is similarly complex. For example, one could characterize #JeSuisCharlie as an expression of condolence and sympathy towards those affected by the fatal shootings that took the lives of twelve people in and around the *Charlie Hebdo* offices. One could also go further and suggest that #JeSuisCharlie implies an endorsement of the values that *Charlie Hebdo* represented and its at times provocative 'bête et méchant' brand of humour. However, this latter approach would not be in keeping with *Charlie Hebdo*'s circulation figures prior to the attacks or the way that their decisions to depict the Prophet Muhammad in the decade prior to the January 2015 attacks often divided opinion in France.

In his work *Je suis Charlie...?*, Michel Duvivier identifies six quite different reasons why someone might decide to declare #JeSuisCharlie.

---

64   As Weston Vauclair and Vauclair note, Todd's methodologies for seeking to analyse the composition of the crowds who were present at demonstrations following the attacks of January 2015 were criticized as being unreliable by several fellow sociologists. See: Weston Vauclair and Vauclair, *De Charlie Hebdo à Charlie*, p. 23.

65   Michel Duvivier, *Je suis Charlie...?* (Paris: CreateSpace, 2015), p. 97.

The first four of these are respectively 'pour [se] lever contre la barbarie aveugle', 'pour defender la liberté d'expression', 'pour défendre la liberté de presse' and 'parce que je n'ai "même pas peur"' ['to stand up against blind brutality', 'to defend the freedom of expression', 'to defend the freedom of the press' and 'because I am "not even scared"'].[66] This group of motivations brings together sentiments of defiance that are based around universal themes, whereas the next two reasons he mentions for stating #JeSuisCharlie are more specific; they are respectively 'parce que je suis juif' ['because I am Jewish'] and 'parce que je suis musulman' ['because I am Muslim'].[67] Duvivier explains that the first of these last two explanations is due to four Jewish shoppers being killed by a gunman during the hostage-taking at the Hyper Cacher supermarket in the Port de Vincennes area of Paris two days after the attack on the offices of *Charlie Hebdo*.[68] He also notes that the twelve people killed in the attack on *Charlie Hebdo* included Ahmed Merabet, a Muslim police officer who was on duty near the offices of the satirical newspaper at the time of the attack. Duvivier further observes that Muslim organizations in France were among those who appealed for their members to attend the national demonstration on 11 January 2015 to pay tribute to those killed in the attacks and 'affirmer leur désir de vivre ensemble dans le respect des valeurs de la République' ['asserts their desire for social cohesion in accordance with the values of the Republic'].[69] As Marie-France Etchegoin et al. have observed, some banners at the 11 January demonstrations sought to simultaneously express solidarity with different groups impacted by the fatal attacks of the week before via slogans such as 'je suis Charlie, je suis flic, je suis juif' ['I am Charlie, I am a cop, I am a Jew'].[70]

The national demonstration in Paris on 11 January 2015 brought with it many paradoxes, not least because it involved many members of the French and international political elite paying tribute to a publication which has long been characterized by its tendency to viciously mock political leaders in France and elsewhere. Although celebrating values such as freedom of the press was one of the

---

66   Duvivier, *Je suis Charlie…?* pp. 16, 18, 45, 50.
67   Duvivier, *Je suis Charlie…?* pp. 52, 56.
68   Duvivier, *Je suis Charlie…?* pp. 52–5.
69   Duvivier, *Je suis Charlie…?* pp. 56, 62.
70   Marie-France Etchegoin et al., *Et soudain ils ne riaent plus* (Paris: Éditions des Arènes, 2016), p. 378.

motivations for the demonstration, the leaders present included several from countries who are not associated with freedom of the press and freedom of expression.[71] Ultimately, it appears that a shared desire to defend somewhat abstract values following a series of horrific attacks seems to have been one of the prime reasons why the 11 January 2015 demonstration brought together so many people from differing walks of life.[72] Pascal Ory notes it has been estimated that 81% of those present at the 11 January 2015 demonstration in Paris were primarily focused on the 'défense des valeurs fondamentales de la République et de la liberté d'expression' ['defence of fundamental values of the Republic and of freedom of expression'].[73] Thus, an attack on a subversive and somewhat niche satirical publication created a situation that led many to celebrate or re-assert the values on which the French state is founded and which serve as the basis of government for the political elite. Although it is clear that *Charlie Hebdo* has a long history of defending freedom of expression and freedom of the press, the support that its efforts have received from politicians and the general public has been far from consistent and its methods have often divided opinion. As Weston Vaulair and Vauclair observe, it is precisely when one focuses on *Charlie Hebdo*'s humour as opposed to its perceived wider symbolic importance that much of the apparent consensus surrounding the demonstration of 11 January 2015 risks evaporating:

> Les questions de ce que représente *Charlie Hebdo* et de l'usage de l'humour vont rapidement déchirer une unanimité qui se reconnaissait dans une douleur et des valeurs communes mais pas forcément dans le journal lui-même. Si une majorité des Français se retrouvent dans les valeurs mises en avant par l'équipe du journal satirique, une minorité en revanche apprécie le style

---

71   See: Alain Gresh, 'D'étranges défenseurs de la liberté de la presse à la manifestation pour "Charlie Hebdo"', *Le Monde Diplomatie*, 12 January 2015, http://blog.mondediplo.net/2015–01–12-D-etranges-defenseurs-de-la-liberte-de-la-presse [accessed 29 March 2017].

72   It should be noted that Emmanuel Todd's *Qui est Charlie? Sociologie d'une crise religieuse* is a work that questions the extent to which French society as a whole – especially working-class people and/or those from the banlieues – were represented among those who attended such demonstrations. However, as previously mentioned, several of his fellow sociologists have in turned called into question the methods used by Todd in order to draw these conclusions.

73   Ory, *Ce que dit Charlie*, p. 135.

d'humour et même l'ensemble des convictions soutenues par l'hebdomadaire. La problématique de l'humour ne simplifie pas les débats, bien au contraire, car être drôle est une expérience plus subjective et contextuelle que l'on croit souvent.[74]

[Questions as to what *Charlie Hebdo* represents and the use of humour quickly destroy a unanimity which emerged from pain and common values but not necessarily the publication itself. Although a majority of French people identify with the values displayed by the satirical publication's writers and cartoonists, it is nevertheless a minority that appreciates its style of humour and the entirety of the convictions held by the weekly publication. The question of humour does not simplify the debates, because being funny is a more subjective and context-based experience than is often believed.]

Although this distinction between those who agreed with the values projected by *Charlie Hebdo* and those who identified with its brand of humour is in many ways valid, it is possible to argue that is hard to dissociate *Charlie Hebdo*'s values and its brand of humour. Indeed, the methods it has used to defend freedom of expression, freedom of the press and laïcité [French secularism] have often been characterized by recourse to provocative humour when representing religion, or indeed depicting many other topics. In other words, many of those who expressed their solidarity with *Charlie Hebdo* following the January 2015 appear to have evoked values that *they* associated with the publication rather than necessarily how *Charlie Hebdo*'s founders and journalists would necessarily seek to define the publication's ethos and modus operandi. Re-asserting the importance of Republican values and national unity became a political imperative in France following the attacks in January 2015, and both President François Hollande and Prime Minister Emmanuel Valls saw their popularity ratings rise significantly in the week following the attacks.[75]

Given *Charlie Hebdo*'s long tradition of ignoring taboos and demonstrating an at times dark and provocative brand of humour,

74   Weston Vauclair and Vauclair, *De Charlie Hebdo à Charlie*, p. 78.
75   Duvivier notes that an Ifop-Fiducial poll carried out on 16–17 January 2015 saw a 21% rise in the approval rating for François Hollande and a 17% increase in that of Emmanuel Valls. Duvivier, *Je suis Charlie...?* p. 75.

many aspects of the treatment of humour in France in the immediate aftermath of the January 2015 attacks seem somewhat paradoxical. Although many people had expressed the notion #JeSuisCharlie, and *Charlie Hebdo* has long been characterized by a desire to laugh about anything and everything, many in France did not seem to endorse the idea that 'on peut rire de tout' ['one can laugh about everything'], despite the regular extolling of the virtues of freedom of expression. Indeed, those who sought to make light of the terrorist attacks – humorously or otherwise – via social media risked facing charged with 'l'apologie du terrorisme' ['excusing terrorism']. In February 2015, a pupil in Seine-Saint-Denis was punished by his school for laughing and saying 'Ahmed Coulibaly', combining the name of the policeman (Ahmed Merabet) killed in the *Charlie Hebdo* attacks on 7 January and the name of the gunman (Amedy Coulibaly) who carried out the hostage-taking and killed four people at the Hyper Cacher store at Porte de Vincennes on 9 January 2015 and killed a policewoman in Montrouge the previous day. The pupil was ordered to write the phrase 'on ne rit pas de choses sérieuses' ['one does not laugh about serious things'] in his school book.[76] What is particularly paradoxical about this phrase is that it is the antithesis of the 'bête et méchant' spirit of *Charlie Hebdo*. The punishment constitutes a dogmatic and arbitrary attempt to police humour, further elements showing it to be at odds with the values on which *Charlie Hebdo* is based. The idea of not laughing at 'de choses sérieuses' ['serious things'] also ignores humour's potential to relieve tension by making light of serious matters, and could be seen as dismissive of any attempts at satire. Furthermore, there is in reality a long tradition of laughing at deeply serious matters and indeed such a practice can be a form of coping strategy. Peter McGraw and Joel Warner argue that this is a key function of many jokes about the Holocaust, and note that Freud argues that humour has a role to play in releasing tension when people are faced with stark scenarios.[77]

The emotion felt in France following the *Charlie Hebdo* shootings was such that many people who regularly use humour to comment on news stories struggled to find a means of expressing their feelings about the events. Several humorous topical shows on French television did not

76　Luca Salza, 'La République mise à nue par sa satire, même', in: Collectif (eds), *Je suis Charlie. Ainsi suit-il...* (Paris: L'Harmattan, 2015), pp. 96–7.
77　McGraw and Warner, *The Humor Code*, pp. 163–4.

air as normal on the day of, or days immediately following, the attacks on *Charlie Hebdo*. These included TF1's *C'est Canteloup*, presented by the well-known comedian and impressionist Nicolas Canteloup, and Canal Plus's *La Revue de presse de Cathérine et Liliane* [*Catherine and Liliane's newspaper review*].[78] The latter show is a mock newspaper review segment of *Le Petit Journal* presented by two male comedians – Alex Lutz and Bruno Sanches – who do so dressed up as female secretaries. On 9 January 2015, the two comedians appeared from behind copies of the 7 January 2015 edition of *Charlie Hebdo* without their make-up before stating 'on est tous Charlie' ['we are all Charlie'].

However, the more acerbic Canal Plus show *Les Guignols* was broadcast as usual on the evening of 7 January 2015 and focused exclusively on the *Charlie Hebdo* attacks. The latex puppet of legendary French newsreader Patrick Poivre d'Arvor (regularly known as PDDA) began the day's show with a health warning provided by a picture of the 7 January 2015 edition of *Charlie Hebdo* to which was attached a label stating 'dessiner tue' ['drawing kills'].[79] The PPDA puppet then dedicated the evening's edition of *Les Guignols* to *Charlie Hebdo* before a series of short items mocked various consequences of the attacks. The puppet of Prime Minister Emmanuel Valls appeared at one stage to announce that the level of security alert under France's *plan Vigipirate* [*National Security Alert System*] would be increased beyond the maximum level of *attentat* [attack alert] to the (fictitious) levels of *sauve qui peut* [save what you can] and then potentially *Chacun pour soi, moi, je m'en fous j'ai une bagnole* [Everyone for themselves, me, I couldn't care less, I've got a car]. Towards the end of the five-minute long show, a puppet of the Prophet Muhammad comments on the fact that the Kouachi brothers who attacked *Charlie Hebdo* shouted 'le prophet est vengé' ['the Prophet has been avenged'] after leaving the newspaper's offices, and indeed the Prophet distances himself from the terrorists. After this denunciation, he is joined on the cloud from which he is speaking by a puppet of the cartoonist Cabu, who was among those killed on 7 January. Cabu introduces himself to the Prophet before

---

78   Pierre Lefébure, 'Rire malgré tout: comment les humoristes d'actualité font face au choc', in Pierre Lefébrure and Claire Sécail (eds), *Le Défi Charlie: les médias à l'épreuve des attentats* (Paris: Lemieux Éditeur, 2016), pp. 63–4.
79   The label in question was very similar in style to those stating 'fumer tue' that appear on packets of cigarettes sold in France.

saying 'on est avec les potes, on peut rentrer?' ['I'm here with friends, can we come in?']. The Prophet's begrudging yet accommodating response is 'franchement, vous vous êtes bien foutu de ma gueule avec vos dessins mais soyez les bienvenus' ['frankly, you really took the piss out of me with your drawings but welcome in'].[80] In a period of just over a week following the *Charlie Hebdo* attacks, six different episodes of *Les Guignols* featured sketches in which *Charlie Hebdo* cartoonists were shown sharing jokes with God in heaven, and the 8 January 2015 episode included a sketch in which Paris Saint-Germain's combative Swedish striker Zlatan Ibrahimovic declares that he will eliminate Daesh.[81]

Les Guignols' use of humour to make light of a serious situation provided a tribute to *Charlie Hebdo* that mirrored the publication's rebellious sense of humour and the concept of 'mauvais goût revendiqué' that has been discussed by Vauclair Weston and Vauclair.[82] The cover of Weston Vauclair and Vauclair's book *De Charlie Hebdo à #Charlie: enjeux, histoires, perspectives* is itself adorned with a cartoon from the website of the comic *Fluide Glacial* that was published in response to the attacks. The image depicts Charb, Cabu, Wolinski, and Tignous in fits of laughter as a fortune-teller looking into a crystal ball announces the following premonition:

> Je vois que vous allez être assassinés par des terroristes... En votre mémoire, le glas de Notre-Dame sonnera, il y aura un grand défilé avec Hollande, Valls, Sarkozy, Copé, Merkel, Cameron et même Netanyahou... Il y aura des drapeaux tricolores et on chantera la 'Marseillaise'... On proposera de vous Panthéoniser, le Nasdaq et l'Académie française diront 'je suis Charlie' et le pape priera pour vous.

> [I see that you will be assassinated by terrorists... In your honour, the bells of Notre-Dame will ring out, there will be a large procession with Hollande, Valls, Sarkozy, Copé, Merkel, Cameron and event Netanyahu... There will be tricolour flags

---

80   This is far from the only time that a puppet of the Prophet Muhammad has appeared on *Les Guignols*, and the programme's depiction of him appears not to have provoked a great deal of debate in France.

81   Lefébure, 'Rire malgré tout', pp. 68, 70.

82   See: Vauclair Weston and Vauclair, *De Charlie Hebdo à Charlie*, p. 90.

and the 'Marseillaise' will be sung... It will be suggested that you are interred in the Pantheon, the Nasdaq Stock Market and the Académie française will say 'I am Charlie' and the Pope will pray for you.]

Conclusions: where the 2015 attack on *Charlie Hebdo* leaves French humour

The aforementioned quotation from a *Fluide Glacial* cartoon encapsulates the highly paradoxical nature of many reactions to the *Charlie Hebdo* shootings, and representations of the publication following the shootings. A niche and subversive publication noted for its highly provocative humour was being not just commemorated but also celebrated by much of mainstream French society, and indeed many of the sorts of figures that it had been unafraid to viciously mock. A relatively marginal publication had become a focus of national grief, and a powerful symbol of the values on which the French Republic was based in the minds of many people.

Following the shootings, there has been considerable discussion in France about the limits of humour and/or freedom of expression and whether or not it is true that 'on peut rire de tout'. These are issues that there is not sufficient space to discuss in depth here, but that will be explored in several stages in the remainder of this book. One of the most emotive questions that has been posed following the events of January 2015 concerns whether or not *Charlie Hebdo* acted irresponsibly in depicting the Prophet Muhammad and thereby provoking the train of events that led to the fatal attacks. However, much discussion of the actions of *Charlie Hebdo* has failed to acknowledge the anarchic nature of a publication that has taken pride in defining itself – or citing criticism of itself – as a 'journal irresponsable' and has been described as exhibiting 'un mauvais goût revendiqué'.[83] However, one could also ask if there are reasonable limits when it comes to how far a publication that defines itself as irresponsible should go. Simone Chambers argues that moral debates about *Charlie Hebdo*'s brand of humour were generally 'not about the right to offend, which is largely

---

83   Jane Weston, '*Bête et méchant*', 109; Weston Vauclair and Vauclair, *De Charlie Hebdo à Charlie*, p. 90.

unquestioned, but about the ethical choice to offend'. Furthermore, she states that 'being free to do something is not the same as having good reasons to do something' and that 'civility' is a concept that 'sets the limits on anger and resentment but does not attempt to suppress or replace these things'.[84] What such comments perhaps fail to adequately acknowledge is that taking offence at a joke that is felt to be of poor taste or be offensive is not always a consequence of the joke teller deliberately setting out to cause offence. In what could be interpreted as Chambers' implied criticism of how *Charlie Hebdo* has sought to exercise its freedom of speech, she does not discuss the publication's long history of effectively taking pride in its own immaturity via its 'bête et méchant' humour.

Discussion of how different groups within society are mocked for comedic purposes at times involves evoking the concepts of 'punching up' and 'punching down'. The former refers to someone making fun of those who are more powerful than the person doing the 'punching' and the latter refers to someone making fun of those who are less powerful than the person doing the 'punching'. Given that most of the leading figures at *Charlie Hebdo* in the years leading up to the 2015 attacks were white, male, and of French descent, the lack of cultural visibility of Muslims in France could be taken to mean that *Charlie Hebdo* were in effect 'punching down' when depicting the Prophet Muhammad. However, it is important to recall that *Charlie Hebdo*'s justification for mocking figures associated with Islam has often been that they have not been caricaturing French Muslims – or indeed Muslims in general – but rather those who have sought to exploit Islam for their own extremist and terrorist objectives. Indeed, Weston Vauclair and Vauclair argue that *Charlie Hebdo* actually has a long history of combating racism in addition to regularly mocking religion, the far right, and consumerism.[85] Mocking those who have sought to pervert the true message of Islam for their own ends could also be said to involve mocking extreme or unethical elements of a religion rather than the religion as a whole. Given *Charlie Hebdo*'s status as a publication that has mocked leading figures associated with many different religions, one

---

84 Simone Chambers, 'Free Speech and Civility in Pluralist Societies', in Edward M. Iacobucci and Stephen J. Toope (eds), *After the Paris Attacks* (Toronto/Buffalo/London: University of Toronto Press, 2015), pp. 15, 17.
85 Weston Vauclair and Vauclair, *De Charlie Hebdo à Charlie*, p. 35.

could perhaps ask if what it does is to 'punch in all directions' rather that 'punch down'. However, one could still ask if doing a sufficient amount of punching up or sidewise provides sufficient justification for indulging in some 'punching down'. The question of how and when people from one group can mock another is an important issue within contemporary debates about humour in France, and one that will be discussed further in the next chapters.

Chapter 2

Dieudonné: from anti-racist activism to allegations of anti-Semitism

Introduction

Although this chapter focuses on a different form of humour compared to the previous chapter – namely that of stand-up comedy rather than the cartoons and articles of a satirical weekly publication – it will maintain the focus on debates about provocative humour and offensiveness. Whereas the last chapter traced ways in which *Charlie Hebdo* has in recent years gone from being perceived as a marginal and controversial publication to one which is now much more widely celebrated, this chapter will focus on an individual who has followed a radically different trajectory. However, it will maintain the focus on media and humour, and in particular media reactions to controversial humour. The French comedian and actor Dieudonné is someone whose brand of comedy and political activism has changed significantly over the last two decades. In the 1990s, he was famous for his double act with Elie Semoun that frequently saw them perform sketches in which they took on the role of *banlieue* teenagers Cohen and Bokassa, the former being Jewish and the latter of West African descent. Their different origins were frequently a key source of humour although generally in a light-hearted and non-threatening manner. Semoun and Dieudonné also released a DVD in 1993 entitled *Une certaine idée de la France*; it took the form of a mock news bulletin and saw them dress up as a range of characters including young people and policemen from a suburban housing estate, former ice skaters, members of the Foreign Legion, a rapping homeless person, academics, a witch doctor, and a sex shop owner. The pair's stage shows were often produced by Pascal Legitimus, a member of the off-beat 1990s comedy group *Les Inconnus* and their act was described as 'a multicultural, *banlieue* version of Laurel and Hardy'.[1]

After Dieudonné and Semoun ceased performing together, Dieudonné increasingly sought to use his notoriety to defend the cause of anti-racism. One of the most high-profile ways he did so was by standing the 1997 legislative elections in Dreux (50 miles west of Paris) in order to help prevent the Front national's Marie-France Stirbois from being elected in the town where her party had gained their first councillor in 1983. The following year, he performed the role of a nightclub doorman in a song about racial discrimination by the Toulouse-based alternative rock group Zebda. In other words, Dieudonné appeared focused on promoting tolerance and challenging discrimination. Although he has continued to do so since the turn of the millennium, his methods have become increasingly divisive and controversial. A series of polemical statements have attracted media attention and debate, and the way in which he has sought to combat racism and campaign for increasing recognition of France's role in the slave trade has led to allegations of anti-Semitism. Dieudonné has always denied being anti-Semitic and instead presented himself as an anti-Zionist who questions Israel's attitudes towards Palestine and its historic links to the slave trade. However, his critics have accused him of using the term anti-Zionism as a cover for what they perceive to be his anti-Semitism.[2] There has been much debate in France about Dieudonné's one-man shows and public declarations, and indeed several attempts by local authorities and the French government to limit his right to perform. This chapter will analyse the trajectory that Dieudonné's career has followed and how he has been portrayed in the media, as well as how Dieudonné has sought to use and pass judgement on the French media. It will also seek to assess what is and is not perceived as an acceptable form of humour in France whilst also examining the justifications and implications of attempting to prevent him from performing.

1   Tom Reiss, 'Laugh Riots: the French Star Who Became a Demagogue', *The New Yorker*, 19 November 2007, http://www.newyorker.com/reporting/2007/11/19/071119fa_fact_reiss [accessed 26 April 2012].
2   Frédéric Haziza, *Vol au-dessus d'un nid de fachos: Dieudonné, Soral, Ayoub et les autres* (Paris: Fayard, 2014), p. 109.

Dieudonné's appearance on *On ne peut pas plaire à tout le monde* (France 3, 1 December 2003)

Although Dieudonné had provoked controversy in 2002 by stating that he preferred the charisma of Osama Bin Laden to that of George W. Bush,[3] a television appearance on Marc-Olivier Fogiel's talk show *On ne peut pas plaire à tout le monde* [*You cannot please everyone*] created even more debate. The fact that the programme itself lasted almost three hours and celebrated the careers of several other leading French humourists has been largely forgotten. It is not the discussions with Shirley et Dino, Jamel Debbouze, Pierre Palmade and Les Nuls that are generally remembered; instead, it is a short intervention by Dieudonné that was supposed to be a homage to Jamel Debbouze that has become the major focal point. Rather than delivering a personal homage to Debbouze, Dieudonné pretended to be a Zionist extremist and delivered a speech whilst wearing the traditional round black hat and curled hair associated with orthodox Jews, as well as a balaclava and military combat gear. In his address, Dieudonné provoked gentle if slightly uneasy laughter from the studio audience when referring to Jamel Debbouze as 'l'humoriste musulman' ['the Muslim comedian'] and a 'mudjahadin du rire' ['a mujahedeen of laughter']. The hosts of the programme, Marc-Olivier Fogiel and Arianne Massenet, initially appeared happy to play along with the unexpected nature of the speech although the former become noticeably uneasy when Dieudonné's character referred to the presence of Jamel Debbouze as 'un acte antisémite' ['an anti-Semitic act']. The speech ended with an appeal for young people living in French housing estates to convert and 'rejoignez l'axe du bien américano-sioniste' ['join the Americano-Zionist axis of good'] and a disputed phrase and gesture. Many of Dieudonné's critics have accused him of closing with a Nazi salute and the phrase 'Isra-heil!'[4] However, Dieudonné has said that he wanted to 'faire entendre quelque chose de nazifiant' ['cause something nazifying to be heard'] but actually said 'Israëlaie' with a German-sounding accent.[5]

---

3   See: Anne Jouan, 'Dieudonné, du rire à la nausée', *L'Express*, 8 September 2018, https://www.lexpress.fr/actualite/societe/dieudonne-du-rire-a-la-nausee_2033680.html [accessed 21 January 2019].
4   See: Anne-Sophie Mercier, *Dieudonné démasqué* (Paris: Seuil, 2009), p. 21.
5   See: Bruno Gaccio et Dieudonné, *Peut-on tout dire?* (Paris: Éditions Mordicus, 2010), p. 70.

This ambiguity rarely featured in the ensuing press coverage, in which it was generally reported without qualification that the comedian had said 'Isra-heil' and given a Nazi salute. In a 2007 court case stemming from his appearance on Fogiel's talk show, in which Dieudonné was found not guilty of public defamation of a racist nature, the judge ruled that what had been said at the moment of the salute was not entirely clear when viewing a video of the programme, but that it was not 'Isra-heil'.[6]

Somewhat surprisingly, the frequently adversarial nature of Marc-Olivier Fogiel's talk show was also largely ignored in debates that took place within the French media. Fogiel has a reputation for being a fast-talking and direct interviewer who is unafraid to interrupt guests and adopt an aggressive line of questioning. Indeed, the title of the chat show *On ne peut pas plaire à tout le monde* alludes to its frequently controversial and divisive nature. Given the nature of his comments on Bin Laden of the previous year, and other declarations reported in the press, it is reasonable to expect that the producers of the show would have been aware of the potential for Dieudonné's presence to provoke controversy. Dieudonné has argued that he was told, presumably by those working on the talk show, that one of the objectives of his sketch was to 'provoque[r] un peu Jamel Debbouze' ['gently provoke Jamel Debbouze'].[7] On the talk show, Debbouze laughed during much of the routine and was effusive in his praise for Dieudonné. He told his fellow comedian 'tu es le meilleur' ['you're the best'] and described himself as 'un fidèle partisan de Dieudo' ['a loyal follower of Dieudo']. Furthermore, he also appeared to criticize negative reactions to some of Dieudonné's stand-up material by stating:

> Il [Dieudonné] règle ses comptes sur scène [...]. Les gens finissent par suivre parce qu'il est drôle, sincère. Il frappe là où ça fait mal et c'est dommage que l'on s'attaque à un mec comme lui parce que l'on a besoin de mecs comme lui.
>
> [He (Dieudonné) settles his scores on stage (...). People end up following him because he is funny, sincere. He strikes where it

---

6   A full copy of this judgement is available online at: http://www.legifrance. gouv.fr/affichJuriJudi.do?idTexte=JURITEXT000007607845&dateTexte= [accessed 26 April 2012].

7   Gaccio and Dieudonné, *Peut-on tout dire?* p. 70.

hurts and it's a shame that people attack a guy like him because we need guys like him.]

The nature of this praise is in keeping with the fact that Dieudonné received a standing ovation from the studio audience of *On ne peut pas plaire à tout le monde* at the end of his sketch despite their relative lack of laughter during his performance. However, Debbouze's attitude to Dieudonné's homage to him on Fogiel's talk show changed rapidly following the widespread criticism of the latter's sketch that appeared in the French media. The day after Dieudonné's controversial television appearance, Jamel Debbouze appeared much more circumspect:

> Dieudonné a beaucoup de talent, mais son sketch était maladroit, voire complètement raté. On peut rire de tout à condition que ce soit drôle. Il se noie dans un discours politique qu'il maîtrise mal. Quand on se risque à ce genre d'exercice il faut être irréprochable. Et vu le contexte politique actuel, mettre de l'huile sur le feu n'est pas forcément une bonne idée. C'était déplacé! Et ma mère m'en a voulu d'embrasser Dieudonné après ce qu'il m'a dit.[8]

> [Dieudonné has a lot of talent, but his sketch was clumsy, even a complete failure. One can laugh about everything as long as it is funny. He gets bogged down in a political discourse that he does not fully understand. When you take on the risk of doing this sort of thing, you need to be irreproachable. And given the current political context, throwing oil on the fire is not necessarily a good idea. It was inappropriate! And my mother was annoyed at me for embracing Dieudonné after what he said to me.]

This criticism is at odds with the way that Debbouze laughed heartily during the sketch and with his comment in the ensuing live discussion that Dieudonné is often unfairly criticized for the nature of his material. Debbouze sought to justify his comments by claiming not to have been able to hear or see the sketch as it was being performed and stating that he only realized what had gone on when watching back the programme after it had been broadcast. He also qualified his praise of Dieudonné by

---

8   Quoted in: Delphine Sloan, *Jamel Debbouze: d'un monde à l'autre* (Saint-Victor-d'Épine: City Editions, 2004), p. 261.

saying 'à mon avis, alors qu'il est sans doute le plus doué d'entre nous, il est devenu fou' ['in my opinion, although he is the funniest of us all, he has gone mad'].[9] It is plausible that a failure to denounce Dieudonné's intervention and explain his own attitude could have created problems for Debbouze given that Dieudonné was in the process of becoming an increasingly marginalized figure from whom others, including his earlier stage partner Elie Semoun, were dissociating themselves.

In seeking to justify his sketch on *On ne peut pas plaire à tout le monde*, Dieudonné has appealed to the concept of universalism by arguing that members of all religions are legitimate targets for comedians and suggested that he was not mocking Jews in general. Furthermore, he has pointed out that he had previously mocked extreme Christian and Muslim figures.[10] In an interview shown on Arte's *Arrêt sur images* [*Freeze-frame*] on 7 December 2003, he also suggested that mocking a Jewish extremist created balance as he had been performing a sketch about a Muslim extremist for the previous two years.[11] By appealing to principles of balance and equality, Dieudonné sought to claim that he was remaining true to his tradition of making fun of a wide variety of people and simultaneously challenging discrimination and prejudice. In other words, he sought to use a similar defence to *Charlie Hebdo* by arguing that his treatment of one specific group should not be isolated from the rest of his humour and his treatment of other groups. However, it is important to place Dieudonné's performances within the context of his offstage political declarations. By 2003, Dieudonné had become a figure whose comments on issues such as Israeli-Palestinian relations had been seen as highly controversial, and who had been criticized due to the nature of comparisons he had made between representations of the Holocaust and memories of the slave trade. For example, he had used an interview in 2002 to blame the attitude of certain Jews for the lack of recognition of the slave trade:

> Les descendants juifs continuent à être indemnisés par rapport à
> ce qui s'est passé durant la Shoah. Nous, les Noirs, n'avons jamais

9   Marie Jocher and Alain Kéramoal, *Jamel Debbouze: la vérité* (Paris: Seuil, 2008), p. 257.
10   See: Olivier Mukuna, *Dieudonné: entretien à coeur ouvert* (Antwerp: EPO, 2005), pp. 30–1.
11   *Arrêt sur images*, Daniel Schneiderman with Dieudonné M'Bala M'Bala (Arte, 7 December 2003) [television interview].

rien eu à cause de certains Juifs qui refusent que notre souffrance soit mise au même niveau que la leur![12]

[Jewish descendants continue to be compensated for what happened during the Shoah. We, black people, have never received anything due to certain Jews who refuse to allow our suffering to be placed on the same level as their own!]

In the same interview, he accused 'le lobby juif' ['the Jewish lobby'] of hating black people due to it feeling that it had a monopoly on feelings of suffering.

Some, such as Jamel Debbouze's long-time producer Kader Aoun, insisted on the need to avoid dissociating Dieudonné's onstage persona from his offstage persona and argued that 'l'insistance [sur les juifs] est quand même dans l'affaire Dieudonné, elle n'est pas anodine' ['the intense focus (on Jews) is actually present in the Dieudonné affair, and it's not insignificant'].[13] This creates a paradoxical situation given that Dieudonné has argued that that some of his comments about Jews have been reported by the press in a manner that has removed them from their context.[14] What Aoun's is suggesting is that it is precisely when Dieudonné's sketch on *On ne peut pas plaire à tout le monde* is placed within the wider context of his public declarations that it becomes more problematic rather than less problematic. Aoun's analysis of what has become known as *l'affaire Dieudonné* [the Dieudonné affair] provides a greater degree of nuance than was present in much of the discussion that followed Dieudonné's appearance on *On ne peut pas plaire à tout le monde*. In many cases, the nature of his performance and the sentiments voiced were themselves frequently criticized for being in poor taste, shocking, or anti-Semitic. Four days after Dieudonné's much discussed appearance, presenter Marc-Olivier Fogiel began the next edition of *On ne peut pas plaire à tout le monde* with an apology. He explained that he shared the sense of shock felt by many viewers, denounced Dieudonné's performance as 'inacceptable' and accused him of performing a sketch

12   Oman D. and K2C, 'Moment, Dieudonné', *Blackmap*, 22 October 2002, http://web.archive.org/web/20021022134311/www.blackmap.com/contenus/ art_culture/moment_dieudo.htm [accessed 26 April 2012].
13   *Zone de libre échange*, Xavier de la Porte et al. with Kader Aoun and Jean-Michel Ribes (France Culture, 6 December 2008) [radio interview].
14   Dieudonné makes this assertion in: Mukuna, *Dieudonné*, p. 15.

that differed from what had been agreed in advance. At the same time, he said that he regretted that he had not denounced Dieudonné during the programme other than by referring to him as 'toujours borderline' ['always boderline'], Fogiel also sought to deflect responsibility by saying 'jamais nous n'aurions le laisser dire ce qu'il a dit si nous avions connaissance de ses propos' ['we would never have left him say what he said if we had been aware of his intentions'].[15] It appears somewhat contradictory that Fogiel thus simultaneously alluded to Dieudonné's reputation for controversy whilst also evoking his own sense of shock at the nature of the sketch that he denounced. Indeed, it was highly paradoxical that the host of a television programme entitled *On ne peut pas plaire à tout le monde* should apologize for a sketch that was not universally lauded.

Anti-racist groups and politicians sought to assert that there was something that was de facto wrong about the nature of Dieudonné's supposed homage to Jamel Debbouze. MRAP denounced 'un sketch qui représente une véritable insulte à toutes les victimes du nazisme, en majorité juive' ['a sketch that constitutes a true insult to all victims of Nazism, of whom the majority were Jewish'].[16] This approach could be called into question given a court judge's ruling that Dieudonné had not said 'Isra-Heil' at the end of his sketch, but the comedian himself did nevertheless acknowledge that 'à la fin, je faisais un salut, et je voulais faire entendre quelque chose de nazifiant' ['at the end, I gave a salute, and I wanted to cause something nazifying to be heard'].[17] In other words, Dieudonné appears to have acknowledged that he played the role of a Jewish extremist in a sketch that concluded with Nazi undertones. He again used terms associated with the Holocaust and the Second World War in an interview with the *Journal du dimanche* to criticize members of Jewish groups who had protested outside one of his one-man shows:

> Ce sont tous ces négriers reconvertis dans la banque, le spectacle et aujourd'hui l'action terroriste qui manifestent leur soutien à la politique Sharon. Ceux qui m'attaquent ont fondé des empires et

---

15   *On ne peut pas plaire à tout le monde*, Marc-Olivier Fogiel and Ariane Massenet (France 3, 5 December 2003) [television programme].
16   Cited in: *Arrêt sur images*, Schneiderman.
17   Gaccio and Dieudonné, *Peut-on tout dire?* p. 70.

des fortunes sur la traite des Noirs et l'esclavage. Ils m'accusent d'être antisémite. Ça n'a aucun sens, personne dans ma famille n'a servi dans la Wehrmacht. Mais c'est Israël qui a financé l'apartheid et ses projets de solution finale.[18]

[They are all slave traders who now work in banking, entertainment and today terrorism who are demonstrating their support for the policies of Sharon. Those who attacked me have established empires and fortunes from the enslavement of black people and the slave trade. They accuse me of being anti-Semitic. It doesn't make sense, nobody in my family served in the Wehrmacht. But it is Israël who financed apartheid and its planned final solution.]

Such declarations meant that the *affaire Dieudonné* swiftly came to concern more than just his appearance on *On ne peut pas plaire à tout le monde*. In other words, it came to encompass his initial sketch, comments that he made following the ensuing protests, and statements he made in other press interviews. Thus, a debate that initially focused on the nature of Dieudonné's brand of humour swiftly encompassed his political declarations. Nicolas Sarkozy (then Interior Minister) had already denounced what he called 'l'antisémitisme de Dieudonné' ['Dieudonné's anti-Semitism'] before the *Journal du dimanche* interview and said that it needed to be 'combattu et sanctionné' ['combatted and punished'] when addressing a meeting of the CRIF (Conseil représentatif des institutions juives de France) in Toulouse on 2 February 2004.[19] Here, Dieudonné's anti-Semitism was taken as a given by a government minister before a court had pronounced a judgement on the matter. Similarly, press articles have been unafraid to refer to him as having been guilty of 'dérapages antisémites' ['anti-Semitic misdemeanours'].[20] Dieudonné was not found guilty of anti-Semitism following his appearance on *On ne peut pas plaire à tout*

---

18   Sandrine Boucher, 'Dieudonné persiste et signe', *Le Journal du dimanche*, 8 February 2004, p. 27.
19   Cited in: *Lundi investigations*, Émile Raffoul and Paul Moreira (Canal Plus, 17 May 2005) [television programme].
20   For example, see: 'Un nouveau dérapage antisémite de Dieudonné', *20 minutes*, 18 July 2008, https://www.20minutes.fr/debats/242288-20080718-nouveau-derapage-antisemite-dieudonne [accessed 27 April 2012].

le monde or his interview in *Le Journal du dimanche*. However, the latter did result in him being fined 5,000 euros for inciting racial hatred by a Parisian court in March 2006. This verdict was confirmed on appeal the following year. Although court verdicts have not pronounced Dieudonné guilty of anti-Semitism per se, the French media has often described the guilty verdicts on charges such as defamation with a racial element or inciting racial hatred as having stemmed from 'des propos antisémites' ['anti-Semitic remarks'].[21]

Although many prominent French Jews and Jewish organizations were swift to brand Dieudonné's sketch on Fogiel's talk show anti-Semitic, not all expressed the same sort of sentiment. In a televised discussion about whether or not France was anti-Semitic in February 2004, the journalist Sylvain Attal described Dieudonné's sketch as 'une caricature antisémite des années 30 version télévisée aujourd'hui' ['a contemporary televised version of a 1930s anti-Semitic caricature'] and the Socialist member of parliament Julien Dray talked of its 'caractère antisémite incontestable' ['unquestionably anti-Semitic nature']. However, the writer, academic, and co-founder of *Médecins sans frontières*, Rony Brauman, did not see Dieudonné's reference to the 'axe américano-sioniste' ['Americano-Zionist axis'] as anti-Semitic and said that although he did not find the sketch funny, he did not feel that it was racist either.[22] Rabbi Haïm Korsia, an advisor to the General Rabbi of France, also took a nuanced view suggesting that 'il [Dieudonné] n'est pas antisémite, il a simplement peu de connaissances du judaïsme' ['he (Dieudonné) is not anti-Semitic, he simply does not have much knowledge of Judaism'] and that 'il n'a pas compris que son sketch pouvait blesser' ['he did not realise that his sketch could cause offence']. Rabbi Korsia also sought to take Dieudonné on a trip to Auschwitz and praised his ability to create dialogue with young people from France's *banlieues*.[23] Any potential for the journey to Auschwitz to alleviate tensions was left unrealized after Korsia's superiors distanced

21   See, for example: 'Dieudonné condamné en appel pour un spectacle avec le négationniste Faurisson', *Le Monde*, 17 March 2011, http://www.lexpress.fr/actualites/1/styles/dieudonne-condamne-en-appel-pour-un-spectacle-avec-le-negationniste-faurisson_973427.html [accessed 27 April 2012].
22   *Ripostes*, Serge Moati (France 5, 22 February 2004) [television programme].
23   Olivier Mukuna, *Égalité zéro: enquête sur le procès médiatique de Dieudonné* (Paris: Editions Blanche, 2005), p. 14.

themselves from the idea. Although Rabbi Korsia seemed keen to engage with the controversy surrounding Dieudonné's remarks in a positive and constructive manner, some of his comments appear quite naïve. Given Dieudonné's provocative nature, it is worth questioning whether he was unaware of the potential for his sketch and subsequent declarations to hurt people. As already discussed, he was seen as a potentially provocative figure prior to December 2003. Indeed, he has stated that 'ce sketch était avant tout censé faire rire Jamel et toucher ceux que j'avais envie de taquiner' ['this sketch was above all intended to make Jamel laugh and to affect those I wanted to tease'].[24] In other words, he was aware of how his routine was likely to be perceived by those with whom he disagreed.

Following his live appearance on *On ne peut pas plaire à tout le monde*, it appears that producers on many French television channels decided that inviting Dieudonné onto their programmes constituted a risk not worth taking. The way that the French media dealt with the controversy provoked criticism from several black intellectuals, notably Belgian journalist Olivier Mukuna. Mukuna has accused the French media of a subtle form of racism and asked why white French people were not previously asked for their views on sketches in which Michael Leeb compared black people to monkeys, and why Jewish figures were not questioned about controversial material referring to the handicapped performed by the Jewish comedian Patrick Timsit.[25] The relative lack of widespread public outrage provoked Michael Leeb to suggest that many in France tacitly accepted that it was acceptable for well-established mainstream comedians – of whom the vast majority are white and male – to build parts of their routines around mocking minorities. Mukuna's comparison between the treatment of Dieudonné and Patrick Timsit is, however, more problematic. It is certainly the case that the controversy surrounding Dieudonné's initial appearance on *On ne peut pas plaire à tout le monde* stemmed from his representation of an admittedly caricatured Jewish figure. However, arguably greater anger stemmed from his subsequent criticism of Jewish discourses of suffering surrounding the Holocaust within the context of calling for greater recognition of how black people were treated during the slave trade. It also appears that Timsit did not evoke his Jewish faith, or Algerian

24   Mukuna, *Dieudonné*, p. 30.
25   Mukuna, *Égalité zéro*, pp. 175–6.

origins, when making his controversial comment 'les trisomiques, c'est comme les crevettes roses: tout est bon, sauf la tête' ['Down's Syndrome sufferers are like prawns, everything is fine apart from the head'] or in the aftermath. A further difference compared with the *affaire Dieudonné* is that Timsit apologized for his comments and sought to reduce rather than inflame tensions. Timsit achieved a form of reconciliation by creating an association to defend those affected by Down's syndrome along with parents of a Down's syndrome sufferer who had initially threatened to take legal action.

Despite the differences between the nature of Dieudonné, Leeb, and Timsit's declarations, they all nevertheless created debates about questions of offensiveness and prejudice within humour. Although Mukuna's comparison between Dieudonné and Timsit is somewhat reductive, he has nevertheless raised important questions about the wider issue of appearances by black intellectuals on French television. At the end of a televised discussion about the visibility of black people on French television on Arte's *Arrêt sur images* on 6 March 2005, Serge Bilé addressed the host to make the following comments:

> J'ai envie de vous dire, Daniel Schneiderman, le jour où on aura l'impression qu'on a avancé, c'est le jour où on ne sera pas surpris de voir des Noirs à la télévision, où on ne sera pas obligé de faire des émissions comme celle-là et le jour où vous inviterez moi, Christiane Taubira et Gaston Kelman pour parler d'autre chose que de Noirs.[26]

> [I want to tell you, Daniel Schneiderman, the day that we will have the impression that we have moved forward will be the day when we will not be surprised to see black people on television. It will be the day when we will not need to make programmes like that one and the day when you will invite me, Christiane Taubira and Gaston Kelman to talk about something other than black people.]

Such a situation suggests that black intellectuals in France are pigeonholed by a two-fold process. Firstly, they are generally invited to discuss issues seen as pertaining to those of their own racial group. Secondly, it appears that the French media were not treating the

---

26   Cited in: Mukuna, *Égalité zéro*, p. 184.

visibility of minorities as a question for the whole of French society (i.e. including those from the white majority) to address. This itself could be seen as a form of *communautarisme* and consequently very much in contradiction with key tenets of Republicanism, and indeed particularly problematic if the practice were to be followed by a state television channel.

The notion that underlying prejudices within the French media affected the reporting of the so-called *affaire Dieudonné* is a major feature of Olivier Mukuna's 2005 book *Égalité zéro: enquête sur le procès médiatique de Dieudonné* [*Zéro equality: an investigation into Dieudonné's trial by media*], and also alluded to in an earlier work in which he interviewed Dieudonné.[27] The former work is highly critical of occasions on which the French media displayed bias or failed to verify information concerning declarations by Dieudonné.[28] Elsewhere, Mukuna has challenged the objectivity and accuracy of other works written about Dieudonné, such as Anne-Sophie Mercier's *La Vérité sur Dieudonné* [*The Truth about Dieudonné*] and *Dieudonné démasqué* [*Dieudonné unmasked*].[29] The books published about Dieudonné within the last decade demonstrate how he has become a highly divisive figure and one whose political viewpoints expressed offstage at times attract more attention that the material he performs onstage. Mukuna's two books remain relatively rare examples of works that seek to evaluate critically the way that he has been represented by the French media, and also portray him as a victim of discriminatory practices and at times inaccurate reporting.[30] The work containing Mukuna's interview with Dieudonné (*Dieudonné: entretien à coeur ouvert*) provides biographical background and discusses Dieudonné's attitude to humour as well as his views on Zionism in France, the commemoration of slavery, and the workings of media and show business circles in France. At the same time as providing a

27 The earlier work was entitled *Dieudonné: entretien à coeur ouvert*.
28 See especially: Mukuna, *Égalité zéro*, pp. 37, 117.
29 Anne-Sophie Mercier, *La Vérité sur Dieudonné* (Paris: Plon, 2005); Anne-Sophie Mercier, *Dieudonné démasqué*. See: P.M., 'Olivier Mukuna: "Ce film s'est réalisé dans des conditions semi-clandestines"', *AgoraVox*, 25 November 2009, http://www.agoravox.fr/tribune-libre/article/olivier-mukuna-ce-film-s-est-65555 [accessed 27 April 2012].
30 There are, nevertheless, some highly partisan works by fans of Dieudonné that seek to examine how he has been portrayed in the media, although not with the same depth or nuance displayed in Mukuna's aforementioned books.

potential means for Dieudonné to challenge the ways in which he has been characterized, reduce tensions, and rectify misunderstandings, it also sees Dieudonné continue to compare Jewish memories of the Holocaust and attitudes to commemorations of slavery. In other words, some of the content risks re-igniting rather than defusing tensions.

At the other end of the spectrum to Mukuna's works are others that seek to provide a much more negative picture of Dieudonné and his motivations. As will be demonstrated later, Anne-Sophie Mercier's *Dieudonné démasqué* (an updated version of *La Vérité sur Dieudonné*) is less centred on his sketch on Fogiel's talk show than on the question of his political activities and those with whom he associates. The same is even more true of Michel Briganti, André Déchot, and Jean-Paul Gautier's *La Galaxie Dieudonné: pour en finir avec les impostures* [*The Galaxy of Dieudonné: putting an end to the deception*], as well as Jean Robin's *Soral et Dieudonné: la tentation antisémite* [*Soral and Dieudonné: the anti-Semitic temptation*] and Frédérifc Haziza's *Vol au-dessus d'un nid de fachos* [*One flew over the fascists' nest*].[31] Although Mercier's updated version of her original book brings together views of a broad range of people who have worked with Dieudonné in film and television, at the same time as primarily focusing on his political activities, the same cannot be said of Briganti, Déchot, and Gautier's work. The trio's book focuses very little on Dieudonné as a comedian and does not provide detailed analysis of the material he has performed. Nevertheless, it provides a context in which some of his onstage material and offstage declarations can be situated. A book combining interviews with the comedy writer Bruno Gaccio and Dieudonné entitled *Peut-on tout dire?* [*Can one say everything?*] contrastingly focuses much more on the limits of comedy and censorship than any of the other works discussed above. The interview with Gaccio provides a balanced assessment of Dieudonné and his material, one that at times criticizes both the artist himself and the way in which others have reacted to him. Although the interview with Dieudonné creates similar problems to Mukuna's extended interview with him, it nevertheless engages in detailed discussion about what are and are not acceptable subjects about which to laugh.

31 Michel Briganti, André Déchot and Jean-Paul Gautier, *La Galaxie Dieudonné: pour en finir avec les impostures* (Paris: Syllepse, 2011); Jean Robin, *Soral et Dieudonné: la tentation antisémite* (Paris: Éditions Tatamis, 2014); Frédéric Haziza, *Vol au-dessus d'un nid de fachos*.

A communication strategy based on provoking controversy?

When reporting on the so-called *affaire Dieudonné*, much of the French press focused on the performer's comments about Jews and Israel. In other words, few engaged in detailed analysis of questions primarily focused on humour and limits as to what is considered acceptable. This, in part, appears to be due to the reporting of several declarations by Dieudonné following his appearance on *On ne peut pas plaire à tout le monde* that were seen as highly controversial. In addition to the interview published in the *Journal du dimanche* on 8 February 2004, many publications were quick to report remarks he made at a press conference in Algiers in February 2005. On this occasion, he criticized what he termed the 'lobby sioniste, qui cultive l'unicité de la souffrance' ['the Sionist lobby, which cultivates the uniqueness of suffering'] and also blamed 'autorités sionistes' ['Zionist authorities'] within the French film industry for preventing him from being able to produce a film about the enslavement of black people. Within this context, he also evoked what he described as 'l'exploitation du souvenir de la Shoah' ['the exploitation of the memory of the Shoah'] and referred to this process as a form of 'pornographie mémorielle' ['memorial pornography'].[32] For some, such declarations formed part of a deliberate communication strategy. Bruno Gaccio argues that 'le seul moyen dont dispose Dieudonné pour continuer d'exister est de faire de la provoc' ['the only means that Dieudonné possesses in order to continue to exist is provocation'].[33] In other words, it would appear that Dieudonné's actions endorse Oscar Wilde's notion that 'there is

---

32   'Dieudonné, star de la semaine judiciaire', *Le Figaro*, 26 June 2008, http://www.lefigaro.fr/actualite-france/2008/06/26/01016–20080626ARTFIG00373-dieudonne-star-de-la-semaine-judiciaire.php [accessed 30 April 2012]. See also: '"Pornographie mémorielle": Dieudonné condamné', *Le Nouvel Observateur*, 11 September 2007, http://tempsreel.nouvelobs.com/societe/20070911.OBS4352/pornographie-memorielle-dieudonne-condamne.html [accessed 30 April 2012]; François Nascimbeni, 'Dieudonné condamné pour des propos antisémites sur la mémoire de la Shoah', *La Dépêche du Midi*, 11 September 2007, http://www.ladepeche.fr/article/2007/09/11/11212-dieudonne-condamne-pour-des-propos-antisemites-sur-la-memoire-de-la-shoah.html [accessed 30 April 2012]. These declarations led to a 7,000 euro fine for defamation with a racial element pronounced by a Parisian court on 11 September 2007 and subsequently confirmed on appeal on 26 June 2008.
33   Gaccio et Dieudonné, *Peut-on tout dire?* p. 41.

only one thing in life worse than being talked about, and that is not being talked about'.[34]

Although Dieudonné's controversial and provocative declarations often receive media coverage, much of this coverage is highly critical and constitutes what many would consider to be negative publicity. This could be taken as a sign that Dieudonné subscribes to the view that there is no such thing as bad publicity, and his own comments suggest that he also derives satisfaction from toying with the press:

> Je connais le régime alimentaire de certains médias [...] il faut leur fournir de la viande crue, sanguinolente. Je leur en donne parfois, et je m'amuse beaucoup à voir leurs réactions.[35]

> [I know the diet of certain parts of the media (...), you need to give them raw meat, dripping with blood. I give them it sometimes, and it really amuses me to see their reactions.]

This suggests that Dieudonné is keen to present himself as being in control, a notion that is very different to the idea that he is a figure who regularly makes counterproductive declarations that merely create negative publicity. Furthermore, the criticism he receives from the mainstream media provides Dieudonné with something to which he can respond – notably via his own social media channels – and also an opportunity to further cultivate a sense of victimhood. This strategy has given Dieudonné a means of seeking to create and maintain a following during a period when the mainstream media in France has generally tended to refer to him rather than enter into dialogue with him. This provides him with the opportunity to present himself as a dissenting voice and someone who is unafraid to present views that others are reluctant to voice. This is a communication strategy that has also been exploited by politicians who have sought to portray themselves as courageous due to their refusal to allow perceived political correctness to prevent them from expressing their opinions in an unabashed manner. The phrase 'je dis tout haut ce que les gens pensent tout bas' ['I say out loud what people think deep down'] has been used many times by the Front national founder and long-time leader Jean-Marie Le Pen.

---

34   Oscar Wilde, *The Picture of Dorian Gray* (Leipzig: Bernard Tauchnitz, 1908), p. 9.
35   In: Gaccio et Dieudonné, *Peut-on tout dire?* p. 84.

Dieudonné has appeared keen to characterize himself as someone who has been made into a pariah by mainstream media, and sought to voice this view via social media and his stage shows in order to maintain a following. This demonstrates the importance of the role of the media – and indeed different forms of media – in creating the highly controversial phenomenon that is Dieudonné.

Media coverage of Dieudonné's controversial and provocative declarations has helped to draw attention to his stand-up shows, notably due to protests against his performances from February 2004 onwards. On 5 February 2004, 200 protesters gathered outside a performance by Dieudonné at the Bourse de travail [Trade Union Centre] in Lyon that local authorities had initially tried to block, due to fears about a potential risk to public order. Inside, the performance was interrupted after a bottle containing an irritant substance was thrown.[36] It was following these disturbances that he took part in the interview with the *Journal du dimanche* that provoked further controversy. These events in Lyon crucially gave Dieudonné an opportunity to present himself as a victim. By designating the Fédération sioniste de France [Zionist Federation of France] as the group responsible for the interruption of his show in Lyon,[37] Dieudonné was able to continue and intensify his criticisms of Zionist groups within France. Here, it is important to note that his initial sketch on *On ne peut pas plaire à tout le monde* did not directly comment on community relations in France or explicitly single out individual groups for criticism. However, this swiftly changed in the aftermath of events in Lyon due to demonstrations that saw visible opponents publicly emerge. These opponents notably included anti-racist organizations (especially *la Ligue Internationale Contre le Racisme et l'Antisémitisme*, LICRA) and a range of French Jewish groups.

Another important moment in the *affaire Dieudonné* was the cancellation of the performer's show at Olympia in Paris that had been scheduled for 20 February 2004. This decision refocused discussions on the question of freedom of expression and his role as a stand-up

36   See report from France 2's 8pm news bulletin of 6 February 2004, available online at: http://www.ina.fr/art-et-culture/arts-du-spectacle/video/2490750001024/echauffourees-lors-d-un-spectacle-de-dieudonne.fr.html [accessed 30 April 2012].
37   Gaccio and Dieudonné, *Peut-on tout dire?* p. 73.

comedian, and fellow comedian Christophe Alévêque argued that 'une société bien portante devrait pouvoir rire de tout et éviter l'humour communautariste' ['a healthy society should be able to laugh about everything and avoid community-specific humour'].[38] Whilst voicing a desire to avoid *communautarisme* appeals to the Republican principle of universalism, what *rire de tout* [laughing about everything] actually entails is rarely stated explicitly in debates about humour. For example, is *rire de tout* about there being no limits to the suitable subject matter for jokes, or does the concept go further, and also refer to laughing at any subject matter in any form? In other words, do those who believe that it should be possible to *rire de tout* implicitly mean that it should be possible to *rire de tout et n'importe comment* [laugh about anything and in any manner]? The need to introduce important nuances when discussing the concept of *rire de tout* was voiced by Pierre Desproges who responded to the question *peut-on rire de tout?* by famously stating 'oui, mais pas avec tout le monde' ['yes, but not with everyone'] before adding 'mieux vaut rire d'Auschwitz avec un Juif que jouer au Scrabble avec Klaus Barbie' ['it is better to laugh about Auschwitz with a Jew than to play Scrabble with Klaus Barbie'].[39] In other words, it is important to remember laughing at jokes can involve groups of people laughing at themselves and also people uniting to laugh at others. Whilst laughing at one's self (or own group) can help to defuse tension, mocking others can be a means of perpetuating hierarchies or seeking to maintain exclusion. In other words, *rire de tout* can potentially be divisive and lead to *communautarisme* rather than constitute a strategy that is opposed to *communautarisme*.

Dieudonné seized upon the cancellation of his show at Olympia in order to describe himself as a 'victime des fanatiques et des intégristes religieux juifs' ['victim of fanatics and Jewish religious fundamentalists'] and argue that he was receiving 'un soutien de plus en plus grand de la part d'un public pour qui j'incarne une certaine idée de la liberté de penser' ['ever greater support from an audience for whom I represent a certain idea of the freedom of thought']; however, it is not clear to what extent the cancellation was actually due to ideological issues

38   Mercier, *Dieudonné démasqué*, p. 137.
39   Quoted in: André Comte-Sponville, 'Peut-on rire de tout?', *Psychologies Magazine*, February 2001, http://www.psychologies.com/Planete/Societe/Articles-et-Dossiers/Peut-on-rire-de-tout [accessed 30 April 2012].

concerning the nature of his material.[40] Several sources cite Olympia's fears for the safety of spectators and its own employees,[41] and the lawyer who represented Dieudonné in his attempts to prevent the cancellation said that the main problem was a disagreement between Olympia and Dieudonné's production company about who should pay for the security measures required.[42] Concerns about public order and safety led to the cancellation of several other shows on his tour in France and Belgium. Although this context could be interpreted as a sign that Dieudonné was not in fact censored due to the nature of his onstage material or political views, it is conceivable that the controversy provoked by Dieudonné's public declarations made local authorities more likely to exploit discretionary powers that could prevent him from performing in their area.

Teasing out whether Dieudonné's controversial comments are a response to intimidation he feels he has suffered, or whether the intimidation is itself a response to his controversial declarations is a complicated issue. On one hand, Dieudonné's 2004 interview with the *Journal du dimanche* came only days after one of his shows in Lyon was interrupted when a bottle of tear gas was thrown. However, the following year saw Dieudonné assaulted in Martinique within weeks of describing the memorialization of the Holocaust as a form of 'pornographie mémorielle' ['memorial pornography']. Both Dieudonné and those who have attacked him – those who have done so physically and those who have protested in a non-violent manner – would likely argue that they were responding to an injustice, creating a situation whereby it becomes difficult to designate the root of such tensions. Dieudonné claimed that one of his attackers in Martinique shouted

40   Hubert Lizé, 'L'Olympia annule le show de Dieudonné', *Le Parisien*, 19 February 2004, http://www.leparisien.fr/loisirs-et-spectacles/l-olympia-annule-le-show-de-dieudonne-19–02–2004–2004768834.php [accessed 30 April 2012].
41   See: Lizé, 'L'Olympia annule le show de Dieudonné'; 'L'Olympia annule le show de Dieudonné', *Libération*, 19 February 2012, http://www.liberation.fr/societe/0101478817-l-olympia-annule-le-show-de-dieudonne [accessed 30 April 2012].
42   *Soir 3 Journal*, Michel Vial and Melissa Monteiro (France 3, 19 February 2004) [television news report], http://www.ina.fr/art-et-culture/arts-du-spectacle/video/2505466001006/annulation-en-refere-du-spectacle-dieudonne-a-l-olympia.fr.html [accessed 30 April 2012].

'sale négro, on va te faire la peau' ['dirty negro, we're going to kill you'] and press reports suggested that his attackers either had Israeli passports or French passports indicating that they had spent significant time in Israel.[43] These details were highly opportune from Dieudonné's perspective given his criticism of Israel's links to apartheid, and his allegations that certain Jewish groups had a dislike for black people illustrated by differing attitudes to the Holocaust and the suffering involved in the slave trade.[44] However, Dieudonné has also become an unwelcome ally of a variety of political organizations. Anne-Sophie Mercier claims that his presence at a high-profile march organized by the anti-racist group Les Indigènes de la République [The Indigenous of the Republic] on 8 May 2005 was not unanimously popular and led to a Green Party politician and one of the Ligue des droit de l'homme's national committee members leaving the march. Furthermore, she quotes the president of Droit au logement (DAL) as having described Dieudonné's support as 'ponctuel et parfois très gênant' ['occasional and sometimes very embarrassing'].[45] Dieudonné has also been shunned by people who have also sought to defend their right to utilize humour that is perceived as being provocative or of questionable taste. In Daniel Leconte's 2007 documentary *C'est dur d'être aimé par des cons*, journalists from *Charlie Hebdo* express frustration at Dieudonné's appearance at a Parisian courthouse where the satirical publication was defending itself in case brought by Muslim groups following the publication of cartoons depicting the Prophet Muhammad. Indeed, *Charlie Hebdo* journalists such as Caroline Fourest can be seen insisting that Dieudonné has misunderstood their reasons for publishing the cartoons. Furthermore, their frustration appears to emanate from their view that Dieudonné is using the court case for his own benefit by attempting to exploit an opportunity to step back into the media spotlight.

In recent years, Dieudonné has reportedly decided that controversy and protests following his public declarations have reduced the need for him to proactively advertise his one-man shows. In an interview with BFMTV's current affairs programme *Grand Angle* [*Wide Angle*] on 12 December 2013, his former producer Christelle Camus described

43   Mukuna, *Égalité zéro*, pp. 121–2.
44   See: Oman D. and K2C, 'Moment, Dieudonné'. This issue is discussed earlier in this chapter.
45   Mercier, *Dieudonné démasqué*, pp. 92–3, 114.

how he had decided against using posters and flyers to publicize his stand-up show, *Foxtrot*, as he was confident that protests against his shows and public declarations from Jewish groups in France would provide him with sufficient publicity. She added that press coverage of attempts to ban his shows often had a significant positive impact on ticket sales.[46] In other words, attempts by protesters and politicians to challenge his legitimacy as a performer – and indeed right to perform at all – have helped to strengthen his following. Indeed, some have suggested that denying Dieudonné publicity by not talking about him at all – rather than criticizing him at the same time as denying him a right to reply – would be a more appropriate response, and indeed one that would make it harder for him to cultivate and maintain as large a following.[47]

Dieudonné 'l'ancien humoriste'

As previously mentioned, media focus on Dieudonné's political declarations has led many to ignore his status as a stand-up comedian and to see him primarily as an agitator or political activist. To state that he is no longer a stand-up comedian is inaccurate given that he continues to perform stand-up comedy shows on a regular basis, and frequently sell out audiences. Those who seek to portray Dieudonné as a former comedian are in effect highlighting a change in the nature of his stand-up material, and the fact that they see his politics as being more significant than his comedy. Critics who have sought to dismiss Dieudonné as a former comedian include Malek Boutih (former head of anti-racist group SOS-Racisme and member of the Parti socialiste) and the American journalist Tom Reiss,[48] as well as authors of several books that criticize his political engagements and the way that he has presented himself. Frédéric Haziza has stated that 'depuis longtemps, Dieudonné n'est plus un humoriste: c'est un agitateur de haine' ['for quite some time, Dieudonné has ceased to be a comedian: he is a stirrer of hatred'].[49] Briganti, Déchot, and Gautier begin *La Galaxie*

46   Robin, *Soral et Dieudonné*, p. 169.
47   Robin, *Soral et Dieudonné*, pp. 99–103.
48   See: *Arrêt sur images*, Schneiderman; Tom Reiss, 'Laugh Riots'.
49   Haziza, *Vol au-dessus d'un nid de fachos*, pp. 118–19.

Dieudonné: pour en finir avec les impostures by stating that 'depuis près de quinze ans, l'humoriste Dieudonné utilise son statut d'amuseur public pour squatter la scène politique française et internationale' ['for almost fifteen years, the comedian Dieudonné has used his status as a public entertainer in order to squat the French and international political scene'].[50] Anne-Sophie Mercier's introduction to *Dieudonné démasqué* similarly suggests that his role and preoccupations have shifted:

> Dieudonné n'est plus un comique, c'est un politique. Certes, son travail d'artiste est évident. Présence sur scène, incroyable capacité à appuyer là où ça fait mal, humour très corrosif. Dieudonné est aussi un grand acteur. Mais aujourd'hui, il est avant tout connu pour ses déclarations fracassantes, ses petites phrases antisémites, et son implication dans la communauté noire et antillaise au service d'une bataille pour la mémoire et la reconnaissance de l'esclavage qui nous concerne tous.[51]

> [Dieudonné is no longer a comedian, he is a politician. Admittedly, his skills as a performer are evident. His presence on stage, his incredible ability to strike exactly where it hurts, his very corrosive humour. Dieudonné is also a talented actor. But today he is above all known for his sensationalist declarations, his little anti-Semitic phrases, and his involvement in the black and Caribbean community in the battle for the memory and recognition of slavery that concerns us all.]

Although Mercier's comments appear contradictory, given that she states that Dieudonné is no longer a comedian before describing the brand of humour that he displays onstage, they nevertheless raise the important question of where the border lies between performing stand-up comedy and utilizing humour within a polemical political presentation. Even amongst those who hold a not entirely negative view of Dieudonné, and criticize how he is represented by the media, there are those who suggest that the blurring of the boundary between Dieudonné the comedian and Dieudonné the political activist and agitator creates problems. For example, Bruno Gaccio appears troubled by what Dieudonné has become:

50   Briganti et al., *La Galaxie Dieudonné*, p. 7.
51   Mercier, *Dieudonné démasqué*, pp. 12–13.

Il est contaminé – et c'est une vraie maladie – par ses nouveaux amis, des gens que je définis, sans bien les connaître, comme profondément antisémites. Je n'ai pas envie de les fréquenter, ni envie de voir Dieudonné en dehors de ses spectacles. J'ai plutôt envie de lui dire: 'fais tes spectacles et tais-toi! Tu fais chier avec ton complot du 11 septembre et tes antisionistes obsessionnels: on peut vivre sans!'[52]

[He is contaminated – and it is a real disease – by his new friends, people who I define, without really knowing them, as profoundly anti-Semitic. I have no desire to spend time with them, nor to see Dieudonné apart from at his shows. I kind of want to say to him: 'do your shows and shut up! You're pissing people off with your 11 September conspiracy theories and your obsessional anti-Zionists: we can live without that!']

In other words, Gaccio has a much more favourable attitude to Dieudonné the comedian than Dieudonné the political activist and agitator. What is somewhat problematic about this stance is that Dieudonné's political viewpoints have, especially since 2003, become an increasingly important part of his one-man shows and it has become ever more difficult to identify where the boundary lies between what Dieudonné declares as a comedian onstage and what he says as an activist offstage. The comedian Jérémy Ferrari has said that Dieudonné's one-man shows 'se sont transformés en meeting politiques' ['have turned into political gatherings'].[53] Ferrari also commented at a debate about humour in September 2017 that Dieudonné has become focused on pleasing his political allies rather than being funny and that he evokes the same political ideas on and offstage.[54] The notion that Dieudonné's expression of polemical

---

52   Gaccio and Dieudonné, *Peut-on tout dire?* p. 39.
53   Thierry De Cabarrus, 'Jérémy Ferrari répond à Dieudonné sur Youtube: comment il démonte la "machine à fric"', *Le Nouvel Observateur*, 18 April 2014, http://leplus.nouvelobs.com/contribution/1191845-jeremy-ferrari-repond-a-dieudonne-sur-youtube-comment-il-demonte-la-machine-a-fric.html [accessed 28 September 2017].
54   Ferrari made these comments at a round table event discussing the theme 'le rire devient-il plus politique?' ['is laughter becoming more political?']. The event was hosted at the Théâtre des Bouffes du Nord on 24 September 2017 as part of a festival organised by the newspaper *Le Monde*.

views has been a consequence of the company he keeps has been evoked by several people who have known him, including the actor and comedian Édouard Baer and the Green Party politician Noël Mamère. Both have questioned the extent to which he possesses clear and coherent political views, and suggested that those he expresses are often the product of external influences.[55] The central argument of Briganti, Déchot and Gautier's *La Galaxie de Dieudonné: pour en finir avec les impostures* is that he has become a figure who has been increasingly defined by his alliances with groups that are far right, ethnically divisive, Holocaust deniers, Muslim fundamentalists, and sectarian.[56] These allegations categorize Dieudonné as someone whose views are incompatible with Republicanism and risks becoming a symbol of the *communautarisme* that he claims to oppose.

Given that Dieudonné remains a performer of stand-up comedy, it is important not just to focus on those who surround him but also on the nature of the material he has performed over the last decade. As previously mentioned, analysis of this is not always a feature of works that concentrate on his political preoccupations. By taking over the running of the Théâtre de la Main d'Or in Paris' 11th arrondissement in the late 1990s, Dieudonné secured himself a space where he was largely free to perform his shows without having to justify himself to producers or directors. The routines that he has performed there from 2004 to 2017 often involved him portraying himself as a victim of censorship and criticizing his treatment by the French media since his appearance on *On ne peut pas plaire à tout le monde* in December 2003. In his 2004 show *Mes Excuses*, he appeared to allude to Jews via phrases such as his opening sarcastic declaration 'Je m'excuse au peuple élu' ['I apologize to the chosen people'] and 'ceux qui ont souffert plus que nous' ['those who have suffered more than us'] but does not regularly use the word *juif(s)* [Jew(s)]. Israël nevertheless constitutes a target that he evoked more explicitly, and he criticized the country for its sales of arms. He added that this is a topic about which it is not permissible to joke in France. Dieudonné frequently uses dark humour and deliberate exaggeration to evoke his sense of victimization, stating for example, 'à un moment j'étais au même niveau que Bertrand Cantat' ['for a time I was on the same

55   Mercier, *Dieudonné démasqué*, pp. 85, 98, 100.
56   See especially: Briganti et al., *La Galaxie Dieudonné*, pp. 63–146.

level as Bertrand Cantat']⁵⁷ and 'j'étais identifié comme la branche humoristique d'Al Qaïda' ['I was seen as the comedic branch of Al-Qaeda']. The Paris-based British journalist John Lichfield argued that his 2006 show *Le Dépôt de bilan* showed him to be 'obsessed with Jews' and that 'when Jews are mentioned – and they are mentioned over and over again – the tone becomes more aggressive, even violent'.⁵⁸

Dieudonné also began his 2012 one-man show *Rendez-nous Jésus!* by alluding to censorship that has restricted where he can perform. In this show, the butt of his jokes included several prominent Jewish figures (e.g. Bernard-Henri Lévy and Dominique Strauss-Kahn) and others with Israeli sympathies (e.g. Francis Lalane). Although this could be seen in part as a form of satire due to the profile of the *affaire DSK*⁵⁹ in France and elsewhere, there are several occasions on which Dieudonné's comments about well-known French Jews appear to adopt a highly stereotypical approach to representing Jews. John Lichfield has suggested that this was a feature of his earlier show *Dépôt de bilan* [*Bankruptcy*], in which he said that 'Dieudonné proceeds by the kind of nudge-nudge, coded provocation that has long been the stock in trade of the anti-Semitic far right in France'.⁶⁰ Michel Wieviorka has argued that this sort of approach is one that Jean-Marie Le Pen has previously adopted, notably during a 1985 speech at a Front national rally in which he singled out a group of French journalists for severe criticism. Although Le Pen did so without alluding to the fact that all of journalists were Jewish, Wieviorka argues that Le Pen's audience would

---

57 Bertrand Cantat is the former lead singer of the French pop group *Noir désir* who was jailed in 2003 for the manslaughter of his girlfriend, the actress Marie Trintignant.

58 John Lichfield, 'Heard the One About the Racist Black Comedian?', *The Independent*, 22 March 2006, http://news.independent.co.uk/europe/article352748.ece [accessed 30 April 2012].

59 The *affaire DSK* refers to allegations that Dominique Strauss-Kahn sexually assaulted and attempted to rape a maid, Nafissatou Diallo, at the Sofitel New York Hotel on 14 May 2011. Although Strauss-Kahn was charged with sexual assault and attempted rape on the day of the alleged offences, prosecutors requested that the charges against Strauss-Kahn be dropped on 22 August. All charges against Strauss-Kahn were formally dropped on 23 August 2011. In 2012, a settlement agreement was reached in a civil case that Diallo brought against Strauss-Kahn. This settlement also brought an end to a counter-lawsuit that Strauss-Kahn brought against Diallo for defamation.

60 Lichfield, 'Heard the One About the Racist Black Comedian?'.

have been likely to have been aware that the journalists concerned were all Jewish.[61]

In *Rendez-nous Jésus* [*Give us back Jesus*], Dieudonné managed to draw a loud laugh from his audience when he said of Dominique Strauss-Kahn's promiscuity 'ce n'est pas des manières de juif' ['that is not the behaviour of a Jew'].[62] Such a comment could be seen as referencing negative stereotypes of Jews as dangerous sexual predators.[63] The philosopher Bernard-Henri Lévy, a high-profile defender of Dominique Strauss-Kahn, is also described within the same show in a way that conjures up the stereotypical notion that Jews exert a controlling influence within the media and circles of power ('il était sur tous les plateaux, en tout cas il a tous les clés' ['he was on all the shows, in any case he has all the keys']). Dieudonné's description of Strauss-Kahn and his wife returning to France from the US and spending large amounts of money in order to try to stage-manage media coverage further appeals to stereotypical discourses that associate Jews with wealth and control of the media. Near the start of the same performance, Dieudonné alluded to his own tendency to talk frequently about Jews by saying that he would not do so that night as he only did so in every second performance. Within minutes, he evoked the Holocaust within the context of a description of topics that one is not supposed to question in France that also included the World Trade Center attacks of 11 September 2001. Towards the end of his show, he made a similar comparison by joking that the Holocaust and Gay Pride are both subjects that cannot be laughed about in France. Whilst such a comment in itself is perhaps not instantly and easily classifiable as an example of anti-Semitism, certain anti-Semitic discourses have nevertheless sought to portray the Jewish man as unmanly or effeminate.[64] Within his shows, Dieudonné often gives the

61   Michel Wieviorka, *L'Antisémitisme est-il de retour?* (Paris: Larousse, 2008), pp. 36–7.
62   Comments made in *Rendez-nous Jésus!* show at the Théâtre de la Main d'Or in Paris on 9 February 2012.
63   For discussion of this stereotype, see: Nathan Abrams, *The New Jew in Film: Exploring Jewishness and Judaism in Contemporary Cinema* (London: I.B. Tauris, 2011), p. 68.
64   See: Ritchie Robertson, 'Historicizing Weininger: The Nineteenth-Century German Image of the Feminized Jew' in B. Cheyette and L. Marcus (eds), *Modernity, Culture and the Jew* (Cambridge: Polity Press, 1998), pp. 25–6, 35.

impression that he is keen to provoke Jews who have criticized him. For example, he alluded to negative reactions to a sketch he performed entitled *Shoananas* (a word that combines 'Shoah' and 'ananas', the French word for pineapple) towards the end of *Rendez-nous Jésus* and dances offstage at the end with a song entitled *Shoananas* playing in the background. The inclusion of this song at a time when he is applauded offstage could be interpreted as an attempt to celebrate his tendency to be provocative, and in particular his provocation of Jews and Jewish groups. Although Serge Uleski has sought to argue that the song was 'destinée à dénoncer l'instrumentalisation du genocide juif dont Dieudonné est une victime collatérale' ['aimed at denouncing the exploitation of the Jewish genocide of which Dieudonné is a collateral victim'],[65] it is important to note that it led to Dieudonné being fined 28,000 euros for 'diffamation, injure et provocation à la haine raciale' ['defamation, slander and inciting racial hatred'] in November 2013 following a case brought due to the song and two videos Dieudonné had broadcast online.[66]

As well as paying attention to Dieudonné's means of representing Jews and Jewishness, it is important to analyse the vision of French society he creates within his shows. Although his earlier career, and the duo he formed with Elie Semoun, saw him evoke themes such as discrimination and prejudice, he did so in a largely unthreatening way. However, it is now the case that many of the views that he expresses within his sketches or while assuming the role of a deliberately exaggerated character are close to the sorts of notion that he espouses in offstage interviews. The idea that France is a country that is racist and accords greater rights to some than others is one example of a view that he has expressed both onstage and in interviews. For example, he joked about France being 'le pays des droits de l'homme, droits de l'homme blanc' ['the country of the rights of man, the right of the white man'] during his 2004 show *Mes Excuses* [*Sorry*] and has argued that 'dans ce pays, on peut stigmatiser les musulmans, les homos, les cathos, les femmes... mais pas les juifs' ['in this country, one can stigmatize Muslims, gays, Catholics, women... but not Jews'].[67]

65   Serge Uleski, *Dieudonné: chroniques d'un succès inespéré* (London: Amazon, 2014), p. 76.
66   Haziza, *Vol au-dessus d'un nid de fachos*, p. 14.
67   These latter comments are cited in: Maurice Bontinck, 'Les bus de

In other words, he suggests that France cherishes Republican values such as equality and universalism but sometimes grants rights in ways that go against the notion that citizenship is based on accessing rights as an unmarked individual.

Although Dieudonné does not appear to discuss the term multiculturalism in detail, his routines and interviews suggest that France is struggling to cope with the presence of different groups of people with potentially competing demands. A recurring example involves his argument that Jewish memories of the Holocaust seek to claim a unique form of human suffering that results in the enslavement of black people not being granted adequate recognition. In his 2012 show *Rendez-nous Jésus,* for example, there were several occasions when he compared one group with another or sought to play one group's interests off against another. This notably occurred after his comment that the Shoah and Gay Pride are two events that it is not acceptable to joke about in France. Following this, he told a story about difficulties he encountered while taking his son to a cinema near the Bastille in Paris on the day of Gay Pride. He recounted how his son asked him why two men were kissing and described seeing one man perform oral sex on another. Dieudonné added that his son and him continued walking for so long that they ended up in the 19th arrondissement, and in an area where Muslims were praying in the street due to mosques being overcrowded. This section concluded with Dieudonné saying that it is possible to face legal action for being a Muslim who prays in the street but that it is acceptable for a man to perform oral sex on another man in the street. This questionable assertion by Dieudonné is also a potential sign of the influence of far-right thinker Alain Soral. Soral shares a similar political trajectory to Dieudonné as he too has gone from being associated with the far left to being identified with the far right. Soral's initial political affiliation was with the *Parti communiste* before he became a member of the Front national's central committee.[68] Soral has sought to argue that both Jews and gays enjoy certain privileges and exert considerable influence within fields

Dieudonné en gare d'Angoulême', *Charente Libre*, 21 March 2010, http://www. charentelibre.fr/article/article-5-le-bus-de-dieudonne-en-gare-d-angouleme, 316086.php [accessed 1 May 2012].
68   In June 2018, the *Front national* re-branded itself *Rassemblement national.*

such as the arts and cinema,[69] and he has been widely accused of anti-Semitism.

In some respects, it could be suggested that Dieudonné establishes comparisons and contrasts between different minority groups as part of an appeal for greater equality in order to defend the importance of key French Republican values such as universalism and equality. Furthermore, French-Algerian historian Benjamin Stora argues that some Jewish intellectuals need to do more with memories of the Holocaust and work with other minority groups in France.[70] However, Stora has been critical of the way that Dieudonné has compared memories of the Holocaust and memories of slavery and stated that:

> La compétition des mémoires devient dangereuse quand elle débouche sur la négation de la souffrance des autres [...]. Je crains que l'on aille vers un durcissement du débat et qu'on assiste au développement d'une forme de communautarisme mémoriel où chacun compte ses morts et refuse d'entendre parler de la douleur de l'autre.[71]

> [Memory battles become dangerous when they lead to the negation of the suffering of others [...]. I fear that we are heading towards an intensification of the debate and that we are witnessing the development of a form of memorial communitarianism where everyone counts their dead and refuses to hear of the pain of the other.]

In other words, it is possible that Dieudonné's approach could be interpreted as *communautariste* rather than a coherent argument for a reassertion of Republican values such as universalism. Comments by the British comedian Mark Steel about how the 2001 attacks on the World Trade Center were used to justify US military intervention in Afghanistan and Iraq raise a further problem. Steel argued that 'anyone who is deeply moved by one set of tragedies while ignoring,

---

69   Marie-France Etchegoin, 'Antisémite, "national-socialiste": comment devient-on Alain Soral?', *Le Nouvel observateur*, 26 January 2014, http://tempsreel. nouvelobs.com/l-enquete-de-l-obs/20140124.OBS3766/antisemite-national-socialiste-comment-devient-on-alain-soral.html [accessed 4 May 2017].
70   Benjamin Stora, *La Guerre des mémoires: la France face à son passé colonial* (Paris: Éditions de l'Aube, 2011), p. 76.
71   Stora, *La Guerre des mémoires*, pp. 83–4.

and even justifying, those on the other side, in reality is not genuinely touched by either' and that this approach becomes 'just an arm of their propaganda'.[72] This implies that Dieudonné's comments about memories of the Holocaust do not provide an effective way of advancing calls for greater recognition of the effects of slavery. Indeed, Patrick Lozès (founder of CRAN, le Conseil représentatif des associations noires [the Representative Council of Black Groups]) has stated that he would have 'mille fois préféré que l'opinion soit invitée à réfléchir et à débattre sur ces questions par d'autres moyens que ceux du scandale' ['Preferred a thousand times over that people were invited to reflect upon and debate these questions by other means than via scandal']. Furthermore, he has said that Dieudonné's approach led to 'une sorte d'impasse' ['a sort of deadlock'] as it provoked 'une sorte de malentendu entre les Noirs et les Juifs de France' ['a sort of misunderstanding between the black people and Jews of France'].[73]

Even among Dieudonné's critics, there are nevertheless those who argue that his focus on questions of memory highlights problems that the French state has created for itself. According to Jean Robin, the *loi Gayssot* [Gayssot law]– which makes Holocaust denial a criminal offence – has created a means for people such as Dieudonné to evoke the supposed influence of Jews on French society due to the lack of laws that ban the denial of other atrocities.[74] Robin argues that the *loi Gayssot* is largely to blame for the emergence of the 'compétition victimaire' ['victim competition'] that is evoked by Dieudonné.[75] As lawyers who have defended Dieudonné's right to perform have pointed out, the way in which the *loi Gayssot*, and three other so-called 'memory laws', have focused on individual atrocities was publicly criticized in December 2005 by a group of nineteen renowned French historians via a declaration that appeared in the newspaper *Libération*. The following year, a group of French lawyers signed a petition that similarly called into question the existence of such laws.[76] It is important to note that

72   Mark Steel, *What's Going On? The Meanderings of a Comic Mind in Confusion* (London: Simon and Schuster, 2008), pp. 24–5.
73   Patrick Lozès, *Nous, les Noirs de France* (Paris: Éditions Danger Public, 2007), p. 155.
74   Robin, *Soral et Dieudonné*, p. 110.
75   Robin, *Soral et Dieudonné*, pp. 241–2.
76   David De Stefano and Sanjay Mirabeau, *Interdit de rire: l'affaire Dieudonné par ses avocats* (Éditions Xenia: Sion, 2014), pp. 143–7.

the signatories of such declarations, and especially the first of the two, included several figures that have left-wing sympathies. In other words, their criticism of memory laws could not be dismissed as a symbol of the sort of anti-Semitism that is associated with the extreme right in France. What distinguishes these two public declarations from the methods that Dieudonné has used, however, is that the signatories sought more explicitly to use reasoned argument than provocative rhetoric.

Dieudonné's evocation of victimhood and victimization at times appears to be somewhat contradictory. On one hand, he criticizes Jews for presenting themselves as eternal victims with a special status; yet, on the other hand, he frequently presents himself as a victim in his performances and media interviews. Since his appearance on *On ne peut pas plaire à tout le monde*, he has begun many of his stand-up shows by referring to the way that he feels that he has been unfairly censored. Indeed, he began his 2012 *Rendez-nous Jésus* show by philos- ophizing about liberty while speaking from behind prison bars, and joked that there is now a standard *arrêté municipal* [municipal decree] that councils use to ban his act. At the end of performances of this show, he returned to the stage to encourage people to buy his DVDs, which he says are *interdits à la vente* [forbidden from being sold]. He has also used this moment to promote a film entitled *Antisémite* that he has made in response to being accused of being anti-Semitic and in which he uses the Holocaust as the basis for often dark and surreal humour. Within this mode of self-presentation, there are certain tensions. Although Dieudonné has claimed onstage that his DVDs are not widely available in mainstream outlets, at the time of writing in autumn 2019, it is still possible to buy DVDs of several of his stand-up shows from major websites such as those of Fnac and Amazon France. Similarly, tickets for Dieudonné's performances were at this time still available from the popular website BilletReduc.com, a site which sells tickets for many stand-up comedy shows across France.

For some of Dieudonné's critics, his cultivation of a sense of injustice constitutes a means of self-promotion. Anne-Sophie Mercier, for example, argues that 'Dieudonné est passé maître dans l'art d'exciter ses troupes pour ensuite mieux faire semblant de les calmer' ['Dieudonné has become a master of the art of working up his troops in order to then do a better impression of calming them down'].[77] Briganti, Déchot, and

77 Mercier, *Dieudonné démasqué*, p. 174.

Gautier see this as 'une logique victimaire' ['a logic of victimisation'] that has stemmed from the threats he has received from radical Sionist groups and led to him 's'acoquine[r] avec l'extrême droite dans un "front des parias" et des "infréquentables"' ['hooking up with the far right in an "alliance of parias" and "undesirables"'].[78] Olivier Mukuna, who is very critical of how Dieudonné has been represented by the French media, argues that 'diabolisé lui-même, il a décidé de provoquer le débat en cessant de participer à la diabolisation de Jean-Marie Le Pen, désigné depuis trente ans comme le "danger raciste exclusive" en France' ['demonized himself, he decided to provoke debate by ceasing to participate in the demonization of Jean-Marie Le Pen, for thirty years designated as the "exclusive racist danger" in France'].[79] To say that Dieudonné no longer participates in the demonization of Jean-Marie Le Pen is arguably an understatement. Dieudonné has made the former leader of the Front national the godfather of one of his children, a daughter who happens to be named Plume (a name that is also used to refer to a sort of pen and therefore references the name Le Pen). He has attended Front national meetings, although it has been reported that Marine Le Pen's public declarations masked her anger at his presence at a party convention in November 2006.[80] Dieudonné has appeared to celebrate the demonization of others at the same time as evoking the ways in which he has been represented. He attracted considerable media attention in December 2008 following a performance at the Zénith in Paris when he presented a *prix de l'infrequentabilité* [a prize for undesirability] to Robert Faurisson, a French historian and Holocaust denier.[81] Dieudonné's interactions with the likes of Jean-Marie Le Pen, Robert Faurisson, and Alan Soral provide a clear sign of the way that he has gone from being associated with anti-racism and left-wing politics in his early career before more recently being characterized by critics as an ally of several individuals associated with the far right.[82]

It is in part due to such associations that Dieudonné has become

78   Briganti et al., *La Galaxie Dieudonné*, p. 35.
79   P.M., 'Olivier Mukuna'.
80   Briganti et al., *La Galaxie Dieudonné*, pp. 83–4.
81   Robert Faurisson also appears in Dieudonné's 2012 fictional film *L'Antisémite* that tells the story of a terminally ill woman who sends her husband to see a Jewish psychiatrist in order to cure his anti-Semitism.
82   See, for example: Briganti et al., *La Galaxie Dieudonné*, pp. 55–61, 65–86.

an ever more controversial and divisive figure. In November 2013, during his time as France's Interior Minister, Manuel Valls described Dieudonné as 'une triste voix qui déchaîne et transpire la haine' ['a sad voice who unleashes and transpires hatred'] during a meeting of the French left to discuss 'Défendre la République contre les extrémismes' ['Defending the Republic against extremisms'].[83] In the months that followed this declaration, Valls sought to utilize legal mechanisms in order to ban Dieudonné from performing his one-man shows. In a manner that is consistent with the actions of many who have sought to categorise Dieudonné as 'un ancien humoriste' ['a former comedian'], Valls stated in December 2013 that 'Dieudonné ne fait plus rire personne depuis bien longtemps' ['It is quite some time since Dieudonné has made anyone laugh'].[84] Although Valls and many of Dieudonné's other critics believe that his one-man shows are no longer amusing, his lawyers observe that ticket sales suggest that there are many who think differently. Furthermore, they suggest that Valls has failed to demonstrate on what basis he feels that Dieudonné is no longer funny and question the extent to which Valls has the competence to make such a declaration.[85] Valls' attempts to use legal mechanisms to prevent Dieudonné from performing proved largely unsuccessful, notably due to judges deciding that Dieudonné's criminal record did not in itself provide reason to believe that he would use his one-man shows to 'tenir des propos pénalement répréhensibles' ['making legally objectionable declarations'].[86] In other words, Valls' attempts to police Dieudonné's humour provided his opponent with greater publicity and a legal victory to celebrate in front of his supporters, as a sign of his ability to successfully challenge those in power and re-assert his supposedly anti-system credentials. In November 2017, however, a court decision to expel Dieudonné from the Théâtre de la Main d'Or in Paris was confirmed, although this decision was officially due to an administrative technicality concerning the procedure by which Dieudonné had been sub-let the venue by a company co-owned by his mother and his wife. Since this time, Dieudonné has faced increasing difficulties when it has come to finding venues willing to host his

83   De Stefano and Mirabeau, *Interdit de rire*, p. 26.
84   De Stefano and Mirabeau, *Interdit de rire*, p. 32.
85   De Stefano and Mirabeau, *Interdit de rire*, pp. 32, 82–3.
86   De Stefano and Mirabeau, *Interdit de rire*, p. 72.

shows, and has performed several on the periphery of Paris in places such as Châtillon and Montreuil. In addition, he has announced venues of several shows in provincial France at the last minute in order to reduce the risk of councils banning his shows. Furthermore several venue owners have accused Dieudonné of renting their venue under false pretences and expressed surprise at seeing the comedian perform at their venue after having rented it out for supposed events organized by a cosmetics firm.[87]

Although Dieudonné seeks to portray himself as espousing a legitimate form of anti-system approach, it is important to explore what being 'anti-system' entails. Being anti-system and anti-Semitic are not mutually exclusive, especially if the 'system' that one opposes is one that is based upon recognizable stereotypes that associate Jews with power and seeking to exercise a controlling influence within sections of society such as the media and the performing arts. In recent years, Dieudonné has sought to defend the *quenelle* salute that has become his calling card as a gesture that is anti-system rather than anti-Semitic in the face of criticism from many who see it as being impossible to dissociate from ant-Semitic connotations.[88]

Conclusion: complications and contradictions?

Dieudonné's way of presenting himself and the evolution of his career provokes many challenging questions and several sources of tension are apparent, as shown by the way he utilizes discourses of victimization. The motivations for his polemical declarations and at times

---

87 See: Coline Renault, 'Comment Dieudonné parvient à contourner l'interdiction de ses spectacles', *Le Figaro*, 18 June 2018, http://www.lefigaro.fr/actualite-france/2018/06/18/01016–20180618ARTFIG00329-comment-dieudonne-parvient-a-contourner-l-interdiction-de-ses-spectacles.php [accessed 10 January 2019].

88 See: Clothilde Chapuis, 'Quenelle de Dieudonné: pourquoi ce geste antisémite est moralement condamnable', *Le Nouvel Observateur*, 8 April 2014, http://leplus.nouvelobs.com/contribution/1185077-quenelle-de-dieudonne-pourquoi-ce-geste-antisemite-est-moralement-condamnable.html [accessed 28 September 2017]; Jonathan Ervine, 'Nicolas Anelka and the Quenelle Gesture: a Study of the Complexities of Protest in Contemporary Football', *The International Journal of the History of Sport*, 24.3–4 (2017), pp. 236–50.

highly controversial humour have been the subject of much debate. In addition to the suggestion that political allies such as Alain Soral have increasingly influenced him, it has been argued that the way in which he presents himself onstage makes him difficult to assess. Bruno Gaccio has stated that Dieudonné's frequent use of irony during his stage shows means that 'on ne sait plus quand il joue au con ou quand il l'est vraiment' ['it is no longer clear whether he is playing the idiot or really being one'] and that this strategy 'envenime un peu plus ses propos' ['makes his declarations a bit more inflammatory'].[89] Thus, his use of irony provides a means by which Dieudonné can seek to distance himself from sentiments attributed to him by his critics aghast at his stage show material. It also provides a way for him respond to accusations of anti-Semitism. However, critics such as Briganti, Déchot, and Gautier argue that this – like his regular insistence that he is anti-Zionist rather than anti-Semitic – is a strategic device that seeks to obscure what they perceive as 'un antisémitisme de plus en plus marqué et violent' ['a more and more marked and violent form of anti-Semitism'] in order to reduce the threat of legal action.[90]

Although accusations of anti-Semitism have brought Dieudonné what many would consider to be negative publicity, they have also helped to keep him and his shows in the public eye during a period when much of the French media has been distinctly wary of engaging with him. It is precisely Dieudonné's ability to court controversy through provocative declarations that explains why the journalist Jean Robin has stated that Dieudonné and his ally Alain Soral, 'n'ont jamais été aussi presents dans les médias que depuis qu'ils en ont été exclus' ['have never been as visible in the media as since they have been excluded from it'].[91] Accusations of anti-Semitism provide him with the opportunity to denounce what he feels to be victimization, censorship, and restrictions to his freedom of expression. Over a decade and a half after his controversial sketch on Marc-Olivier Fogiel's talk show, this context is one that he continues to evoke frequently in his one-man shows and in press interviews. At the same time, denying the allegations of anti-Semitism and arguing that courts have never found him to be guilty of anti-Semitism provides a means of both countering critics and legitimizing his stage material and

89   Gaccio et Dieudonné, *Peut-on tout dire?* p. 55.
90   Briganti et al., *La Galaxie Dieudonné*, pp. 35–6.
91   Robin, *Interdit de rire*, p. 99.

public declarations. To argue that Dieudonné has never been convicted of anti-Semitism masks the fact that verdicts in court cases in which he has been convicted of inciting racial hatred have at times seen judges conclude that he has made statements that have exploited anti-Semitic sentiment. For example, in March 2006 Dieudonné was fined 5,000 euros for 'incitation à la haine raciale' ['inciting racial hatred'] following comments he made about the role of Jews in the slave trade. The verdict stated that the views expressed by Dieudonné were 'directement inspirés de l'imagerie antisémite' ['directly inspired by anti-Semitic imagery'] and that his declarations involved 'recourant à des stéréotypes antisémites' ['recourse to anti-Semitic stereotypes'].[92]

As already stated, judging where Dieudonné the comedian and Dieudonné the political activist and agitator begin and end, or indeed overlap, is far from easy. Furthermore, the fact that there are those among both his critics and former colleagues who suggest that his declarations may be affected by personal issues further complicates matters. Ariel Wizman has speculated that 'deep psychological problems' may have led to his political shift towards more divisive and polemical stances, and Anne-Sophie Mercier suggests that 'certaines des déclarations de Dieudonné, passées inaperçues, font même franchement craindre pour la santé mentale de son auteur' ['some of Dieudonné's declarations, which have gone unnoticed, make one frankly worry about his mental health'].[93] Similarly, situating Dieudonné in relation to Republican values is no easy task. From one perspective, Olivier Mukuna argues that 'Dieudonné est un véritable Républicain' ['Dieudonné is a true Republican'] as he is 'un citoyen qui défend les utopies que sont l'universalisme, le refus du communautarisme et de la hiérarchisation de traitement selon les origines de chacun' ['a citizen who defends the utopias that are universalism, refusing communitarianism at the hierar-chisation of treatment according to one's origins'].[94] However, asserting that Dieudonné is a defender of universalism does not sit easily alongside his highly divisive comparisons between minority groups such as Jews and black people, or gays and Muslims. Indeed, several of his critics argue that this compartmentalization of minority groups constitutes a form of

---

92   Haziza, *Vol au-dessus d'un nid de fachos*, p. 103.
93   Reiss, 'Laugh Riots'; Mercier, *Dieudonné démasqué*, p. 172.
94   P.M., 'Olivier Mukuna'.

communautarisme.[95] What is somewhat clearer is that Dieudonné's brand of humour and public declarations suggest that he is keen to capitalize on the fact that increasing numbers of people in France appear ill at ease with the diversity that he previously celebrated as an anti-racist activist.[96] His argument appears to be that France is struggling to apply its Republican principles in everyday life and is not effectively managing an increasingly diverse society. However, Dieudonné no longer appears to celebrate diversity in the manner that he did when he was a left-wing anti-racist activist. Now, he increasingly seeks to play the concerns of one minority group off against another in order to cultivate a following. For the historians Nicolas Bancel, Pascal Blanchard, and Ahmed Boubeker, his scapegoating of Jews constitutes a highly reductive attempt to pinpoint a cause of inequalities within France (and elsewhere) that frequently involves representing the Jew as a symbolic 'ennemi intérieur' ['internal enemy'] that encourages 'le rélégué issu des immigrations postcoloniales' ['the excluded who are the product of postcolonial migrations'] to 'construire, en miroir, son propre ennemi' ['construct, as a mirror image, their own enemy'].[97] Although his initial sketch on *On ne peut pas plaire à tout le monde* did not make many explicit references to French society per se, it led to much debate about Dieudonné's brand of humour within the context of exploring matters such as freedom of expression, offensiveness, and diversity. In recent years, attempts by the French state to police Dieudonné's humour, and the French media's general tendency to talk *about* rather than *with* Dieudonné, have often proved counterproductive and created precisely the conditions that have helped him not just to cultivate an online following but also continue to attract large numbers of people to his stand-up shows.

95   See, for example: Stora, *La Guerre des mémoires*, pp. 83–4.
96   Surveys cited by the historians Nicolas Bancel, Pascal Blanchard and Ahmed Boubeker suggest that between 2009 and 2015 the proportion of people in France who felt that there were too many immigrants in the country increased from 46% to 73%, and the percentage who felt that children of immigrants born in France are not 'vraiment français' rose from 37% to 66%. See: Nicolas Bancel, Pascal Blanchard and Ahmed Boubeker, *Le Grand Repli* (Paris: La Découverte, 2015), p. 120.
97   Bancel et al., *Le Grand Repli*, p. 21.

Chapter 3

Jamel Comedy Club: stand-up comedy
à la française?

Introduction: the origins of the *Jamel Comedy Club*

Jamel Comedy Club has played a major role in helping to increase the popularity and prominence of stand-up comedy in France. It has taken on additional cultural significance due to the ways in which many of its leading performers have sought to articulate visions of Frenchness. This chapter will explore the origins of the *Jamel Comedy Club* and the role that it has played in redefining comedy in France as well as the visions of French society that it has projected. Given that one of the often-cited objectives of the programme was to provide a launch pad for the careers of up-and-coming stand-up comedians in France, it will examine the career trajectories of the cohort of comedians that featured in the first two television series broadcast in 2006 and 2007, and analyse what these tell us about humour in France. This chapter will show that many of the influences on performers who were part of the initial television series of the *Jamel Comedy Club* were American or British rather than French. It will again examine relations between the media and comedy, both by assessing how and why Canal Plus helped to launch the *Jamel Comedy Club* and also by discussing media reactions to the initiative.

Just as the concept of multiculturalism is often seen as being un-French,[1] it can also be said that socio-political and cultural issues mean that a large part of the *Jamel Comedy Club*'s significance stems from adopting an approach that challenges key tenets of French

1 See: Jennings, 'Citizenship, Republicanism and Multiculturalism in Contemporary France', p. 589.

Republicanism. Republicanism's universalist ethos means that it does not generally identify the presence of different groups within society based on criteria such as ethnicity or social class. It instead focuses on people having a relationship with the state as individual citizens; furthermore, its egalitarian principles mean that it is not possible to officially quantify the number of people from different ethnic or racial groups. However, the *Jamel Comedy Club* celebrates diversity and socio-ethnic identities in a manner that is not fully consistent with some of the aforementioned aspects of France's egalitarian Republican ethos. Indeed, it does so by utilizing an art form that is considerably more associated with American and British culture than it is with French culture.

Jamel Comedy Club was initially broadcast as a weekly Saturday evening half-hour-long television show on Canal Plus featuring a succession of aspiring French comedians, many of whom were from France's *banlieues* and/or the descendants of immigrants. The shows broadcast on Canal Plus were compered by the well-known stand-up comedian and actor Jamel Debbouze, and the comedians involved regularly performed under the *Jamel Comedy Club* name at the Théâtre de Dix Heures in Pigalle before moving to a theatre on the Boulevard de la Bonne Nouvelle that Debbouze converted into a comedy club. The initial troop of comedians from *Jamel Comedy Club* television series also went on a national tour and released a DVD of their show at the Casino de Paris. Further DVDs of the initial television series were also released. Within the televised shows, many of the performers explored precisely the types of themes that have dominated Debbouze's own stand-up routines. These included life in France's *banlieues* as well as reflections on diversity and stereotypes in contemporary France. Furthermore, the topics focused upon by the performers sought to create a sense of identification among a predominantly young audience.[2] As stated in this book's introduction, this created a good fit with the significant youth-focused element of Canal Plus's cultural output, and also represented a form of continuity within the context of the role that the channel has played in helping to boost the prominence of French comedians since its inception in the 1980s. By focusing on stand-up

2   Laurent Béru, 'Un humour ethnoculturel et socio-générationnel: L'exemple du programme télévisuel Jamel Comedy Club', *French Cultural Studies*, 22.2 (2011), p. 164.

comedy, and predominantly young stand-up comedians, Canal Plus was furthering its association with edgy and new cultural forms.

The precise time at which Canal Plus sought to launch such a programme was far from a coincidence. In autumn 2005, a wave of suburban unrest in France followed an incident in which two ethnic minority youths were electrocuted after a police chase on a housing estate in Clichy in the Seine-Saint-Denis area north of Paris. In the aftermath of events in Clichy, and the more widespread protests, discussions within the French media took place about the need to ensure greater visibility of ethnic minorities on French television. By 2006, Jamel Debbouze had already achieved considerable notoriety following acting roles in films such as *Le Fabuleux destin d'Amélie Poulain* and *Astérix et Obélix: Mission Cléopatra*, and also from the success of his stand-up shows in terms of both ticket and DVD sales. Several aspects of Jamel Debbouze's background meant that he was well suited to a project aimed at boosting and celebrating diversity. As Isabelle Vanderschelden argues, Debbouze's 'physical features hardly evoke the male French star stereotype' and he is 'small, of slim build, dark-skinned and has a physical disability'.[3] Having been brought up by Moroccan parents in Barbès and Trappes, he is a clear example of someone from a minority and largely under-privileged background who has achieved considerable success. Although wary of political recuperation, especially by right-wing politicians, Debbouze has acknowledged the significance of his status by stating 'Je suis politique de par mon parcours' ['I am political by virtue of my journey'] and that 'pour un petit Rebeu qui a un bras dans la poche, monter sur la scène de l'Olympia et enchaîner des Zénith, c'est politique' ['For a little Arab guy who has a hand in his pocket, being on stage at Olympia and performing lots of times at the Zénith, that's political'].[4] Debbouze's rise to fame in the 1990s and immediately after the turn of the millennium demonstrate what constitutes a prime example of a trend described by the sociologist Nelly Quémener:

Les années 1990-2000 amorcent un tournant plus radical encore

---

3   Isabelle Vanderschelden, 'Jamel Debbouze: a New Popular French Star?', *Studies in French Cinema*, 5.1 (2005) p. 63. Debbouze lost the use of his right arm after he was hit by a train while crossing train tracks at a station in Trappes when he was a teenager. A friend of his, Jean-Paul Admette, died in the accident.
4   Pierre Siankowski, 'Jamel, un homme intègre', *Les Inrockuptibles*, 30 March 2011, p. 32.

vers une figure d'humoriste, participant actif des rapports de pouvoir et porteur d'une vision du monde forgée par l'expérience de domination. Ce tournant s'incarne tout particulièrement chez les humoristes femmes et ceux issus des minorités ethnoraciales émergeant par la voie télévisuelle.[5]

[The 1990s and 2000s saw the beginning of an ever more radical shift towards comedians becoming active participants in power relations and the bearers of world views forged by the experience of domination. This shift is embodied especially by female comedians and those from ethno-racial minorities who emerged thanks to television.]

Quemener's characterization illustrates how French comedy and comedians have in recent decades certainly not been as depoliticized as Lipovetsky argued they were in the late 1980s.[6] Jamel Debbouze initially rose to fame by performing short sketches and film reviews on various shows on Canal Plus and Radio Nova, which means that his involvement with *Jamel Comedy Club* constituted a return to his roots by as it involved him again collaborating with Canal. Furthermore, Debbouze's role as the leader of a project aimed at boosting the careers of emerging comedians – of whom many shared his *banlieue* roots or foreign descent – saw him take on a role similar to that of one of his own teenage role models in Trappes. One of Debbouze's main influences during this period was a teacher named Alain Degois who introduced him to improvisational theatre, and who used this genre as a means of involving young people from the area in positive cultural activities. In his late teenage years, Jamel's role as an *animateur culturel* [youth worker/teaching assistant] at a collège in Trappes saw him take on the role of mentor as he coordinated several projects that involved pupils, and sometimes staff, performing musical or theatrical shows for friends and parents.

Following his initial success as a stand-up, Jamel has continued to support projects for emerging local artists in Trappes coordinated by Alain Degois, and evoked the wealth of talent that is present in the

---

5   Quemener, *Le Pouvoir de l'humour*, p. 22.
6   See: Lipovetsky, *L'Ère du vide*, p. 200. See discussion of Lipovetsky's views on French comedy and comedians in the introduction to this book.

banlieues.[7] His stand-up shows have also been described as creating an opportunity to 'porter un autre regard sur la banlieue' ['look differently at the banlieues'],[8] something that he would have doubtlessly been keen to promote after the events of autumn 2005 had seen many French journalists and politicians focus on negative aspects of life in suburban France. On his first French television appearance during the 1993 *Téléthon* as an eighteen-year-old, Debbouze was already keen to point out that 'les banlieues ne sont pas ce qu'on croit' ['the banlieues aren't like people think'] and that 'y vivent aussi des gens qui ont du coeur, qui sont généreux, qui sont solidaires' ['there are also people who live there who are kind-hearted, generous and supportive'].[9]

Promoting such a vision of France's *banlieues*, and celebrating the existence of diversity in France as a whole, appears to have been one of the main aims of the *Jamel Comedy Club*. The remit for its initial emergence as a television programme influenced its modus operandi, as demonstrated by the fact that the three criteria used to select performers were 'la mixité sociale, faire marrer le public, et avoir un rire intelligent' ['social diversity, making the public laugh, and having an intelligent form of humour'].[10] Although the second of these elements is highly unsurprising, the presence of the other two is of greater significance. The explicit reference to 'mixité sociale' makes clear the socio-political focus of the project and the last one appears to symbolize a desire to engage in or create socio-political debates. The increased desire of French television channels to feature a more diverse range of presenters, including more from visible ethnic minorities, stemmed from the aftermath of the 2005 *banlieue* unrest. Despite the fact that Canal Plus's *Jamel Comedy Club* certainly played a role in this process, its relationship with France's *banlieues* is often discussed in an overly reductive manner. Although it was described as a symbol of 'la comédie des banlieues' by some journalists when it started,[11] insufficient attention has been

---

7   Jocher and Kéramoal, *Jamel Debbouze*, pp. 180–1.
8   From review of Jamel Debbouze's initial one man show that appeared in *Le Parisien* on 31 October 1995. Cited in: Jocher and Kérmoal, *Jamel Debbouze*, p. 122.
9   Bernard Violet, *Jamel Debbouze: l'as de coeur* (Paris: Fayard, 2008), p. 143.
10   Elisha Karmitz, 'La Comédie des banlieues', *L'Express*, 21 July 2006, http://www.lexpress.fr/culture/scene/la-comedie-des-banlieues_459349.html [accessed 1 June 2017].
11   See: Karmitz, 'La Comédie des banlieues' ['banlieue comedy'].

devoted to the fact that several leading performers from the first series were not actually from France's *banlieues*. Indeed, there was a tendency within much of the French media to conflate the *banlieue* and ethnic minority roots of the performers.[12] Although performers such as Thomas Ngijol, Fabrice Éboué, and Le Comte de Bouderbala grew up in the *banlieues* of Paris and exploited their *banlieue* roots in their stand-up material, others such as Dédo and Blanche Gardin did not evoke their *banlieue* upbringing as explicitly. Little was made of the provincial upbringing of Claudia Tagbo (born in Abidjan, Ivory Coast, but who spent the majority of her secondary school education in the Lozère and Gard areas of southern France), or Alexis Macquart (originally from the Pas-de-Calais in northern France). Indeed, Noom Diawara has been critical of the way that the original group of *Jamel Comedy Club* performers was categorized by the French media:

> On est passé pour des jeunes de banlieue, anciens délinquants qui ont arrêté de faire des histoires pour faire de l'humour. Ce n'était pas du tout ça en fait, c'est juste que l'on était des jeunes – de minorités, certes – qui faisaient de l'humour et ce n'était pas communautaire. C'est générationnel et c'est un nouveau type d'humour avec de nouveaux codes.[13]

> [We were seen as young people from the banlieues, former criminals who had stopped getting in trouble in order to be funny. It wasn't that at all in fact, it's just that we were young people – admittedly from minorities – who were being funny and it wasn't community-specific. It was generational and it was a new type of humour with new codes.]

In other words, the socio-political context that made French broadcasts receptive to broadcasting a programme such as *Jamel Comedy Club* also informed the – at times inaccurate – categorization of the initial group of performers. In a broader examination of 'l'humour des minorités' in France during the 1990s and 2000s, Nelly Quemener argues that this period actually saw a shift from 'réhabiliter la figure du "jeune de

---

12   Of the fifteen comedians who performed in the first series of the *Jamel Comedy Club*, nine were from France's *banlieues* and thirteen were either of foreign descent or mixed race.

13   Noom Diawara, interviewed by Jonathan Ervine (unpublished), 25 March 2017.

banlieue" en prenant du contre-pied le stéréotype négatif qui lui est associé' ['to re-appropriate the figure of the "young person from the banlieues" by adopting the opposite view to the negative stereotype which is associated with it'] towards instead 'insiste[r] bien advantage sur la multiplicité des constructions identitaires' ['place much greater emphasis on the plurality of forms of identity'].[14] *Jamel Comedy Club* exemplifies this trend through the myriad ways in which different stand-up comedians present themselves and their experiences, using humour to intervene in debates about the opposition (or interaction) between Frenchness and foreignness and represent their daily life.

When one looks at the biographies of the performers who partic-ipated in the initial series of *Jamel Comedy Club*, an examination of their parents' professions and their level of educational attainment suggests that several of the comedians from the *banlieues* of Paris are actually from relatively middle-class backgrounds. Fabrice Éboué, although born in Maisons-Alfort, attended private Catholic schools during a childhood largely spent in Nogent-sur-Marne; his father was a gynaecologist and his mother a history teacher. Both Blanche Gardin and Thomas Ngijol have fathers who were sociologists; Gardin's mother was a writer and translator and Gardin herself completed a postgraduate degree in sociology. Sami Ameziane, whose stage name is Le Comte de Bouderbala, studied applied foreign languages at l'Université Paris 8 after passing a *baccalauréat littéraire* [literary school leaving exam] and spent a year at the University of Connecticut in the United States. Of the performers who did not grow up in the *banlieues* of major French cities, Claudia Tagbo obtained a master's degree in Performing Arts from Université Paris 8. In addition, Mamane – who was born in Niger and is the son of an ambassador – arrived in France to study for an advanced postgraduate degree in Plant Physiology at l'Université de Montpellier after having also lived in the Ivory Coast and Cameroon.

14   Quemener, *Le Pouvoir de l'humour*, p. 87.

Margins and the mainstream: exploring the significance of *Jamel Comedy Club*

The significance of *Jamel Comedy Club* extends far beyond the diversity provided by the material and socio-ethnic mix of the performers. It was also novel in cultural terms as it brought stand-up comedy to a major French television channel, and thus helped a great many French viewers to familiarize themselves with this form of comedy. Although Canal Plus 'has constituted a stepping stone for many emerging artists, including Jamel Debbouze',[15] *Jamel Comedy Club*'s format was something new and different for French audiences. The succession of new artists performing short routines based on their own lives and involving interaction with the audience constituted a departure from the more rigid structures, and generally depoliticized nature, of stage shows by more well-established French comedians who symbolized what Quemener terms 'la tradition du café-théâtre français' ['the tradition of the French café-theatre'].[16] Indeed, Jamel Debbouze explained the principles of stand-up on some of the first episodes of the television show and also several of the stage shows. Press articles about the programme adopted a similar approach in order to establish a cultural context. In so doing, both Debbouze and the many French journalists that wrote about the *Jamel Comedy Club* frequently evoked what they saw as the American roots of stand-up comedy. Articles regularly mentioned black American comedians such as Richard Pryor and Eddie Murphy – both of whom Debbouze has cited as influences – and treated the genre as one dominated by artists from minority backgrounds. Although the point was not always explicitly made in press coverage of the launch of the *Jamel Comedy Club*, a parallel can be drawn between the arrival (and subsequent re-appropriation) of originally American hip-hop culture – especially rap music and breakdancing – in 1980s France and the increased visibility of stand-up comedy in France to which *Jamel Comedy Club* contributed. Nevertheless, this chapter will also show that several press articles over-simplified the performers' links with urban culture, and in particular rap culture.

Although the notion that *Jamel Comedy Club* involved an American cultural form becoming more prominent in France was discussed in

---

15   Vanderschelden, 'Jamel Debbouze', p. 62.
16   Quemener, *Le Pouvoir de l'humour*, p. 107.

several press articles around the time of the initial television broadcasts, a more detailed exploration of the main performers' relationship with American stand-up comedy could have been provided. For example, there was very little discussion of the way that certain leading comedians from *Jamel Comedy Club* have sought to re-appropriate – or arguably re-use – jokes from the repertoire of leading British or American comedians. Several of the leading performers in the initial series of *Jamel Comedy Club* were familiar with performers such as Richard Pryor and Eddie Murphy, and this appears to have influenced their material. For example, Thomas Ngijol's imagining of a black Superman (broadcast in the first television series, and evoked in several of his theatre shows) re-used a familiar starting point for black North American comedians such as Pryor. However, it is important to note that Richard Pryor is not just a reference point for black comedians in *Jamel Comedy Club*. Indeed, he has been described as a major influence by non-black comedians such as Dédo. Dédo has talked of having 'découvert le stand-up par Richard Pryor' ['discovered stand-up thanks to Richard Pryor'] and how, as a teenager, he marvelled at the American comedian's way of 'casser le quatrième mur théâtral' ['break the theatrical fourth wall'] in order to 's'adresser directement aux gens' ['speak directly to people'].[17] In other words, the appeal of comedians such as Richard Pryor to members of *Jamel Comedy Club* went beyond a sense of identification based on race and representing minority status and was also derived from his comedic or storytelling style.

The fact that Debbouze was following an American model when launching *Jamel Comedy Club* is further demonstrated by the way that he launched the television programme after buying the rights to a format and logo associated with the American television show *Def Jam Comedy*. This programme is widely credited with having helped to launch the careers of many African-American comedians. In addition to copying an American approach, Debbouze also effectively took over the lesser-known pre-existing Paris-based Comic Street Show comedy nights by basing *Jamel Comedy Club* around several of its leading performers. In addition to evoking Richard Pryor and Eddie Murphy in media interviews, leading black American singers such as Barry White, James Brown, and Stevie Wonder were regularly

17   Dédo, interviewed by Jonathan Ervine (unpublished), 24 March 2017.

referenced by Jamel Debbouze while compering the television shows. Debbouze himself, as a comedian, has tended to focus more on personal experiences and observational material than other older and more traditional French performers whose routines are more explicitly scripted, character-based, or sketch-based. A recurring joke alluded to this in one of his early stand-up shows and involved the repetition of the line 'après j'vous fais des sketches' ['later I'll do some sketches for you'] in the middle of anecdotes he was recounting to the audience. He has also joked onstage about how his audiences are different to those of older French comedians such as Pierre Palmade and Muriel Robin.[18] As has been observed by Jérôme Jeanjean, Jamel Debbouze's brand of humour 'se moque des conventions ronron-nantes du comique [et] le spectacle est bâti à la mesure d'un set de rap, tout en ruptures de rythme et en mimiques évocatrices' ['mocks the monotonous conventions of the comic (and) the show is constructed in the manner of a rap set, composed of breaks in rhythm and evocative gestures'].[19] Such an approach helps to explain why so many young and urban-based French people have identified with Debbouze, although it is important to acknowledge that his popularity extends beyond such groups.[20] Comedians from *Jamel Comedy Club* have also sought to position their approach as something novel within the context of French humour, as demonstrated by these sentiments voiced by star performer Thomas Ngijol:

> L'existence même de cette émission [Le *Jamel Comedy Club*] est une revendication. C'est de revendiquer le fait qu'il y a un autre humour, c'est de revendiquer le fait qu'il y a d'autres personnes qui sont capables de prendre la parole et qui ont des choses à dire. C'est la seule revendication qu'il y ait...[21]

---

18   Frédéric Chau, who performed in the second and third series of the *Jamel Comedy Club,* has nevertheless said that seeing Palmade and Robin perform on consecutive nights during a family holiday as a teenager played a role in his decision to become a comedian. See: Frédéric Chau, *Je viens de si loin* (Paris: Philippe Rey, 2015), p. 150.
19   Jérôme Jeanjean, 'Un Show rêvé', *Les Inrockuptibles*, 17–23 mars 1999, p. 21.
20   This is a point acknowledged by Vanderschelden in 'Jamel Debbouze', p. 63.
21   *Génération éclectique, le magazine des cultures urbaines*, Chakib Lahssaini with Thomas Ngijol, Fabrice Éboué and Patson (France Culture, 28 July 2006) [radio interview].

[The very existence of this programme is a statement. It's making a statement about there being another humour, making a statement about the fact that there are other people who are capable of having their say and who have things to say. It's the only statement there is…]

Ngijol's comments suggest that performing stand-up comedy can itself be empowering, particularly for those who have not previously had the opportunity to perform to large television audiences. Jamel Debbouze also made this point in media interviews when the Canal Plus television series was being launched.[22] The inclusionary potential of stand-up comedy has also been evoked by Debbouze's long-time collaborator Kader Aoun, who believes that it is an art form that involves 'désacraliser la scène, la rendre moins inaccessible' ['demystify the stage, make it less inaccessible'].[23] In other words, Aoun identifies stand-up comedy as an art form whose relative lack of hierarchies and conventions means it has the potential to achieve a broad appeal.

Whilst Ngijol, Debbouze, and Aoun are right to point towards the way that stand-up comedy can be progressive and inclusive, it would be wrong to assume that it is always one of its defining characteristics. Such a characterization is problematic for two main reasons. Firstly, it is wrong to assume that all French comedians from racial, ethnic, or other minority groups base their routines around these roots. Indeed, it is noticeable that half of the performers on a list of mainstream traditional French comics that Laurent Béru sees as very different from those involved with the *Jamel Comedy Club* are of foreign descent.[24] Secondly, it is important to remember that there are well-established popular comedians who seek to perpetuate stereotypes or prejudices based on factors such as gender, race, or ethnicity. Certain comedians in France have gained a reputation in part through performing routines based on imitating racial stereotypes associated with minority groups; Michel Leeb's famous *L'Africain* sketch from the 1980s provide a prime

22   See: Karmitz, 'La Comédie des banlieues'.
23   In: Jocher and Kéramoal, *Jamel Debbouze*, p. 273.
24   Béru's list of French mainstream performers is as follows: Jean-Marie Bigard, Michel Boujenah, Chevallier et Laspalès, Franck Dubosc, Eric et Ramzy, Florence Foresti, Jean-Luc Lemoine, Titoff, Michaël Youn. See: Béru, 'Un humour ethnoculturel et socio-générationnel', pp. 169–70.

example.[25] Indeed, Maxime Cervulle et al. argue that the emergence of projects such as the *Jamel Comedy Club* should not obscure the way that much contemporary mainstream comedy in France has been shaped by a period of social crisis in which there is often a 'backlash néocon-servateur' ['neo-conservative backlash'].[26]

Although the referencing of stereotypes by the performers in the *Jamel Comedy Club* has at times been somewhat problematic, the power dynamics in play have generally been different from those in the examples cited above. The comedians in the *Jamel Comedy Club* are from a diverse range of backgrounds and have generally used comedy to make light of their differences and effectively promote tolerance within a multicultural society. This is very different to what happens when a comedian from a racial majority performs material in which they mock members of racial minorities. In a 2011 interview with the cultural magazine *Télérama*, Jamel Debbouze described how he has sought to demystify topics such as immigration that he feels have been manipulated by politicians and the media:

Les Français ne connaissent pas leur immigration, ils en ont peur. C'est normal parce que c'est TF1 qui a fait les présentations! Et puisque, à chaque veille d'élection présidentielle, on leur ressort le meilleur argument : la peur de l'étranger... J'essaye juste de faire connaissance avec la France et de faire en sorte que la France fasse connaissance avec nous. C'est la même chose au Jamel Comedy Club, le théâtre où je programme des jeunes comiques, beaucoup issus de l'immigration...[27]

[French people are not familiar with their country's immigration, they are scared of it. It's normal because it's TF1 that has presented it! And since, in the run-up to every presidential election, they are presented with the best argument: the fear of the foreigner... I am just trying to get to know France and make sure that France

---

25   In Judith Sibony's 2015 documentary film *Chocolat: une histoire du rire*, Patson – who performed in the first three series of the *Jamel Comedy Club* – tells of being mocked in the school playground due to this sketch's portrayal of people who shared his African roots.

26   Cervulle et al., 'Du Rire aux armes', p. 7.

27   Aurélien Ferenczi, 'Jamel Debbouze: l'entretien', *Télérama*, 19 January 2011, p. 18. TF1 is the most-watched television channel in France.

gets to know us. It's the same thing at the Jamel Comedy Club, the theatre where I put on young comedians, many of whom have immigrant roots...]

In his stand-up shows, Jamel Debbouze has evoked his dual French-Moroccan heritage without seeking to privilege one over the other. In *Jamel Comedy Club*, many of the comedians mention similar themes such as the challenges of being *métisse* and several draw upon the experience of visiting their ancestors' country of origin. Cultural differences are often held up as something that can be laughed about and several comedians deliberately play up to stereotypes associated with their own ethnic/racial group, and this sometimes involves them deliberately adopting exaggerated accents for parts of their routines. Almost all draw on personal experience although a degree of exaggeration and imagination is used to embellish certain anecdotes. As Laurent Béru argues, concentrating on such themes is notable given French Republicanism's reticence to approach racial issues.[28] Furthermore, Nelly Quemener argues that the decade before the launch of *Jamel Comedy Club* – the 1990s – saw 'l'avènement à la television d'un humour basé sur le récit de soi, la parole expérientielle et "authentique", qui n'hésite pas à apposer un regard parfois critique sur l'universalisme républicain' ['the emergence on television of a humour based on first-person storytelling, personal experience and "authenticity", which does not hesitate to cast a sometimes critical eye over Republican universalism'].[29] In other words, the *Jamel Comedy Club* needs to be understood not uniquely as a response to debates about the visibility of minorities following the *banlieue* unrest of autumn 2005, but also as a symbol of continuity when it comes to humour on French television. Despite the show's apparent socio-cultural mission, Debbouze has repeatedly asserted that he does not want to be seen as someone carrying out a task similar to that of a social worker.[30] In other words, he has sought to reduce the extent

---

28 Béru, 'Un humour ethnoculturel et socio-générationnel', p. 169. This reticence stems from the way that French Republicanism is based on universalism and the notion that people have a relationship with the state as individual citizens.
29 Quemener, *Le Pouvoir de l'humour*, p. 86.
30 See: Sloan, *Jamel Debbouze*, p. 129; Pierre Siankowski, 'La Force d'en rire', *Les Inrockuptibles*, 31 July–6 August 2002, p. 27.

to which evoking socio-political issues deflects attention away from his status as a performer. This is quite different from the way that Dieudonné is a comedian who has both evoked socio-political issues and sought to involve himself in mainstream politics by standing for election on several occasions. Although Debbouze draws upon his North African roots in some of his routines, he has presented himself as both French and Moroccan via his stage shows and said during these performances that his audiences are a symbol of France's diversity. Indeed, the journalist Pierre Siankowski argues that focusing on Jamel's ethnicity risks obscuring the importance that his innate sense of humour has played in his success.[31]

Despite the distinctions mentioned above, there is nevertheless a tension between how Debbouze sometimes plays up his non-French roots and at other times appears to minimize their importance. This is symptomatic of the complexities involved in negotiating a hybrid identity. It is also worth recalling that the inclusive and progressive ethos of *Jamel Comedy Club* is not seen by its originators as being purely to do with racial and ethnic issues. In explaining the significance of the stand-up comedians chosen to participate in the *Jamel Comedy Club,* its artistic director Kader Aoun appealed to more universal concepts by stating that 'notre société est très verrouillée lorsqu'on est le fils de personne, et c'est plutôt inhabituel de voir à la télévision de nouveaux artistes qui ne viennent pas du sérail' ['our society is very closed when you are not the son of someone well-known, and it's quite unusual to see new artists on television who are not part of the inner circle'].[32] Even though these words do not explicitly suggest that racial or ethnic issues are the basis for the exclusion described, the existence of such barriers suggests that France is not as egalitarian as its Republican principles suggest that it should be.

Problems and criticisms concerning the *Jamel Comedy Club*

Although the majority of the press coverage that followed the launch of the *Jamel Comedy Club* was positive, certain criticisms emerged due to both its format and the way that the performers discussed questions

31   Cited in: Sloan, *Jamel Debbouze,* pp. 200–1.
32   Violet, *Jamel Debbouze,* p. 339.

of identity. For some cynics, the project and especially the television series meant that it was a sort of 'Star Academy de l'humour'.[33] In other words, its format was seen as mirroring that of a popular musical reality television show in which young contestants competed against each other to win a recording contract. This criticism is, however, open to question for several reasons. Firstly, *Jamel Comedy Club* did not involve the performers competing against each other and it did not use telephone voting in order to boost its profits. In addition, *Jamel Comedy Club* was not as aggressively marketed towards young people as *Star Academy* was by TF1. Several of the comedians who participated in the *Jamel Comedy Club* at its inception underlined that they felt justified in asserting that they had greater artistic legitimacy than contestants on a musical reality television show. Fabrice Éboué emphasized this point during a radio interview on the station France Culture:

> Nous, on est là depuis X temps, on sait ce que c'est la galère de comédien sans revenir sur le classique 'j'ai galéré'. Je veux juste dire que si on a un CV à poser sur la table, on l'a comme tout le monde et on n'est pas là par hasard.[34]

> [Us, we have been present for a certain time, we know what it's like to struggle as a comedian without having to just come out with the cliché 'I struggled'. I just want to say that if we have a CV to put on the table, we have one like everyone else and we are not there by chance.]

Éboué thus rejected the idea notion that the *Jamel Comedy Club* performers had been plucked from obscurity. He had, himself, previously performed at several Parisian comedy venues. These included the Théâtre du Point-Virgule in Le Marais, a venue at which many well-known (and more traditional) French comedians such as Jean-Marie Bigard and Pierre Palmade performed during their early careers. It is also a venue that rejected Jamel Debbouze when he auditioned there in 1995.

Although questions have been raised about the Jamel Comedy Club and what it represents, it is debates around the content of the comedians'

---

33   *Génération éclectique* [radio interview].
34   *Génération éclectique* [radio interview]. Amelle Chahbi expressed similar sentiments during this programme when discussing the same topic.

performances that have been the most contentious. For some critics, the show has focused on urban culture to such an extent that it has produced a form of *humour communitaire*. For example, Pascal Girbig characterizes its approach as one where 'on sectionne les choses, chacun s'isole, alors qu'il serait plus intéressant d'avoir une approche globale des choses' ['things are catergorized, everyone isolates themselves, when it would be more interesting to see a broader approach to things'].[35] In addition to calling into question its breadth of appeal or relevance, the notion of *humour communitaire* characterizes the *Jamel Comedy Club's* approach as incompatible with the universalism enshrined in French Republicanism. Whilst adopting an American model of stand-up comedy has been something that the proponents of the project have been keen to vaunt, they have sought to challenge the notion their performances constitute a form of *humour communitaire*. This adjective *communitaire* tends to be used in France to be dismissive of something that is perceived as being specific to an individual community rather than society as a whole. Given that the *Jamel Comedy Club* aims to comment on contemporary French society, labelling it as *communitaire* would suggest that it is producing a restricted and overly selective vision. Jamel Debbouze has, however, argued that the form of humour in which he believes is one that plays a role in breaking down barriers created by *communitarisme*:

> Le communautarisme me rend dingue, ça me fait régresser. Ça fait baisser le niveau. Je serai heureux le jour où je verrai des Juifs 'se foutre de la gueule' des homos; ou des femmes qui chambrent des Arabes. Bref, le jour où on pourra caricaturer tout le monde sans avoir de problèmes, et c'est à cela que j'aimerais contribuer.[36]

> [Communautarianism drives me crazy, it makes me go backwards. It lowers the level. I will be happy the day when I see Jews 'take the piss out of' gays; or women who tease Arabs. In short, the day when it will be possible to caricature everyone without having any problems, and I would like to contribute to that.]

---

35   Pascal Girbig, 'Communautarisme: peut-on rire de tous?', *Atlantico.fr*, 14 July 2011, http://www.atlantico.fr/decryptage/humour-laique-communautaire-stand-jamel-correzien-128888.html [accessed 18 April 2012].

36   In: Pauline Person, 'Interview Jamel Debbouze', *Télé 2 semaines*, http://www.tele-2-semaines.fr/contenu_editorial/pages/echos-tv/7651-jamel-debbouze-je-serai-heureux-quand-on-pourra-caricaturer-tout-le-monde [accessed 22 February 2011].

The way in which Debbouze evokes caricaturing in the above comments is however potentially problematic due to issues concerning the use and re-use of stereotypes. One could also ask whether a situation involving groups mocking each rather, than reflecting on society as a whole, produces a form (or forms) of *humour communautaire*. Certain critics of the *Jamel Comedy Club* would certainly argue that it does. Jamel Debbouze clearly aspires towards acceptance that crosses boundaries of race, ethnicity, and class, and the extent of the success of his one-man shows and levels of DVD sales suggest that he has in many ways achieved this. Nevertheless, he has joked onstage about being offered film roles where he is asked to play characters who constitute negative stereotypes of North African men.[37] He has talked, more seriously, about aspiring towards greater universality and in an interview with *Les Inrockuptibles* said that 'un jour, dans mes films, je m'appellerai Arthur ou Jean-Philippe' ['one day, in my films, I will be called Arthur or Jean-Philippe'].[38] Debbouze has re-asserted his dislike of *communautarisme* in interviews about the *Jamel Comedy Club*, including one in *Télérama* in 2006:

> Je m'adapte toujours. Et je hais tous les communautarismes. La seule communauté est celle de l'homme. On m'a trop exclu pour que j'exclue aujourd'hui. Je suis plus proche d'un Juif intelligent qu'un Arabe con.[39]

> [I always adapt. And I hate all forms of communitarianism. The only community is that of man. I have been too often excluded to exclude people myself. I am closer to an intelligent Jew than a stupid Arab.]

One could again suggest that Debbouze's opposition to *communautarisme* – as it is expressed above – is somewhat problematic. When evoking universalism after expressing his dislike of *communautarisme*, he refers to two groups that are not mutually exclusive (*les Juifs, les*

37   Noom Diawara, who participated in the first three series of the *Jamel Comedy Club,* has used his stand-up shows to joke about some of the similarly stereotypical West African roles he has been asked to play in films.
38   In: JD Beauvallet, 'Farces à Trappes', *Les Inrockuptibles*, 17–23 March 1999, p. 25.
39   In: Fabien Pascaud, 'Ouvrir la brèche pour les autres, c'est le kif du kif', *Télérama*, 19 July 2006, p. 15.

Arabes) in order to try to reinforce his point. Furthermore, talking of *la communauté de l'homme* [the community of man] paradoxically uses gender-specific language to evoke a sense of community.

Several of the comedians that were part of the *Jamel Comedy Club* when it was launched have, however, evoked their belief in the importance of universalism in less problematic terms. Claudia Tagbo has said that the main principle of the club was 'être au plus près de soi-meme tout en abordant des thèmes universels pour concerner le plus de monde possible' ['to be as true to oneself as possible while dealing with universal themes in order to reach as many people as possible'].[40] Similarly, Fabrice Éboué said in 2006 that 'l'amour de l'être humain' ['love for the human being'] is a crucial principle when it comes to making people laugh, and this comment suggests that jokes need to be grounded in a form of universalism.[41] However, in another interview five years later, Éboué employed terms that are less compatible with Republican values by describing *Jamel Comedy Club* performers as symbolizing 'une génération en France qui se trouve être multiculturelle et multiréligieuse' ['a generation in France who happens to be multicultural and multireligious']. Unlike several of his fellow performers, he also admitted that 'parfois le *Jamel Comedy Club* s'égare dans des penchants trop communautaires' ['sometimes the *Jamel Comedy Club* gets lost in overly community-specific tendencies'] and stated that being *communautaire* at the start of one's career is possible if one decides to 's'ouvrir par la suite' ['subsequently broaden one's focus'].[42] The comments cited above illustrate that the performers involved with the *Jamel Comedy Club* have not all sought to discuss *communautarisme* in the same manner, and also that the ways in which they have done so have at times been problematic. If there is a specific demographic targeted by the *Jamel Comedy Club*, it appears to be that which is traditionally associated with the Canal Plus comedy output – in other words, young people living in urban or suburban areas. As

40 In: Florence Broizat, 'La Griffe Jamel', *Télérama*, 13–19 January 2007, p. 22.
41 In: *Minuit Dix*, Laurent Goumarre with Fabrice Éboué, Thomas Ngijol and Patson (France Culture, 27 September 2006) [radio interview].
42 In: Julien Le Gros, 'Fabrice Éboué: "parlons d'une nouvelle génération qui a la couleur d'aujourd'hui"', *Africultures*, 25 November 2011, http://www.africultures.com/php/index.php?nav=article&no=10498 [accessed 18 April 2012].

Laurent Béru points out, the show's valorization of youth culture and youthfulness is one of its defining features.[43]

A potentially more damaging criticism of the *Jamel Comedy Club* concerns the argument that some of its performers use stereotypes in a manner that negates some of the universalist aspirations mentioned above. Before examining specifics, it is first worth considering how stereotypes function within comedy. Considering inherent power dynamics is particularly important, not least due to the way that Andrew Stott argues that 'watching a parade of stereotypes [...] affords the comfort of confirming an audience's prejudices'.[44] It is worth qualifying this by adding that such a process will only take place if an audience shares the same prejudices, as a lack of shared prejudices would not create the same sense of identification between the audience and the performers. When it comes to minority artists, Alec Hargreaves suggests that reproducing stereotypes is to be expected as 'it is unquestionably difficult to penetrate mainstream markets without adjusting in some degree to the codes and expectations of majority ethnic consumers'.[45] Moving more explicitly into the realm of power relations, Jimmy Carr and Lucy Greeves see the stereotyping of groups within jokes as a means for the joke teller to 'overcome anxieties about [their] own shortcomings and reaffirm [their] own community identity'.[46] In other words, evoking stereotypes has the potential to reinforce hierarchies. Despite this, theorists such as Erving Goffman and Mireille Rosello see the re-appropriation of stereotypes by members of stigmatized groups as something that can create a sense of empowerment and challenge hegemonic discourse.[47] However, how one goes about doing so can involve a careful balancing act. As Rosello observes, a stereotype needs to be re-uttered if it is to be challenged by tackling it head-on and this re-utterance, or 'meta-utterance' can be taken to be an 'unavoidable element of allegiance'.[48]

43   Béru, 'Un humour ethnoculturel et socio-générationnel', pp. 164–5.
44   Stott, *Comedy*, p. 44.
45   Alec Hargreaves, 'The Contribution of North and Sub-Saharan African Immigrant Minorities to the Redefinition of Contemporary French Culture', in C. Forsdick and D. Murphy (eds), *Postcolonial Studies: a Critical Introduction* (London: Arnold, 2003), p. 154.
46   Carr and Greeves, *The Naked Jape*, p. 210.
47   See: Erving Goffman, *Stigma: Notes on the Management of Spoiled Identity* (London and New York: Penguin, 1968); Rosello, *Declining the Stereotype*.
48   Rosello, *Declining the Stereotype*, pp. 13, 36.

Several further accusations have engaged with stereotypes, several accusations have been levelled at the initial group of *Jamel Comedy Club* performers that featured in the two television series broadcast on Canal Plus concerning their evocation of stereotypes. As Laurent Béru points out, the performers aimed to 'stigmatise[r] certains poncifs socioculturels tout en les réutilisant pour faire rire leur public' ['stigmatize certain socio-cultural clichés whilst re-using them to make their audiences laugh'].[49] In other words, they sought to re-appropriate stereotypes in the manner described by both Goffman and Rosello (see discussion above). However, as Béru later observes, the existence of such stereotypes within French society reveals 'la difficulté de vivre ensemble que peut rencontrer la population d'un quartier connaissant une situation multiconfessionnelle, pluriethnique et multiculturelle' ['difficulty in achieving social cohesion that can be encountered by a population from an area that experiences a multi-faith, multi-ethnic and multicultural situation'].[50] What is problematic about this form of representation is that it counters the way that the *Jamel Comedy Club* largely seeks to evoke diversity within French society as an issue that lends itself to humorous observations rather than one which pinpoints social and racial inequalities that the state has failed to adequately address.

For Fabrice Éboué, growing up with and accepting diversity within French society confers a sense of entitlement when it comes to dealing with stereotypes and questions of racial difference. He has said of the comedians initially involved with the *Jamel Comedy Club* that 'on est la première génération à pouvoir se permettre de plaisanter sur les Noirs, les Blancs, les Jaunes' ['we are the first generation that is able to allow itself to joke about people who are black, white or yellow'] and adding 'on a la légitimité' ['we have the legitimacy']. He then established a contrast by stating that 'si Bigard faisait les mêmes blagues, on le taxerait de raciste' ['if Bigard did the same jokes, he would be branded racist'].[51] Jean-Marie Bigard's differing roots, as a white French comedian born in the 1950s who is often seen as being somewhat right-wing, would thus mean that his mocking of the same groups would be more likely to cause offence and seen as an endorsement of discriminatory practices. Whilst there is something potentially empowering about members of

49   Béru, *Un humour ethnoculturel et socio-générationnel*, p. 163.
50   Béru, *Un humour ethnoculturel et socio-générationnel*, p. 167.
51   In: Broizat, *La Griffe Jamel*, p. 22.

minority groups re-appropriating and re-using stereotypes that have been exploited in more aggressive and explicitly discriminatory ways by members of majority groups, this does bring with it certain problems. When talking about being black and living in France, Thomas Ngijol has joked that 'l'équipe de France de football ressemble de plus en plus à l'équipe du Zimbabwe' ['the French football team is looking more and more like the Zimbabwe team']. To understand how race and ethnicity affect the power dynamics of such statements, it is worth remembering that the long-time Front national leader Jean-Marie Le Pen criticized the French national football team for not truly representing the French nation due to the high proportion of black (and North African players).[52] Here, it is important to draw a series of distinctions. Firstly, Le Pen's comments were made in all seriousness and are in keeping with the way that the Front national has often been accused of advocating racial discrimination and contributing to the stigmatization of racial and ethnic minorities in France. What Ngijol is doing is taking the same characteristic (the high number of black players in the French football team) and celebrating, and normalizing, it in a light-hearted manner. He is celebrating not just this charac-teristic but effectively also the fact that he is allowed to joke about it. However, Rosello's discussion of re-utterances of stereotypes suggests that this re-utterance may be problematic. One potential consequence of Ngijol's jokey comments is that they may remind some viewers of Le Pen's comments on the French football team and the fact that some see the number of black players in the French football team as a problem.

The way in which jokes are told by the various members of *Jamel Comedy Club* suggests not only that they believe that people can create humour by laughing at themselves and those like them, but also that they can do so by laughing at those who are from different minority groups. For example, two French-born comedians of West African descent, Fabrice Éboué and Thomas Ngijol, have performed routines that mock those from the French Caribbean on the basis of the stereotype that such people are excessively laid-back or lazy.[53] In one

---

52   See: Mogniss Abdallah, '"L'Effet Zidane", ou le rêve éveillé de l'intégration par le sport', *Hommes et migrations*, 1226 (2000), pp. 5–14.
53   Éboué and Ngijol were born in Paris. Both parents of the latter are from Cameroon whilst the former is the son of a Cameroonian father and French mother, and uses his *métisse* roots as the basis for much of his stand-up material.

of the early television programmes, Ngijol joked about how a French-Caribbean branch of Al-Qaeda would be unlikely to be effective by caricaturing its potential members as being too laid-back and easy-going to possess sufficient focus and determination to carry out an attack. In his own stand-up show, *Faites entrer Fabrice Éboué* [*Bring in Fabrice Éboué*], Fabrice Éboué has described the notion of people in the French Caribbean going on strike as 'un pléonasme' ['a pleonasm'] before imitating a very leisurely protest taking place whilst Zouk music played in the background. In a show at the Théâtre de Dix Heures in 2006, Ngijol also once responded to some Moroccans' negative reaction to a joke about Algerians with the phrase 'il y a de la solidarité maghrébine ce soir, c'est Couscous United dans ce coin' ['there's Maghrebi solidarity tonight, it's Couscous United in this corner']. Although the laughter of those targeted by this comment suggested that it was taken in good humour, it is nevertheless clear that Ngijol's words reduced a group of audience members to a simple and easily recognizable stereotype.

Where the use of such stereotypes is potentially most troubling is when they are used by members of one minority group to mock members of another group that is perceived as less well integrated or that lacks the same sort of presence and visibility within French society and culture. When this occurs, the degree of balance stemming from one group mocking another is reduced. What happens in such cases is that hierarchies are endorsed by virtue of members of a more visible or well-integrated group mocking those who are in a less favourable position. In keeping with Jamel Debbouze's desire to see a society where minority groups (or those subject to discrimination and prejudice) are able laugh at each other, it seems that many of his fellow performers have taken the view that members of all minority groups are fair game. Bruno Icher is able to cite one performance where a comedian asked a member of the audience if she was Pakistani before following up with 'vous pouvez dire à vos cousins d'arrêter de nous vendre des roses dans les restaurants? Merci' ['can you tell your cousins to stop selling us roses in restaurants? Thanks'].[54] One-man shows involving the protagonists of *Jamel Comedy Club* have involved jokes based on a similar premise. In his most recent solo DVD entitled *Tout*

54   Bruno Icher, 'Jamelting potes', *Libération*, 9 February 2007, http://www.liberation.fr/culture/010193469-jamelting-potes [accessed 23 January 2012].

sur Jamel [*All about Jamel*], Jamel Debbouze reflects on what it would be like to have a player of Romanian descent representing France at football, and imitates the stereotypical figure of the Romanian beggar while doing so. Immediately after this routine, Debbouze comments that 'on est tous les racistes de quelqu'un' ['we are all someone else's racists']. What is problematic about such an assertion is that it could be seen as a means of downplaying racial prejudice, which is somewhat paradoxical given Jamel Debbouze's criticism of negative ways in which the *banlieues* and immigration are represented in the French media. The way in which Pakistanis and Romanians are freely mocked using particularly crude stereotypes may also be a consequence of the fact that such depictions do not evoke a sense of (post-)colonial guilt. The situation would be quite different if the targets of such jokes were from groups lacking cultural visibility that were from former French colonies. This has parallels with Christie Davies's discussion of jokes about Polish Americans in the United States, who he argues 'have not received the same degree of protective and indignant censorship [from offensive jokes compared to Black Americans] because the ultra-liberals do not feel the same guilt, concern, and anger on their behalf'.[55]

Thomas Ngijol and Fabrice Éboué's first solo DVDs see them both mocking members of minority groups lacking cultural visibility in France through their portrayal of *Asiatiques* [East Asians] as being more different than other minorities. Ngijol states 'un Asiatique, pour un comique c'est un cadeau de dieu' ['an East Asian, for a comedian is a gift from God'] before joking about how they are mysterious and difficult to read. Éboué concludes the live show recorded for his DVD by expressing his desire for French society to be as multicultural as his audience before light-heartedly adding that they should unite 'pour niquer la gueule aux Asiatiques' ['to get one over on the East Asians'].

Within these examples, it is worth differentiating between how stereotypes are used by the performers. The majority of the comments are based on the assumption that members of certain groups will correspond to certain recognizable stereotypes (e.g. the lazy *Antillais*, the rose-selling Pakistani, the begging Romanian, the mysterious *Asiatique*, etc.). However, the last example from the end of Fabrice Éboué's show involves a comedian making himself that butt of

55 Davies, *Mirth of Nations*, p. 191.

the joke due to his contradictory assertions (expressing his love of multiculturalism at the same time as jokingly encouraging people to unite against *Asiatiques*). However, this last example only works in this manner when the audience is aware that this is the performer's intention and laughs at the evident contradiction, rather than the idea of people ganging up on *Asiatiques*. In other words, context is again the key. Éboué's already mentioned belief that he is entitled to mock racial and ethnic differences, whilst not unproblematic, underpins why he uses such a joke. However, there remains the danger that this sort of humour can also appeal to those of a different standpoint, who view diversity and multiculturalism much less favourably and prefer to simply laugh at the evocation of a recognizable stereotype. Indeed Eric Macé argues that one of the main challenges involved exploiting stereotypes with jokes is 'savoir comment rire des stéréotypes sans que l'ironie ou le second degré ne soit pris pour du racisme ou de la stéréotypisation' ['knowing how to laugh about stereotypes without the irony or off-beat humour being taken for racism or stereotyping'].[56] The example of Ngijol's comments about the number of black players in the French football team illustrates the importance of the relationship between the joke teller and the subject(s) of the stereotype(s) evoked.

Potential problems concerning the evocation of stereotypes in *Jamel Comedy Club* stem from not just how racial and ethnic differences are represented, but also how gender and sexuality are treated. Although Macha Séry, writing in *Le Monde*, rejected the argument that the comedians produce a form of 'humour communautaire' she was nevertheless critical of 'les fréquentes allusions à l'homosexualité appuyées par force mimiques' ['the frequent allusions to homosexuality which are accompanied by gestures'].[57] As none of the performers chose to identify as gay, lesbian, or transgender, the problem here is that an absent minority who has no right to reply is being mocked. Consequently, jokes about people who are lesbian, gay, bisexual, or transgender cannot easily be explained away by saying that within *Jamel Comedy Club* everyone makes fun of everyone else. Where gender is

56   Macé, 'Rions ensemble des stéréotypes, p. 23.
57   Macha Séry, 'Jamel assure sa relève', *Le Monde*, 9 July, https://www.lemonde.fr/vous/article/2006/07/07/jamel-assure-sa-releve_793032_3238.html [accessed 24 February 2012].

concerned, a lot of Jamel Debbouze's routines as a stand-up since he started out have revolved around codes and behaviours in a strongly macho *banlieue* environment. However, such themes are not present as often in the routines of the male comedians in the *Jamel Comedy Club* as they were in many of Debbouze's early stand-up shows. However, the way in which the female comedians present themselves and are represented by others within the *Jamel Comedy Club* is significant. Nelly Quemener argues that the Ivory Coast-born Claudia Tagbo 'revisite [...] l'image d'une féminité noire exotisée et hypersexualisée héritée de la période coloniale' ['revisits (...) the exoticized and hypersexualized image of black femininity inherited from the colonial era'] via a performance on the *Jamel Comedy Club* broadcast on 15 July and in which she exhibits 'un corps dansant, se trémoussant et montrant ostensiblement ses fesses' ['a dancing body, grooving and ostensibly emphasizing her buttocks'].[58] Although several of the other comedians do a few dance moves whilst arriving onstage, none of them present what could be described as an 'eroticized' image even if it is one that they are reproducing for the purposes of comedy. Female comedians (notably Claudia Tagbo and Amelle Chahbi) perform more material that involves reflections on femininity than male comedians do about masculinity. Tagbo's entrance onstage, although positively seen by Quemener, reinforces notions of difference rather than normalizing that fact that she is female and a comedian. Similarly, Amelle Chahbi is introduce by Jamel Debbouze as 'l'atout charme du *Jamel Comedy Club*' ['the most charming feature of the *Jamel Comedy Club*'] before she appears onstage at the performance recorded for the 2007 *Jamel Comedy Club* DVD. This again involves highlighting femininity as if to suggest that the presence of female comedians points towards a further element of inclusivity within a show that focuses on diversity. However, the simplistic way in which this is done does little to suggest a truly progressive attitude to gender. Consequently, it appears that the progressive ethos of the *Jamel Comedy Club* is partially negated by the way that it deals with sexuality and gender.

When discussing comedy and stereotypes, it is important to appreciate the frequency with which one can identify stereotypes within stand-up comedy. This is not just relevant to the material

---

58   Quemener, *Pouvoir de l'humour*, p. 113.

that is performed but also to how performers present themselves. By assuming a caricatured or stereotyped role, performers can create both a context for their humour and represent themselves in a way with which their audiences can identify. Many comedians often wear specific types of clothes or style themselves in a manner that either fits with their brand of humour or the image of themselves that they are seeking to create. For example, those who perform a traditional or more dated brand of humour are often traditionally and smartly dressed while those who are more modern and off-beat often reflect this by the way they style (or do not style) their hair and by loud clothes. Where *Jamel Comedy Club* is concerned, François Reynaert has said of the performers that 'chacun campe un stéréotype' ['each one plays a stereotype'].[59] Laurent Béru goes further by observing that 'les genres musicaux diffusés et les looks vestimentaires mis en valeur sont utilisés comme autant de marqueurs identitaires' ['the genres of music used and the fashion styles showcased are used as markers of identity'].[60] Although this is not unusual in stand-up comedy, it is rendered more problematic by the context in which the *Jamel Comedy Club* was created. It is important to recall that Jamel Debbouze has frequently been critical of how French *banlieues* are represented in the media, both onstage and in media interviews. Furthermore, his comedy club sought to respond to a context where young people from visible minorities and/or the *banlieues* are largely absent from French television. Given these elements, it is somewhat paradoxical that many of the performers present themselves in a way that evokes many recognizable stereotypes.

Beyond *Jamel Comedy Club*: career trajectories of the first generation of comedians

Some members of the initial troop of comedians have seen their careers progress more rapidly than others in terms of launching their own solo shows and DVDs. Jocher and Kéramoal argue that several members of the group (Fabrice Éboué, Thomas Ngijol, and Patson) quickly became

59   François Reynaert, 'La France multiculturrire', *Le Nouvel Observateur*, 5 November 2009, p. 94.
60   Béru, 'Un Humour ethoculturel et socio-générationnel', p. 165.

the stars who occupied top billing whilst others received what some felt was scant remuneration for their involvement in non-televised shows that played to packed audiences at the Théâtre de Dix Heures. The authors observe that this led to one comedian, Le Comte de Bouderbala (real name Sami Ameziane) leaving after being refused a pay rise.[61] Although performing in *Jamel Comedy Club* appears to have opened up many opportunities for the individual performers to pursue new projects, Ameziane actually decided to temporarily pursue a stand-up comedy career in the United States due to his frustration at what he saw as a lack of opportunities in France.[62]

In terms of career progression, it is at times hard to assess the extent to which all the members of the *Jamel Comedy Club* gained from the experience and how much of this was due to Jamel Debbouze himself. Although Debbouze was the instantly recognizable face of the project, the television shows, and the national tour, he generally did not appear at the regular – and untelevised – comedy nights at the Théâtre de Dix Heures. It should also be remembered that his collaborator and producer Kader Aoun played a major role in selecting and preparing the performers. Several performers suggest that it was in many ways the name of Jamel Debbouze that played a big role; for example, Claudia Tagbo has said of the troop that 'le label "Jamel" a accéléré notre notoriété' ['the "Jamel" label made us known more quickly'].[63] Thomas Ngijol, however, sought to play down the impact of Jamel Debbouze in a radio interview in 2006 during which he stated that 'Jamel n'a rien libéré [...], il a mis juste un deuxième coup de pied à une porte entre-ouverte et c'est vrai qu'un coup de pied de Jamel est plus efficace qu'un coup de pied de Laurent Gerra parce que lui c'est un contre-sens, il ferme la porte' ['Jamel didn't unleash anything (...), he just gave a second kick to a half-open door and it's true that a kick from Jamel is more effective than a kick from Laurent Gerra because he would be the opposite and close the door'].[64] The way that he compares Debbouze with Laurent Gerra (a well-known impersonator and comedian) suggests that Ngijol values a form of comedy that is

---

61 Jocher and Kéramoal, *Jamel Debbouze*, pp. 273, 276.
62 He mentions this in an interview that is included as a bonus feature on the self-titled DVD he released in 2014.
63 Florence Broizat, 'La Griffe Jamel', p. 22.
64 *Minuit Dix* [radio interview].

new, young, and dynamic rather than one that corresponds to a more traditional model.

The success of *Jamel Comedy Club* on Canal Plus has allowed several of the leading performers not just to have more opportunities to perform stand-up comedy, but also to appear on other more mainstream television and radio programmes. For example, Fabrice Éboué regularly appeared on Marc-Olivier Fogiel's talk show *T'empêches tout le monde de dormir* on M6 from 2006 to 2008 and Thomas Ngijol did likewise on Canal Plus' *Le Grand Journal* during the same period. Although this represented a progression towards more general and mainstream programmes, it at times involved the two comedians assuming a role similar to that of a jester and commenting on discussions from a position that isolated them from other guests and greater participation in the debates.[65] Both Éboué and Ngijol have occupied regular roles on well-known and more explicitly humorous radio discussion shows, respectively Laurent Ruquier's *On va s'gêner* on Europe 1 and Stéphane Bern's *Les Fous du roi* on France Inter. Like many of their collaborators in the initial *Jamel Comedy Club*, they have also been involved in many theatrical and cinematic projects. Noom Diawara has written and performed in several successful plays that he co-directed with fellow comedians such as Amelle Chahbi. One of these, *Amour sur place ou à emporter* [*Take-Away Romance*], was released as a film in 2014 and in the same year Diawara starred in the highly successful film comedy *Qu'est-ce que l'on a fait au bon dieu?* [*Serial Bad Weddings*] Thomas Ngijol and Fabrice Éboué wrote and directed a 2011 film comedy entitled *Case départ* and the two appear together in the 2015 comedy *Le Crocodile de Botswanga* that was co-written by Fabrice Éboué and Blanche Gardin. Blanche Gardin has herself had acting roles in several films and television programmes, notably including the Canal Plus drama series *WorkinGirls*. Despite the ways in which several of the initial members of the *Jamel Comedy Club* have been able to embark on projects in theatre and cinema rather than remain solely within the field of stand-up comedy, some are keen to insist that they see stand-up comedy as a lot more than just a means to move on to other projects. Dédo provided a prime example of this when describing the process of planning a new solo stand-up show in March 2017:

65   Quemener, *Pouvoir de l'humour*, pp. 178–9.

Cela a toujours été un vrai moteur pour moi, cela n'a jamais été un moyen en soi, entre guillemets. Cela a toujours été une finalité, le stand-up. Je ne me suis pas dit je vais passer par là pour aller ailleurs. Je me suis toujours dit que ce que j'ai envie de faire est de parler aux gens et essayer quelque part de leur transmettre des idées. Voilà, le but du jeu c'est de continuer à faire en sorte que le public m'apprécie, continuer d'être là, et que ce public-là grossit.[66]

[It has always been a real driving force for me, it has never been a so-called means to an end. Stand-up has always been an end in itself. I did not say to myself that I was going to use it to get somewhere else. I always thought that what I wanted to do was to speak to people and try in some way to convey my ideas to them. So really, my aim is to continue to ensure that the audience appreciates me, to continue to be present, and that the audience increases.]

Within the field of stand-up comedy, several of the performers from the initial series of *Jamel Comedy Club* have released DVDs of their solo performances. Several of the solo stand-up shows and DVDs are notable due to the way in which their titles and publicity materials explicitly reference American culture. This is particularly true of performers of West African descent who have sought to reference Afro-American culture. One of the most explicit examples of this trend is provided by Patson's 2012 solo stand-up DVD, *Yes We Can Papa!* The title evokes the campaign slogan associated with Barack Obama's election as American president in 2008, and the presence of a series of stars on a DVD cover on which blue, white, and red dominate further highlights the Americanness. In addition, it is noticeable that all three of Claudia Tagbo's solo stand-up shows have had English titles (*Claudia Comedy Gospel*, *Crazy*, *Lucky*) and the first of these clearly references a musical genre – gospel – that is heavily associated with African Americans. However, cultural genres associated with African-Americans have also been referenced by performers of North African descent as is demonstrated by the decision of D'Jal to entitle his 2007 solo show *One Man Groove*. However, references to American culture

---

66   Dédo, interviewed by Jonathan Ervine (unpublished), 24 March 2017.

are not just evident in the projects undertaken by performers from the initial series of *Jamel Comedy Club* who are from visible minorities. For example, Alexis Macquart has performed alongside other stand-up comedians in stage shows entitled *Desperate Housemen* and *Ex in the City* that reference popular American television series (respectively, *Desperate Housewives* and *Sex in the City*).

When one looks at the solo stand-up DVDs released by members of the initial *Jamel Comedy Club* cohorts, it is clear that many focus on similar material to that which they presented in the television series. This is largely true of the Patson's 2012 DVD *Yes We Can Papa!*, the self-titled solo DVD released by Le Comte de Bouderbala in 2014, Claudia Tagbo's DVD *Crazy* (also released in 2014), and Dédo's *Le Prince des ténèbres* (2015). The fact that all three performers released these DVDs at least six years after the start of the *Jamel Comedy Club* suggests that participating in the show was not in itself sufficient in order to be able to swiftly progress with certain types of solo projects. However, both Thomas Ngijol (*Thomas Ngijol à block* in 2010, *Thomas Ngijol 2* in 2015) and Fabrice Éboué released their first solo DVDs slightly earlier than the aforementioned trio; *Thomas Ngijol à block* appeared in 2010 and *Faites entrer Fabrice Éboué* appeared the following year. Ngijol and Éboué indeed both released follow-up DVDs in 2015, respectively entitled *Thomas Ngijol 2* and *Levez-vous*. Éboué's solo DVD material is generally similar to that which he performed in *Jamel Comedy Club* although there are perhaps more examples of dark humour. However, there is a clear difference between how Ngijol presents himself in his first and second solo DVDs. His first DVD begins with him leaving a tower block in Maisons-Alfort (the area where he grew up) before getting a suburban train to La Cigale to perform his show. The fact that he listens to a song featuring the lyrics 'nothing really changed' during the train journey suggests that he is presenting himself as still being in touch with his *banlieue* roots despite having achieved notoriety as a performer. However, the Ngijol that we see in his second solo DVD from 2015 focuses less on France's *banlieues* and more about regional specificities in different parts of France. He also reflects in an at times sentimental manner about getting engaged and becoming a father, thereby furthering the extent to which his material is based on more universal or mainstream topics.

The *Jamel Comedy Club* was often described as an urban cultural project at the time of its launch, not least due to the previously discussed context established by the *banlieue* unrest of 2005. However, both within the *Jamel Comedy Club* television series and their subsequent stand-up material, several comedians seek to mock – rather than celebrate – what is often referred to as urban culture. In his appearances on *Jamel Comedy Club* shows, Le Comte de Bouderbala mocked the ways in which rappers use and abuse the French language and this trend continues in his solo DVD. Noom Diawara has also made fun of rappers in his solo stand-up material and argues that this is part of the way in which *Jamel Comedy Club* performers have sought to laugh both at themselves and society in general.[67] Fabrice Éboué's first solo DVD actually subtly challenges the notion that the areas surrounding Paris conform to the array of negative stereotypes about France's *banlieues*. For example, he jokes about the Seine-et-Marne being a rural and uncultured area and describes his native Nogent-sur-Marne as being a '*ZEP*' by virtue of being a *zone d'euthanasie prioritaire* [priority euthanasia area] rather than a *zone d'éducaiton prioritaire* [priority education area].[68]

Conclusions: the evolution and continued significance of *Jamel Comedy Club*

The success of the *Jamel Comedy Club* has extended well beyond its status as a television series, as is demonstrated by the career trajectories of several of the leading comedians who performed in the initial series. In addition, the regular – and untelevised – stage shows that are part of the *Jamel Comedy Club* brand no longer take place at the somewhat cramped initial venue of the Théâtre de Dix Heures on the Boulevard de Clichy. In 2008, Jamel Debbouze took over a disused cinema in the Boulevard de la Bonne Nouvelle and turned it into a more spacious comedy club very much on the American model; there is a bar at one end of the room and the audience sit around small tables.

The progression of the initial *Jamel Comedy Club* performers towards new projects has left a gap for new up-and-coming comedians.

---

67 Noom Diawara, interviewed by Jonathan Ervine (unpublished), 24 March 2017.
68 *Zones d'éducation prioritaire* were areas identified by the French Education Ministry as requiring special efforts and additional resources in order to address problems such as low levels of educational attainment.

Although few appear to have received the same career boost as those from the original troop, the *Jamel Comedy Club* events at the Comedy Club in the Boulevard de la Bonne Nouvelle were still regularly playing to packed audiences in autumn 2019. Although the focus on urban culture and diversity still dominates much of the material, there has been a greater variety of forms of humour in recent years. For example, Redouanne Harjane has added a more surreal form of comedy that involves songs and one-liners that evoke absurdity and involve random reflections on everyday life. Tony Saint-Laurent has brought a somewhat more off-the-wall humour than most of the original performers, with the possible exception of Fabrice Éboué. There is also sketch-based comedy, which represents an interesting direction given that the more personalized and Americanized style of stand-up of the initial *Jamel Comedy Club* represented a break with France's long tradition of comedians whose material is mainly sketch-based. The comedy club still acts as a career launching-pad and its website invites performers to send it short videos if they wish to be considered for what are close to open-mic events. These evenings are known as Debjam Comedy, bearing the name of a company created by Jamel Debbouze whose name is very close to that of the American *Def Comedy Jam* from which he bought the rights to the format of *Jamel Comedy Club*.

In general terms, what *Jamel Comedy Club* has achieved goes beyond normalizing the presence on television of a greater number of comedians of ethnic minority and/or *banlieue* roots. Its initial television programme and continued stage shows in Paris have led to an upsurge in interest in comedy, which has become both increasingly popular and increasingly mainstream. This can be seen by the increasing numbers of comedy events that now take place in cities such as Paris, and the prominence of such events on billboards in the French capital. There were nine series of *Jamel Comedy Club* on Canal Plus between 2006 and 2016 as well as a spin-off series *Jamel Comedy Kids* in 2016 that involved children aged five to ten performing sketches by their favourite comedians.

The success of *Jamel Comedy Club* on Canal Plus appears to have inspired other French television channels to attempt to profit from the rising popularity of stand-up comedy in France. In 2010, the public channel France 2 launched *On n'demande qu'à en rire* [*We're only asking to laugh at it*]. The show was created by the television presenter, actor, and comedian Laurent Ruquier and set out to boost the profile of up-and-coming comedians in France. Unlike *Jamel Comedy Club*, it did not set out to respond to a specific socio-cultural issue such as the lack of visibility of young people from minority groups and/or the *banlieues* on French television.[69] Furthermore, *On n'demande qu'à en rire* adopted a noticeably different format to *Jamel Comedy Club* that was not based on the same type of stand-up comedy. Laurent Ruquier's programme involved comedians performing sketches on designated topics and then being graded by a group of judges. This task-focused approach thus meant that it replicated elements that one might associate with television or radio panel shows rather than the much less sketch-based aspect of *Jamel Comedy Club*.

When it comes increasing diversity within what is referred to as *le paysage audiovisuel français* [the French audiovisual landscape], it appears that the *Jamel Comedy Club* has played a role. Nelly Quemener argues that the period up until 2007 was one during which it was generally white comedians who would engage with political issues on French television and radio. However, she argues that increasing numbers of comedians from minority groups have taken on this role since 2007; indeed, she cites Thomas Ngijol as a prime example.[70] In addition to helping to launch the careers of a range of new and more diverse young performers, initiatives such as the *Jamel Comedy Club* also play a role in the democratization of culture by making it more accessible to a wider audience. Spike Boukambou, one of the organizers of Comic Hall Stars (a similar but lower profile and non-televised project to the *Jamel Comedy Club*) has stated that urban stand-up comedy makes it possible to 'amener au coeur de la ville un public qui ne va jamais dans les théâtres parisiens' ['bring to the heart of the city an audience who never go to Parisian theatres'].[71] This dynamic has parallels with the way the growth in popularity of hip-hop in France during the 1980s and 1990s led to young people from the *banlieues* performing, or watching, breakdancing in city centre locations. What remains to be seen is the extent to which France's relatively recently developed interest in

---

69   It should also be noted that Laurent Ruquier is a presenter whose shows on French television and radio are generally not targeted at the same young and urban demographic as much of Canal Plus's comedy output.

70   See: Quemener, *Le Pouvoir de l'humour*, pp. 161–2.

71   Karmitz, 'La comédie des banlieues'.

stand-up comedy will result in the establishment of a comedy circuit that extends to provincial cities and consequently beyond the current range of Parisian comedy venues. Although popular well-established comedians often go on national tours of large theatres and arenas in France, there is a distinct lack of venues outside of Paris where regular comedy evenings take place.

The most significant element of the *Jamel Comedy Club* stems not just from its mainstreaming of stand-up comedy, but they way that it has achieved this via an approach that challenges traditional French forms of stage humour and also the nation's Republican ideology. Whereas Republican universalism has the potential to mask difference, the *Jamel Comedy Club* has made racial and ethnic differences highly visible at the same time as presenting them in a way that paints a largely positive picture of a multicultural French society. It is noticeable that few performers focus predominantly on perceived injustices or inequalities and that direct criticism of the French state's policies on immigration and the *banlieues* is relatively rare. Sarkozy was at times the victim of put-downs from Jamel Debbouze when he compered some of the early episodes of *Jamel Comedy Club*, but other comedians' mocking is generally fairly gentle. For example, Mamane (who was born in Niger and has also lived in Cameroon and the Ivory Coast) began one appearance onstage by dancing *la valse musette* [a traditional Parisian waltz] and saying that he did so as a response to Sarkozy's widely reported comment on immigration 'La France, tu l'aimes ou tu la quittes' ['France: you like it or you leave'].

The ways that several of the performers engage with stereotypes may at times be problematic, but it is in part symptomatic of the complexities of dealing with hybrid identities in a society that traditionally takes a largely strict and inflexible approach to such matters. Via the material performed onstage, Quemener argues that the comedians 'publicise[nt] différents répertoires identitaires, dont on peut supposer qu'ils dissonant avec un projet de République uniforme et homogène' ['perform their cultural belonging and their identities, they "decolonize" the notion of identity, appropriate it and redefine it'].[72] In other words, the images of a diverse France that they project are not dictated by the ideological straight-jacket of French Republicanism's focus on a vision of universalism and citizenship that often obscures difference.

72   Quemener, *Le Pouvoir de l'humour*, p. 104.

Chapter 4

Islam and humour: more than just a debate about cartoons

Historically, Islam is not a religion that has been always been associated with humour; for example, much more has been written about Jewish humour than Muslim humour. In article for the *Guardian* in 2007, Sarfraz Mansoor stated that 'Muslim comedy sounds, to many, like an oxymoron'.[1] Furthermore, Khalid Kishtainy began his 1985 book *Arab Political Humour* by recalling that several of his friends 'felt a shudder at the thought of tackling the sense of humour of the Prophet Muhammad and the holy imams of Islam'.[2] Despite the nature of these comments, recent decades have provided much reason to challenge the idea that humour is less compatible with Islam than it is with other religions. Indeed, Jean-Jacques Schmidt argues in *Le Livre de l'humour arabe* that Muslims in Arab societies are more humorous than is often imagined:

> Les Arabes, musulmans et chrétiens, que certains parmi nous imagineraient austères, puritains et rigides, fermés au rire et à la plaisanterie, ont accumulé, en la matière, au cours du temps, un patrimoine qui n'a rien à envier aux autres civilisations et prouve que le rire est bien le propre de l'homme comme l'avaient dit Rabelais, et Aristophane bien avant lui.[3]

> [Arabs, Muslims and Christians, that some of us would think of as austere, puritanical and rigid, and unreceptive to laughter and

1 Sarfraz Manzoor, 'Funny Old World', *The Guardian*, 6 April 2007, https://www.theguardian.com/stage/2007/apr/06/comedy.religion [accessed 20 July 2017].
2 Khalid Kishtainy, *Arab Political Humour* (London: Quarter Books, 1985), p. ix.
3 Jean-Jacques Schmidt, *Le Livre de l'humour arabe* (Paris: Actes Sud, 2005), p. 10.

jokes, have actually, over time, accumulated a richness in this area that is no less significant than that of other civilizations and which shows that laughter is indeed unique to man, as was said by Rabelais and Aristophanes many years previously.]

As this chapter develops, we will see that the universality of humour is a topic evoked by several leading Muslim comedians when discussing their performances. This will show that many Muslim performers are seeking to articulate their vision in a means that is in keeping with French Republican values rather than the more problematic *humour communautaire* discussed in this book's introduction. Before proceeding further, however, it is worth asking how it has come to be that Islam is at times perceived as a religion lacking in humour. Among the prime reasons are many non-Muslims' lack of awareness of Islam, and a tendency for the media in many non-Muslim countries to focus on the sensational by concentrating on the actions of the most extreme followers of Islam.[4] Hans Geybels has argued that 'the affair surrounding the Mohammed cartoons has strengthened the image of a humourless Islam even further'.[5] Although such debates are of great social, cultural, and political significance – not least in France given the attacks on the offices of *Charlie Hebdo* discussed in Chapter 1– to use them as the sole means to assess Islam's relationship with humour creates a highly skewed picture. A major problem about using debates about cartoons depicting the Prophet Muhammad to assess Islam's relationship with humour is that such discussions tend to focus almost exclusively on Muslims as subjects of humour without seeking to adequately assess the ways in which Muslims themselves use humour. This typifies a trend identified by Ulrich Marzolph, who states that 'if Western audiences discuss Muslim humour at all, public opinion focuses on the perceived

4   Nilüfer Göle argues that 'les medias, dans leur manière de traiter la presence de l'islam, exacerbent les traits visuels dans les débats' ['the media, due to their way of covering the presence of Islam, exacerbate visual elements in debates'] and that 'les visibilités islamiques sont représentées dans leurs formes excessives, prises dans une spirale d'aberration de l'altérité' ['the visibility of Islam is represented by its excessive forms, which occupy a spiral from aberration to alterity']. Nilüfer Göle, *Musulmans au quotidien: une enquête sur les controverses autour de l'islam* (Paris: La Découverte, 2015), p. 284.
5   Hans Geybels, 'The Redemptive Power of Humour in Religion', in *Humour and Religion: Challenges and Ambiguities*, eds. Hans Geybels and Walter Van Herck (London and New York: Bloomsbury, 2012), pp. 12, 18.

lack of an adequate reception of Western humorous expression in the Muslim world'.[6] Such an approach is not merely skewed but also somewhat out of date given that in 2012 Diletta Guidi argued that the previous fifteen years had seen Islam's relationship with humour change as 'l'objet du rire se transforme en "fabriquant" du rire' ['the object of laughter transforms into a "manufacturer" of laughter'], and that 'on constate l'apparition d'un nouveau genre de rire où l'islam est à la fois l'objet et le véhicule' ['we have seen the emergence of a new form of laughter where Islam is simultaneously the object and the vehicle'].[7] This chapter will seek to advance the long overdue analysis of how Muslims have used humour in France.

As discussed in the introduction to this book, jokes and humour can reveal much about the status of a minority group within a society.[8] Lawrence Mintz has argued that being the subject of jokes is an early stage in the evolution of how a minority group uses humour. To recap, Mintz argues that this is a stage that is followed by others where a group internalizes the jokes before creating a type of 'self-critical humour', then the group develops a form of humour that is closer to 'realism, and finally mocking those who have created jokes that stigmatize the minority group.[9] What this means is that focusing primarily on non-Muslims' representations of Muslims when exploring Islam's relationship with humour risks not just creating a partial or skewed picture, but also risks not fully acknowledging the status and confidence of Muslims with countries such as France. In many places where they are a minority group, Muslims face challenges such as dealing with prejudice, stigmatization, and discrimination. However, humour is a tool that Muslims are increasingly using to make light of difference and demystify stereotypes.

In international terms, there has been a rise in the profile of Muslim comedians in countries such as the United States of America in the years following the 2001 World Trade Center attacks. Indeed, Haroon

6   Ulrich Marzolph, 'The Muslim Sense of Humour', in Hans Geybels and Walter Van Herck (eds), *Humour and Religion: Challenges and Ambiguities* (London and New York: Bloomsbury), p. 171.
7   Diletta Guidi, 'Rire et Islam', in Dorra Mameri-Chaambi (ed.), *L'Islam et la France: chroniques d'une histoire commune* (Paris: Chronique Éditions, 2012), pp. 174–5.
8   Rappoport, *Punchlines*, pp. 65–6.
9   Rappoport, *Punchlines*, pp. 99–100.

Siddiqui goes as far as arguing that 'the events of 11 September [...] cracked open the market for Muslim comics', and focuses in particular on North American Muslim comedians who sought to demystify stereotypes associating Islam and terrorism via their stand-up routines.[10] A prime example of Muslim performers who have sought to do so is the group Allah Made Me Funny. Originally founded by African-American Muslim convert and comedian Preacher Moss in 2003, the act became a trio the following year as Moss embarked on a tour along with fellow comedians Azhar Usman and Azeem Muhammad. In 2006, Azeem Muhammad was replaced by Mohammed Amer. Usman has described the referencing of Allah in the group's name as a being a means of 'recognizing, and appreciating, and thanking God for the gift which he has given us, which is that he has made us funny'.[11] In another interview, he told of how the placing of Allah within the group's name in part a means of challenging negative stereotypes. Usman told *Guardian* journalist Sarfraz Manzoor in 2007 that 'the word Allah has been hijacked – people hear it and think it's part of a war cry that terrorists say when they are about to cut somebody's head off', also adding that 'but for Muslims it's the most beautiful word in existence so I wanted to take that word back'.[12] Azhar Usman has also talked about how the status of Muslims in many parts of the world, and the challenges they face, makes comedy an appealing artistic vehicle:

> Stand-up is a protest art and actually the people who take up protest art are the underdogs. It is people who are disenfranchised, people who are lower in the power dynamic. If there is a power disparity in the world, those who have been given the shorter stick are often going to be the ones who use satire, who use humour.[13]

Much of the material performed by Allah Me Funny tackles Islamophobia and negative stereotypes of Islam, notably to do with terrorism, but it also touches upon more mundane aspects of daily

---

10   Haroon Siddiqui, *Being Muslim* (London: A&C Black, 2010), pp. 36–7. See also: Guidi, 'Rire et Islam', p. 174.
11   Jonathan Ervine. '(Re-)presenting Islam: a Comparative Study of Comedians in the United States of America and France', *Performing Islam*, 2.1 (2013), p. 92.
12   Sarfraz Manzoor, 'Funny Old World'.
13   Ervine, '(Re-)presenting Islam', p. 92.

life as experienced by Muslims. Given challenging situations faced by French Muslims – such as high unemployment rates[14] and sensationalist portrayals of Islam in the media[15] – one would perhaps expect France to be precisely the sort of country in which a comparable group to Allah Made Me Funny would emerge. However, France's different relationship with stand-up comedy compared to the United States and the United Kingdom (see discussion of this in previous chapter) in an important factor that needs to be acknowledged. In addition, comedians in France who explicitly place their faith or ethnicity at the heart of their comedy risk being branded examples of *humour communautaire*, a designation discussed in this book's introduction that characterizes them as displaying attributes that are incompatible with key elements of France's Republican ideology. Despite these additional challenges that face Muslim stand-up comedians in France, there have nevertheless been some significant developments during the last decade in France that merit analysis. This chapter will take as its starting point and prime focus a web series entitled *À part ça tout va bien* [*Apart from that, everything's fine*] that uses humour to portray the lives of predominantly young Muslims in France. After exploring the objectives of the series and its key themes, and attempts to develop follow-up projects, this chapter will examine what the series shows about attitudes to Islam and humour within France. This will involve analysing the nature of jokes performed in the web series, media reactions to the project, and also its creators' feelings about how the project was received. It will then examine subsequent projects undertaken by the creators of *À part ça tout va bien*.

This chapter will also discuss other Muslim comedians in France, as well as French comedians who have evoked Islam within their stand-up material. This will include discussing the *Comédie Muslim* shows performed by Nabil Zerrouki as well as Mustapha El Atrassi's recent stand-up shows. It will also involve discussing the way in which non-Muslim comedians, such as Sophia Aram and Jérémy Ferrari, have depicted Islam within their stand-up shows in recent years. This analysis will help to provide a more rounded picture of the extent to which stand-up comedy in France is playing a role in challenging stereotypes about Islam and redefining images of French Muslims.

---

14 See: Siddiqui, *Being Muslim*, p. 38.
15 See: Göle, *Musulmans au quotidien*, p. 284.

À part ça tout va bien: a tale of online laughter

In 2008, the writer and director Sylvain De Zangroniz (widely known simply as Zangro) started working with the actor and comedian Hassan Zahi to produce a humorous web series about French Muslims that appeared on a site named *À part ça tout va bien*. The site's motto was 'qui a dit que les musulmans n'avaient pas d'humour' ['who said that Muslims didn't have a sense of humour'] and made clear the group's intention to use humour to respond to what it saw as tensions created by the French media's portrayal of Islam and Muslims.[16] The *raison d'être* of the project was made clear via the following statement:

> à l'heure du repli communautaire d'un côté et de l'islamophobie de l'autre, nous voulons à travers des films de comédie faire le lien entre des mondes qui s'éloignent et qui pourtant devront apprendre à vivre ensemble. Rétablir le dialogue, détendre les esprits pour faire du 'choc des civilisations' une farce plutôt qu'un drame, telle est l'ambition de tous les comédiens et artistes qui participent à ce site. Des comédiens de toutes confessions que le rire rassemble. Rire de nos peurs, de nos différences et de nos faiblesses, rire de nous-mêmes et rire des autres. Car c'est sans doute cela vivre ensemble : pouvoir rire de son voisin autant que de soi-même.[17]

[At a time of withdrawal back into one's own community on the one hand and Islamophobia on the other hand, we want to use our humorous films to create a link between worlds that are growing apart but will have to learn to live together. Re-establish dialogue, calm tensions by turning the 'clash of civilizations' into

---

16   The website specifically mentions 'foulard à l'école, divorce pour non virginité, caricatures danoises, mosquées interdites en banlieues' ['veils in schools, divorce due to not being a virgin, Danish cartoons, mosques forbidden in the banlieues'] and describes these issues as 'événements repris par la presse nationale et internationale [qui] nous révèlent les crispations qui divisent les citoyens français' ['events covered by the national and international press (that) reveal the tensions that divide French citizens']. 'En savoir plus', *À part ça tout va bien* [n.d.], http://comediemuslim.apartcatoutvabien.com/en-savoir-plus-sur-a-part-ca-tout-va-bien.php [accessed 20 July 2017].
17   'En savoir plus', *À part ça tout va bien* [n.d.], http://comediemuslim.apartca-toutvabien.com/en-savoir-plus-sur-a-part-ca-tout-va-bien.php [accessed 20 July 2017].

a farce rather than a tragedy, that is the ambition of all the actors and artists who are participating in this site. Laughing about our fears, our differences and our weaknesses, laughing about ourselves and laughing about others. Because this is what social cohesion is about: being able to laugh about one's neighbour as much as about one's self.]

In other words, the web series provided a further example of humour being used to both demystify stereotypes and unite people of different origins. Such an ethos means that *À part ça tout va bien* initially appears to have significant similarities with the *Jamel Comedy Club*. However, the fact that it originated online rather than on television – and lacked the presence of a nationally celebrated star such as Jamel Debbouze – meant that *À part ça tout va bien* did not receive comparable media interest within France. It was, however, the subject of television reports in Switzerland and Canada and also received coverage in several local and national newspapers in France as well as on radio stations such as France Culture and Radio France Internationale as well as the television channels France 3 and Arte.

The sketches – most of which were under five minutes long – focused predominantly on the daily life of young Muslims in France, and the subject of the jokes include both people who mis-use Islam for their own benefit and those who have an irrational fear of Islam based on ignorance. The most popular video was viewed over one million times, and the second most popular was watched over half a million times. Many of the sketches were filmed in the Bordeaux area, although a series of eight episodes entitled *Islam School Welkoum* was shot in Morocco, as were two short videos entitled *Le Cousin*. In addition, a sketch called *Sweet Home* was filmed in Chicago and another was shot in Brazil. Most of the sketches are based around at least one of the four objectives listed below:

1. Mocking fears of Islam that are irrational or imagined rather than real;

2. Mocking individuals who seek to portray themselves as being more Muslim than they actually are for their own benefit;

3. Challenging the idea that a true and pure form of Islam is necessarily to be found in countries of the Maghreb such as Morocco;

4. Suggesting that the version of Islam followed by those in the West is not always as enlightened or progressive as might be thought.

Among the sketches that can be placed in the first category were ones entitled *Le Côté obscur* [*The Dark Side*] and *Le Corbeau* [*The Anonymous Letter*]. In the first of these two sketches, two French women sitting on a park bench look on in concern when they notice a father – played by Hassan Zahi – reading a book to his daughter, who appears to be about three or four years old. Their fear stems from the fact that they believe the daughter's black outfit, which includes a veil, to be a form of traditional Islamic dress and interpret the father reading to her as a sign that he is attempting to radicalize his young child. The pair of women say that seeing such a young girl wearing veil is 'un-French' and something that would never be allowed at school, and imagine that she is not allowed to play at home. They voice their fears that the father is in the process of 'lobotomiser une petite' ['lobotomizing a young girl'] and comment that within Islam 'si tu es une fille, tu es programmée pour te taire pas pour réfléchir' ['if you're a girl, you're programmed to keep quiet and not to reflect']. Before leaving the park in frustration, the pair consider contacting a social worker. As the sketch draws to a close, it becomes apparent that the father has been reading a fairytale to his daughter and that her black clothes are in fact part of a Darth Vader fancy dress costume that she is wearing for a birthday party.

A sketch entitled *Le Corbeau*, which is set in a school, also focused on fears surrounding Islam. It sees the apparently distressed teacher of a diverse secondary school class tell the head teacher that her class have branded her a whore as they feel that skirts she has been wearing are too short. She tells of receiving an anonymous note from a pupil about this matter along with a hijab that she was invited to wear in order to help her to dress more modestly. In her discussion with the distressed colleague, the head teacher says that she will seek out 'le petit Ben Laden' ['the little Bin Laden'] responsible for sending the note and threatens to cancel the class's upcoming ski excursion and trip to Italy if no-one takes responsibility for the sending the note. The head decides to grant the victimized teacher two weeks of leave due to the stress that she has experienced. At the end of the sketch, the teacher meets her boyfriend – played by Hassan Zahi – outside the school and tells him that his plan worked and she now has two weeks of holiday to enjoy. The fact that the white teacher's boyfriend appears to have been responsible for the idea is highly significant given that he is visibly from an ethnic minority background; this detail means that the sketch ultimately does not revolve around a strict dichotomy between Islamophobic or racist French teachers and the unfairly blamed ethnically diverse pupils in the class.

The jokes in the *À part ça tout va bien* sketches did not merely focus on non-Muslims' prejudices concerning Islam; several focus on ways in which Muslims seek to present themselves. A sketch entitled *La Perle rare* [The Rare Pearl] began with a girl being given a headscarf to wear by a friend before going on a date with a boy. The dialogue between the girl and her friend reveals that the girl going on the date is not a particularly devout Muslim and indeed fears being asked about Islam by the boy she plans to meet. However, she wears the headscarf in order to impress her date, who is reportedly more devout and also seen as a particularly worthy potential boyfriend for this reason. When we see footage of the date, the girl responds 'Inch'Allah' when asked by the boy if they will meet up again and the boy replies 'je suis vraiment heureux que dieu t'ait mise sur mon chemin' ['I am truly happy that God placed you on my path'] before they both say 'Hamdullah'.[18] Once the pair head their separate ways at the end of the date, the boy removes his traditional Islamic headcovering and replaces it with a baseball cap. He then phones a friend to proclaim 'ça y est, ça a marché!' ['done it, it worked!'] and express his delight at having secured a second date with the girl. An important element of what sketches such as those just discussed above demonstrate is the ability of the Muslims who perform in them to both laugh at themselves and laugh at non-Muslims' stereo-typical negative perceptions of them.

The *À part ça tout va bien* sketches do more than just concentrate on issues faced by French Muslims in France as some of the sketches – in particular an eight-part collection entitled *Islam School Welkoum* – were filmed in Morocco. This specific group of sketches focused on a group of wayward French teenagers who have been sent to Morocco by their parents in order to discover 'le vrai islam' ['the true Islam']. However, the running joke in the *Islam School Welkoum* videos is that the person

---

18   'Inch'Allah' means 'God willing' and 'Hamdullah' means 'Praise be to God'.

charged with explaining 'le vrai islam' to them is not particularly knowledgeable about the religion himself and that his motivation for teaching them appears to be uniquely financial. When the young French Muslims start to engage in conversations that could potentially help them to discover the true nature of Islam, the teacher curtails discussion that risk exposing his own ignorance. He presents a narrow and very stereotypical view of Islam and is shown to use what could diplomatically be termed somewhat rudimentary teaching methods. When the school is about to be inspected, he is seen teaching the students the first few letters of the alphabet in Arabic and doing a short '*haram* or *halal*' quiz.

Among the other sketches shot outside of France is one entitled *Sweet Home* that was shot in Chicago. This sketch involves a young French Muslim named Salim visiting his older cousin Omar (played by Hassan Zahi) in the United States. Throughout the video, Salim is keen to experience American life and taste a hamburger whilst his cousin Omar repeatedly seeks to restrict his younger cousin to visiting a small range of places within Chicago's Arab quarter. Omar displays a suspicion of other minority/immigrant groups in the area that frequently verges on paranoia. He berates Salim from talking to a pair of black American girls in a park because he says it was clear that the girls were high on cocaine. The way Omar talks to the girls leads to him being called both a racist and a terrorist. Omar also tells Salim to be wary of the Polish and prevents his younger cousin from eating the hamburger he craves by picking it up and giving it to a homeless man. Towards the end of the sketch, Omar apologizes for judging his cousin and failing to understand him. As a conciliatory gesture, he tells Salim that he has bought two tickets for an amazing concert to make up. Despite Omar mentioning that he knows Salim is passionate about soul music, the performer he describes as 'un mec du coin, la plus belle voix de Chicago' ['a local guy, the greatest voice in Chicago'] turns out to be a Middle Eastern-looking performer who is wearing traditional oriental dress and has a long black beard.

The sketches discussed so far make light of potentially sensitive issues surrounding Islam, either mocking those who hold prejudices or making fun of people whose attempts to be a good Muslim are based on deception or taking things to extremes. The fact that the sketches send up both Muslims and non-Muslims is in keeping with the project's aim to bring people together through laughter since it encourages viewers to laugh at people from different ethnic or religious groups for a variety of reasons. The way in which many of the *À part ça tout va bien* videos appear to be constructed in response to a specific pre-existing stereotypes about Islam mirrors the structure of many episodes of the Canadian television sitcom *Little Mosque on the Prairie*.[19] Diletta Guidi argues that *À part ça tout va bien*'s humour stems from 'une sorte de mise en avant du stigmate, [où] les comiques le renversent et en dédramatisant les traits' ['a means of highlighting the stigma, where the comedians invert and dedramatize its characteristics'], adding that 'barbe, voile et burqa deviennent alors les accessoires du rire' ['the beard, the veil and the burqa thus become accessories to the laughter'].[20] In her work *Declining the Stereotype*, Mireille Rosello suggests that tackling stereotypes head-on in this way is potentially problematic as it gives a certain degree of power to a pre-existing stereotype.[21]

The creators of the *À part ça tout va bien* appear to have exploited existing stereotypes in order to make it easier for audiences to relate to the sketches, and ultimately lead them towards focusing on wider and more universal issues. Zangro has suggested that the stereotypes in the sketches acted as a hook, recognizable elements that helped the sketches to bring together people around a universal message:

> Je pense que l'on rit d'une grande partie des stéréotypes qui sont véhiculés, de peur des gens, des phantasmes des gens, des mépris aussi, comme on le précise sur le site, des petites faiblesses humaines. L'idée c'est que tout le monde se retrouve dans des petites faiblesses que l'on partage tous, que ce soit la lâcheté, l'hypocrisie, la méchanceté par moment, la trahison, l'appât du gain... Voilà c'est finalement essayer de nous rassembler en parlant de nos travers communs.[22]

> [I think that to a large extent we are laughing about stereotypes that are conveyed, people's fears, people's fantasies, also people's disdain, as we explain on the site, about little human weaknesses. The idea is that everyone identifies with these little weaknesses

---

19   This North American show was produced for the Canadian Broadcasting Corporation (CBC) from 2007 to 2012, and is based around events that take place in a mosque located in a (fictional) rural Canadian town called Mercy.
20   Guidi, 'Rire et Islam', p. 175.
21   See: Rosello, *Declining the Stereotype*, p. 36.
22   Ervine, '(Re-)presenting Islam', p. 97.

that we all share, whether it's cowardice, hypocrisy, occasional nastiness, treason, avarice... So it's about ultimately trying to bring everyone together by talking about our common failings.]

This focus on shared values, and shared failings, presents *À part ça tout va bien* as more than just a Muslim comedy project. This more universalist focus helps to place it in a context that is more suited to both France's traditions of *laïcité* [French secularism] and the concept of republican universalism. Furthermore, the universalist ethos provides a counter argument to those tempted to categorise *À part ça tout va bien* as an example of '*humour communautaire*', a label that Zangro and Zahi have been keen to avoid.[23] The way in which Zangro described the humour and ethos *À part ça tout va bien* in the 2011 interview cited above is very similar to the way in which Azhar Usman sought to characterize his comedy trio Allah Made Me Funny in an interview two years previously:

> We are human beings and like any human being each of us has our personal struggles, our personal shortcomings and our own personal challenges, spiritual or otherwise. And so [...] what you are getting is three comedians who are going to lay bare their soul for you, and do so in a funny way. And guess what happens? People connect with it because people in the audience go through the same thing.[24]

Although Allah Made Me Funny and *À part ça tout va bien* are using slightly different forms of comedy – respectively stand-up comedy and sketch-based comedy – they are both seeking to use humour to combat sensationalist discourses, and discourses of otherness, that concern Muslims. Furthermore, they are seeking to establish their attempts to do so as highly meaningful and relevant to both Muslims and non-Muslims. The conception of humour described by Zangro and Azhar Usman above provides a prime example of what Ulrich Marzolph sees as one of the main functions of Muslim humour, namely the existence of 'humour as the expression of a tolerant and appreciative position towards the difficulties and vicissitudes of social existence and towards the human foibles regarded as imperative'.[25]

---

23   See: Ervine, '(Re-)presenting Islam', p. 98.
24   Cited in: Ervine, '(Re-)presenting Islam', p. 95.
25   Marzolph, 'The Muslim Sense of Humour', p. 183.

Within the humour of *À part ça tout va bien*, and indeed that of many Muslim comedians, there are certain limits to what is and is not joked about. For example, Hassan Zahi has emphasized that in the online sketches he and Zangro wrote for the series 'nous rions *avec* l'islam et non pas *de* l'islam' ['we laugh *with* Islam and not *about* Islam'] (own emphasis added).[26] Their focus is on finding humour within Islam challenges the notion that Islam is a humourless religion.

Although Zango and Zahi's use of humour to explore potentially sensitive issues concerning Muslims was seen as novel within France, it not only followed in the footsteps of projects in the Anglophone world that ultimately achieved a greater degree of mainstream diffusion but also occurred at a similar time to significant projects in other European countries. The year in which *À part ça tout va bien* was launched (2008) also saw the German Central Council of Muslims encourage young Muslims in Germany to make light-hearted videos about being Muslim as part of a competition that sought to challenge stereotypes. Just like *À part ça tout va bien* had done, the German competition acknowledged the existence of the notion that Muslims lack a sense of humour:

> Be Muslim and funny? Is that possible? Muslims don't understand fun, are always serious and grim. Right? That, in any case, is the widespread image, that many people – and often we too – have of us. So it's no surprise that the question comes up: as a Muslim, can you laugh or even laugh *about* Muslims? Is that allowed?[27]

The competition encouraged young German Muslims to 'shoot a funny video, make a Muslim joke, tell an authentic Islam-related experience that had you rolling on the floor laughing, be one of the first Muslim comics, write a humorous song or draw a cartoon'.[28] It is particularly significant that a Muslim organization has listed cartoons among the possible forms of entry given that the word would, for many people, evoke controversies and tensions arising from depictions of the

---

26   Guidi, 'Rire et Islam', p. 175.
27   This English translation of the context in which the German competition was launched is provided in the following article: Gisèle Kuipers, 'The Politics of Humour in the Public Sphere: Cartoons, Power and Modernity in the First Transnational Humour Scandal', *European Journal of Cultural Studies*, 14.1 (2011), p. 75.
28   See: Kuipers, 'The Politics of Humour in the Public Sphere', p. 75.

Prophet Muhammad that were published in the Danish newspaper *Jyllands Posten* and subsequently reprinted in publications such as *Charlie Hebdo*. Although the aspirations of the German Central Council of Muslims were in many ways similar to those of *À part ça tout va bien*, it is important to acknowledge several significant differences between the two projects. The fact that a Muslim organization led the German initiative is a particularly noticeable difference given that the person who came up with the initial idea for *À part ça tout va bien*, Zangro, is in fact an atheist. Indeed, one can also say that the German competition involved a cultural organization encouraging performers to use their art(s) with a specific socio-cultural goal in mind, whereas the French project involved performers coming together to focus on a similar objective without any prompting from Muslim organizations in France. Despite the fact that Zangro and Zahi have both suggested that the public and the media in the English-speaking world appear more receptive to comedy projects that have an explicit focus on Muslims,[29] their humorous web series actually pre-dates two Anglophone online equivalents – the American series *Halal in the Family* and the British series *Diary of Badman* – that are discussed in an article about Muslim online comedy by Tim Miles.[30]

The aforementioned initiatives demonstrate a shared desire on the part of Muslims in several different countries at a broadly similar time to tackle the notion that Islam and Muslims are humourless. Furthermore, they highlight humour's potential to act as both a means of self-expression and also a tool to be exploited in order to challenge negative stereotypes. The extent to which all the performers discussed above know of each other is unclear, although Zangro and Zahi have referred to their awareness of both the *Little Mosque on the Prairie* series and the American comedy trio Allah Made Me Funny when interviewed. Indeed, they have cited Canadian sitcom as one of the inspirations for their own web series.[31] Although interviews with the protagonists of *À part ça tout va bien* and Allah Made Me Funny show that the two groups shared many preoccupations, there are some subtle differences when it comes to the subjects of their jokes. One

29   See: Ervine, '(Re-)presenting Islam', p. 102.
30   Tim Miles, 'Halal? Ha! LOL: An Examination of Muslim Online Comedy As Counter-Narrative', *Comedy Studies*, 6.2 (2015), pp. 167–78.
31   Ervine, '(Re-)presenting Islam', pp. 98–9.

of the most noticeable is that *À part ça tout va bien* appears to focus less on tackling stereotypes that associate Islam and terrorism, or Islam and violence. A potential reason for this is that Allah Made Me Funny started touring only a few years after the World Trade Center attacks of 2001, a spectacular event of global importance that led to an increased focus on violence, terrorism, and radicalism within the Muslim world. Although the consequences of this were felt internationally, they had a particular impact in the United States due to it being the country where the attacks took place. When *À part ça tout va bien* started in 2008, memories of major terrorist attacks by Muslim groups on French soil were not as fresh. However, this has changed following events such as the firebombing of the *Charlie Hebdo* offices in November 2011, the Toulouse shootings committed by Mohammed Merah in March 2012, the January 2015 shootings in Paris at the *Charlie Hebdo* offices and the Hyper Cacher supermarket, and the July 2016 attacks in Nice.

Shortly after the November 2011 firebomb attack on the *Charlie Hebdo* office in Paris, *À part ça tout va bien* creator Zangro described how he felt the news of the attack and controversy surrounding *Charlie Hebdo*'s depictions of the Prophet Muhammad had taken place at a particularly unfortunate time. He argued that these events occurred at a stage when the public and the media in France had been becoming increasingly receptive to the humorous sketches from the group's web series. However, he believed that the attacks led to 'dix pas en arrière' ['ten steps backwards'] when it came to French people's receptiveness to humour focused on the daily life of French Muslims. Furthermore, he felt that the attack on *Charlie Hebdo* led many people in France to believe that Muslims did not possess a sense of humour. With an air of resignation, he lamented that 'on se demande quel peut être l'effet de nos vidéos maintenant sur un public qui est de plus en plus crispé' ['we're wondering what the potential effect of our videos is now going to be on an audience that is more and more tense'].[32] Despite the fact that the videos aimed to challenge negative stereotypes about Islam, Zangro felt that the events of November 2011 meant that the mindset of many people in France became less open to representations

---

32 Ervine, 'Re-presenting Islam', p. 97. Interview originally conducted in Bordeaux on 7 November 2011.

of Muslims and Islam that was diametrically opposed to stereotypical depictions.

Perhaps somewhat counter-intuitively, the chances of being able to make a spin-off television programme of a similar nature to *À part ça tout va bien* seemed to be increasing again five years later despite the fact that France had suffered several major terrorist attacks committed by Muslim extremists in the intervening period. In September 2016, Zangro contacted Hassan Zahi about a project that involved making a short film for France Télévisions about a group of Muslims. Despite the fact that it was ultimately shown late in the evening, Zahi nevertheless considered this to constitute 'une petite porte qui a été franchie' ['a small step forwards'].[33] Indeed, this pilot episode resulted in France Télévisions buying the rights to a four-part series. This series appears more similar to the Canadian sitcom *Little Mosque on the Prairie* than to *À part ça tout va bien* sketches as it was based around 24 hours in the life of an imam. In the earlier online sketches, mosques and religious figures were very rarely visible. Furthermore, the France Télévisions series involves four episodes lasting 26 minutes and is thus more comparable to *Little Mosque on the Prairie* in terms of its format.

Limits to the success of *À part ça tout va bien*

Zangro's comments about the events of November 2011 make clear his sense of frustration about the difficulties that he and Hassan Zahi encountered when trying to use the online success of *À part ça tout va bien* as a starting point for other projects. The desire of Zangro and Hassan Zahi to create similar projects on television suggests that they believe that there was a limit to what could be achieved by their sketches remaining a purely online phenomenon. For the sociologist Éric Macé, the fact that *À part ça tout va bien* was broadcast online via sites such as YouTube and DailyMotion constitutes a significant difference from the Canadian sitcom *Little Mosque on the Prairie*:

> Si en effet on trouve ici le même type de verve comique d'autodérision et de déstabilisation des clichés et des stéréotypes

---

33   Hassan Zahi, interviewed by Jonathan Ervine (unpublished), 23 March 2017.

réciproques que dans la série canadienne, la différence principale tient cependant au fait qu'en France ce type de fiction ne passe pas sur les chaînes de télévision mainstream comme CBC [Canadian Broadcasting Corporation, une chaîne publique nationale au Canada], mais qu'elle ne trouve à s'exprimer que dans la web-fiction – elle-même financée par un groupe de presse spécialisé visant le public musulman (Saphir News).[34]

[We indeed find here the same type of comic flair for self-mockery and challenging the same clichés and stereotypes as in the Canadian television series. However, the main difference stems from the fact that in France this type of fiction is not appearing on mainstream television channels like CBC (Canadian Broadcasting Corporation, a national public channel in Canada). Instead, such projects only find an avenue of expression in web-fiction – indeed web-fiction financed by a specialized news agency that targets the Muslim audience (Saphir News).]

It could be argued that being supported by a media organization whose target audience is composed of Muslims reduced the likelihood of *À part ça tout va bien*'s sketches reaching a wider non-Muslim audience. However, the videos' availability on sites such as YouTube and DailyMotion facilitated their dissemination and resulted in interest from a variety of media outlets in France and internationally. However, one must consider the extent to which videos disseminated via the likes of YouTube and DailyMotion have the same impact as similar material that is broadcast by more traditional branches of the media. In an article that discusses Anglophone comedians' responses to controversies involving Islam, Hirzalla, Van Zoonen, and Müller argue that 'YouTube has been acknowledged as one of the most potent places where people can perform and contest identity'. However, they also state that comments posted on YouTube in reaction to comedians' interventions in socio-political debates are often 'hard to qualify as contributions to "civic culture"'.[35] This, in itself, suggests that influencing civic culture through YouTube videos needs to involve debates that take place outside YouTube and within other media.

The fact that Zangro and Zahi struggled to make the transition from

34 Macé, *Rions ensemble des stéréotypes*, p. 35.
35 Fadi Hirzalla, Liesbet van Zoonen, Floris Müller, 'How Funny Can Islam

filming online sketches to producing similar material for television or a longer film was a considerable source of frustration to both of them. Zangro stated in November 2011 that producing a web series was a necessary starting point as he felt that French television channels would be unlikely to broadcast the sort of material that he and Zahi produced for *À part ça tout va bien*, a situation that he described as 'une particularité française' ['a distinctively French characteristic'] given the success enjoyed by *Little Mosque on the Prairie* in Canada and the number of views accumulated by the videos at apartcatoutvabien.com. He argued that this reluctance would have been unlikely to have occurred in many other European countries.[36] In the same interview, Zahi argued that *À part ça tout va bien* was a project ahead of its time in France and expressed cautious optimism by stating that he felt 'la comédie humoristique ethnique religieuse' ['ethnic and religious comedy'] would become successful in France over time.[37] However, he suggested in the same interview that this would only occur once there had been a change of mindset in France as he felt that *À part ça tout va bien* was 'un bout de puzzle qui ne rentre pas dans le puzzle pour les Français' ['a jigsaw piece that doesn't fit into the jigsaw from French people's perspective'] and that 'ça va rentrer mais il faut changer de puzzle' ['it's going to fit but we need to change the jigsaw'].[38]

Stand-up comedy and Islam in France

As previously mentioned, it is extremely important to pay attention to who is telling the joke when discussing representations of Islam and Muslims within French comedy. Questions of hierarchies and power relations influence how jokes may be received. There can be an element of self-deprecation involved in joking about one's own religion, but mocking an often stigmatized minority religion could be perceived as taking aim at an easy target or further contributing to its stigmatization. In recent years, several comedians in France – both

Controversies Be? Comedians Defending Their Faiths on YouTube', *Television and New Media*, 14.1 (2013), p. 59.

36   Ervine, '(Re-)presenting Islam', p. 99.
37   Ervine, '(Re-)presenting Islam', pp. 101–2.
38   Ervine, '(Re-)presenting Islam', p. 102.

Muslim and non-Muslim – have performed stand-up shows in which a key element has been discussing Islam. During roughly the same period as Zangro and Hassan Zahi were filming sketches for apartca-toutvabien.com, Nabil Zerrouki started presenting a stand-up show with similar aspirations. Flyers advertising his *Muslim Comédie* shows illustrated this by stating 'ne vous fiez pas aux apparences, oubliez les préjugés et venez découvrir un nouveau style d'humour' ['don't rely on appearances, forget your prejudices and come to discover a new style of humour']. They also evoked a desire to 'mettre de côté les stéréotypes et de mettre en avant la compréhension et la tolérance par le rire' ['cast aside stereotypes and showcase understanding and tolerance through laughter']. However, one could question the extent to which his shows actually involved a new *style* of humour as opposed to a *conventional* style of comedy that evoked a somewhat less familiar *subject matter* (i.e. the day-to-day life of Muslims in France). As I have stated elsewhere, however, it appears that these shows were not entirely successful when it came to attracting non-Muslim spectators and involved some jokes that appeared to depend on a greater understanding of Muslim daily rituals than the *À part ça tout va bien* sketches.[39]

More recently, the comedian Mustapha El Atrassi has achieved a notable level of success performing stand-up shows in renowned Paris comedy venues such as le Théâtre du Point-Virgule. He first performed at this celebrated venue as a teenager in 2001 and has subsequently performed at the newer Grand Point-Virgule Montparnasse. By 2006, he was a regular guest on the popular television and radio shows of the broadcaster and comedian Laurent Ruquier. El Atrassi also appeared on the first season of *Jamel Comedy Club* on Canal Plus in 2006, although he was not one of the more high-profile performers. Although he has not explicitly marketed his shows on the basis that they provide a humorous insight into life as a Muslim in contemporary France, he has talked during several of his shows about being a Muslim and how Muslims are perceived in France. Much of his material in certain shows has focused on growing up in a housing estate on the outskirts of Tours and moving to Paris whilst still in his teens. El Atrassi's humour is also a lot more provocative than that which features in *À part ça tout va bien* or is performed by the Allah Made Me Funny trio. Indeed, El Atrassi

---

39   See: Jonathan Ervine, 'L'Islam et l'humour: du rire libérateur au rire communautaire', *Temps des Médias*, 28 (2017), pp. 153–4.

began his 2017 show *Sans modération* [*Without moderation*] by stating 'La France va mal [...] il y a beaucoup de blagues que l'on ne peut plus faire en France' ['Things are going badly in France (...) there are many jokes that one can no longer tell in France'] and then embarking on a mission to tell as many jokes as possible that he felt fitted into this taboo category.

In several of his stand-up shows, Mustapha El Atrassi has discussed terrorism. This has often involved him playing with stereotypes that associate Muslims and terrorism via dark humour, and on other occasions he has sought to make more direct points about associations between Islam and terrorism that are not couched within a deliberately ironic approach. A joke that falls into the former category is the following comment he made near the start of a set he performed in English at the Comedy Cellar in New York:

> I'm a regular Muslim. I pray five times a day, I give money to
> homeless people and I'm training to become a pilot. I'm kidding,
> I don't give money to homeless people.

What this shows is El Atrassi is unafraid to acknowledge the existence of negative stereotypes about Muslims, and seeks to defuse them by taking ownership of them and undermining them via deliberately ironic comments. He has also adopted a similar approach concerning more recent terrorist attacks in France, such as the 2016 Bastille Day attack in Nice. In one of his routines, he talked about receiving criticism for not having waited long enough before joking about the attacks, adding 'j'avais fait des blagues la veille de l'attentat' ['I had been telling jokes the day before the attack']. He follows this up by declaring 'à Nice j'ai perdu un très bon ami à moi, j'en ai pas envie d'en parler parce que les gens me posent des questions de merde du genre "il était où? À la plage? La Promenade des Anglais?"; mais non, il était dans le camion' ['in Nice, I lost a very good friend of mine, I don't really want to talk about it because people ask me crap questions like "where was he? On the beach? The Promenade des Anglais?"; no, in fact he was in the truck'].[40]

---

40   The 14 July 2016 terrorist attack in Nice involved Mohamed Lahouaiej-Bouhlel, a Tunisian national who had been living in France since 2005, driving a lorry into a crowd of people who had gathered on the Promenade des Anglais to celebrate Bastille Day and watch the traditional firework display.

El Atrassi also alluded to the attacks when approaching the topic of humour and Muslims in the same show by stating 'on est très susceptibles et je crois que l'on a prouvé plusieurs fois ces derniers temps' ['we're very sensitive and I think that we've proved it several times recently']. However, this led into a monologue about who has the right to joke about Islam that was not constructed in order to provide the same sort of shock value as the previously cited jokes:

> Si moi je parle de l'islam on va dire que je suis communautaire et c'est là le problème. Moi je suis français, tu vois, je crois... Je suis français mais je suis marocain, tu vois ce que je veux dire, tu ne peux pas te débarrasser du Maroc [...] J'ai fait une prise de sang, il y avait de l'huile d'olive, tu ne peux pas te débarrasser de ça [...] Tout le monde, surtout les non-musulmans parlent de l'islam en France. C'est dans la bouche de tout le monde, il n'y a rien qui me rend plus français que de parler de l'islam. C'est injuste parce que s'il y a un comique qui s'appelle Maxence [...] S'il fait des blagues sur le terrorisme, tout le monde va faire la même chose, les gens vont avoir la même réaction en France, 'Oh la la la, quel courage, oh la la la, il est Charlie!' Alors que moi, avec ma gueule, je peux faire exactement les mêmes vannes et les gens vont dire 'oh la la la, il est avec eux, il est avec eux'.

> [If I talk about Islam people are going to say that I am communitarian and that's the problem. I am French, you see, I believe... I am French but I am Moroccan, you see what I mean, you can't rid yourself of Morocco (...) I had a blood test, there was olive oil in it, you can't rid yourself of that (...) Everyone, especially people who aren't non-Muslim, talk about Islam in France. The words are on everyone's lips, there's nothing that makes me more French than talking about Islam. It's unfair because if a comedian called Maxence (...) If he does the same jokes about terrorism, people are all going to have the same reaction in France, 'Oh la la la, what courage, oh la la la, he is Charlie!' But if I, with my face, tell exactly the same jokes, people are going to say 'oh la la la he is with them'.]

Rather than seeking to reclaim a stereotype used to stigmatize Muslims, the comments cited above raise serious issues about attitudes towards both humour and freedom of expression in France. The implicit rules that El Atrassi denounces are clearly regressive as he is effectively suggesting that Islam and Muslims can be the *subject* of jokes told by non-Muslims whereas Muslims cannot be the *tellers* and *creators* of jokes about Islam as that would be *communautaire*. Indeed, one could argue that taking the view that not all groups are equally free to joke about certain topics is incompatible with key republican concepts such as universalism and freedom of expression. It is also highly problematic to argue that Muslims should not joke about terrorist attacks specifically when they have been perpetrated by a 'fellow' Muslim. Such an attitude effectively holds an entire community – or arguably several communities given the diversity of beliefs, races, and ethnicities among those referred to as French Muslims – responsible for acts of extremists with whom the vast majority of the community may well feel that they have little in common. Indeed, several of the perpetrators of terrorist attacks in France committed in the name of Islam in recent years have been reported to have been isolated figures who have become radicalized outside of France. Furthermore, it is important to remember that Muslims have been among the direct and indirect victims of terrorism in France during recent years; several have lost their lives in terrorist attacks in Paris and Nice and others have been the victims of physical or verbal abuse in the aftermath of such attacks.

When discussing religion and humour in recent stand-up shows such as *Troisième degré* [*Third degree*] and *Sans modération* [*Without Moderation*], El Atrassi does not just talk about French Muslims. He refers to the term 'un Juif drôle' ['a funny Jew'] as being the biggest joke of the evening before recounting how Jewish spectators have told him after his shows that they appreciate the way he has demonstrated that it is possible to laugh about Jews without being anti-Semitic. He expands on this by saying that Jewish spectators have thanked him for showing that Jews *do* have a sense of humour and have actually encouraged him to go further in his routines that deal with Jews. El Atrassi thus seems to believe that anyone can joke about anyone else, and implicitly that his status as a member of an ethnic minority gives him greater freedom to joke about members of other ethnic minorities. In his show *Sans modération*, he joked that black French people's tendency to exaggerate means that slavery probably only lasted about a year and a half. In several shows, he has asked the audience in dimly lit venues 'est-ce qu'il y a des noirs dans la salle?' ['are there any black people in the room?'] before adding 'je ne vous vois pas' ['I can't see you'] and suggesting 'il fallait mettre une veilleuse' ['you should have brought a night-light']. This joke is very similar to one that resulted in the former English footballer Paul Gascoigne pleading guilty to a charge of racially abusing a black security guard; at an event in Wolverhampton during November 2015 Gascoigne admitted saying to the security guard 'can you smile so I can see you?'. The fact that Gascoigne is not a member of visible ethnic minority could be argued to change the dynamics of the joke somewhat, and El Atrassi stated before making the joke about black people that 'il faut se moquer les uns des autres' ['we all need to make fun of each other'] and described black people in France as 'les plus drôles' ['the most funny']. However – as I argued in the chapter about the *Jamel Comedy Club* – it is somewhat simplistic to argue that members of minority groups mocking each other is necessarily unproblematic. The prosecuting lawyer in the court case involving Gascoigne stated that the security guard 'felt the crowd go quiet' after the joke,[41] which contrasts with the way that El Atrassi's use of a very similar joke provoked laughter. The 'je ne vous vois pas' ['I can't see you'] line, however, produces significantly more laughter than the follow-up comment 'il fallait mettre une veilleuse' ['you should have brought a night-light']. Following the latter comment, El Atrassi sought to defend himself during the version of the *Sans Modération* show he made available via his YouTube channel by commenting 'le seul qui golri fort c'est un renoir, les autres sont gênés' ['the only person who's laughing lots is a black guy, the others are embarrassed'].[42]

In addition to re-appropriating discourses used to stereotype and stigmatize French Muslims, El Atrassi also evokes what he sees as positive aspects of Islam and French Muslims during shows such as *Sans modération*. For example, he talks about how overcrowded mosques are a sign of how well Islam is doing and says that this contrasts with low levels of attendance in French churches. El Atrassi jokes that Muslims suffer prejudice in France due to jealousy and expresses pity at the way that so many people are ignoring Christianity; he suggests that churches should

41   Steven Morris, 'Paul Gascoigne Admits Racially Abusing Black Bodyguard', *The Guardian*, 19 September 2016, https://www.theguardian.com/uk-news/2016/sep/19/paul-gascoigne-pleads-guilty-to-racially-aggravated-offence [accessed 25 July 2017].
42   'Golri' and 'renoir' are both terms used in a form of French slang called *verlan* that involves swapping syllables of words; the former is derived from the word 'rigole' ['laugh'] and the latter from 'noir' ['black']. The YouTube video

counter this by listing themselves on Airbnb and equipping themselves with WiFi. He also suggests that Muslims in France are well integrated, adding that alcohol is 'l'un des premiers vecteurs d'intégration en France' ['one of the main means of integration in France'] and that members of his parents' generation started drinking alcohol on arriving in France in order to integrate. His recent shows *Troisième degré* and *Sans modération* have also ended with him challenging negative stereotypes about Islam such as the idea that women are subjugated and the wearing of the headscarf impinges on freedom of expression. Overall, it is important to note that Mustapha El Atrassi does not present his stand-up shows as being specifically about being a Muslim and the extent to which he is explicitly seeking to use laughter to bring people together is unclear. With respect to this latter point, there is a significant degree of ambiguity. On one hand, he takes pride in telling jokes that one is apparently supposed not to tell, and deliberately employs an ironic tone when describing Islam in France as 'un sujet léger et rassembleur' ['a light and unifying subject'] during *Sans modération*. On the other hand, he evokes the need to 'se moquer les uns des autres' ['make fun of each other']. There is, however, a clear difference between Mustapha El Atrassi and examples of Muslim comedy such as *À part ça tout va bien*, Nabil Zerrouki's *Muslim Comédie*, the American trio Allah Made Me Funny and the Canadian sitcom *Little Mosque on the Prairie*. It is highly noticeable that El Atrassi takes considerable pride in exploiting a brand of humour that is both more provocative and more likely to provoke debates about the limits of humour or questions about what constitutes good or bad taste when it comes to jokes. However, the way that several of his jokes involve him seeking to reclaim and re-appropriate stereotypes that have been used to stigmatize Muslims is in keeping with the approach of the aforementioned acts.

When discussing Muslim comedians in France, it would be remiss not to mention Jamel Debbouze given that he is both Muslim and arguably the leading stand-up of his generation in France. However, as Guidi notes 'Jamel n'utilise toutefois le mot "musulman" qu'à l'intérieur de ses sketches et de manière ironique' ['Jamel however only uses the word "Muslim" within his sketches and in an ironic manner'] via statements such as 'Moi, je suis musulman pratiquant... heu...

of *Sans Modération* is available on YouTube at the following address https://www.youtube.com/watch?v=Vsk0Ahu7qwA&t=46s [accessed 25 July 2017].

pratiquement' ['Me, I'm a practising Muslim… well… practically'] that downplay the importance of Islam in his daily life.[43] It is certainly the case that Debbouze's stage material makes much less frequent reference to being from a Muslim family than to his Moroccan roots or childhood in the Parisian *banlieues*. The ways in which Debbouze alludes to his relationship with Islam highlights how it can be potentially complicated deciding who are or are not examples of Muslim comedians. Should the term 'Muslim comedian' be applicable to any comedian who is Muslim? If not, how Muslim do they have to be and how should one determine this? Furthermore, how should one categorize comedians whose religious beliefs and/or identity is unclear? Diletta Guidi has argued that term 'humour musulman' ['Muslim humour'] is subject to a 'double exploitation' ['dual usage']; she argues that 'certains humoristes se définissent eux-mêmes en ces termes, alors que pour d'autres la description est extérieure, indépendante de leur volonté' ['some comedians define themselves in these terms, while for others this description is an exterior one, independent of their will'].[44] Guidi mentions that Sophia Aram – a contemporary of Jamel Debbouze who also went to school in Trappes and is a child of Moroccan immigrants – is at times referred to as Muslim despite having declared that she is atheist.[45] In an interview-based article that appeared in *Télérama* in 2013, the journalist Valérie Lehoux described Aram as being 'de culture musulmane mais viscéralement athée' ['culturally Muslim but strongly atheist'].[46]

Sophia Aram has described herself in similar terms to those used by Valérie Lehoux, notably in her second stand-up show *Crise de foi* [*Crisis of Faith*]. In this show that she first performed in 2010, Aram stated 'je suis de culture musulmane […], je suis à l'islam ce que les Ferrero Rocher sont à la diplomatie internationale […], je suis athée d'origine musulmane' ['I am culturally Muslim (…), I am to Islam what Ferrero Rochers are to international diplomacy (…), I am an atheist of Muslim descent']. The third part of this description is somewhat paradoxical as it simultaneously evokes a sense of identity based on a lack of religious faith in the present and one that is also rooted in having been religious

---

43   Guidi, 'Rire et Islam', p. 176.
44   Guidi, 'Rire et Islam', p. 175.
45   Guidi, 'Rire et Islam', p. 176.
46   Valérie Lehoux, 'Sophia Aram: "Contrairement aux apparences, je ne suis pas une petite chose fragile"', *Télérama*, 5 January 2013, http://www.telerama.

in the past. Aram's attitude to religion is significantly different to that of the creators of the *À part ça tout va bien* sketches. Whilst the latter have talked about using humour as a means of focusing on religion in a manner that promotes the idea of *vivre ensemble* [social cohesion], Aram states that she is pleased to hear religions evoking the idea of *vivre ensemble* but feels that they actually 'servent plutôt à diviser' ['are actually in fact divisive'].[47] In *Crise de foi*, Aram focused on Islam as well as both Christianity and Judaism, setting out to tackle the three main monotheistic religions. Aram began her shows by declaring 'ce spectacle est sensible de heurter la sensibilité de ceux qui mettent leur foi au-dessus de leur sens d'humour' ['this show is liable to offend the sensitivities of those who place their faith before their sense of humour']. In interviews Sophia Aram has often mentioned the importance of being free to tackle whichever topics she pleases in her performances and the importance of 'le droit au blasphème' ['the right to blasphemy'] within the context of freedom of expression.[48] During the first few minutes of *Crise de foi*, Aram appeared as a burqa-wearing Muslim, a nun, and then an orthodox Jew while dancing across the stage. She made clear her general suspicion of religious teachings, notably near the start via a comparison between 'la transmission de foi' ['the transmission of faith'] and 'la vente triangulaire' ['pyramid schemes']. Throughout the show, she ridiculed religious conservatism. Where Islam is concerned, she mocked a Muslim football team from Créteil who cited their religious beliefs when seeking to justify their decision not to play a match against Paris Foot Gay, a team that has campaigned against homophobia since its founding in 2003. Towards the end of the show, she imagined a scenario involving Islam, Judaism,

fr/radio/sophia-aram-contrairement-aux-apparences-je-ne-suis-pas-une-petite-chose-fragile,91447.php [accessed 25 July 2017].

47   Michel Bourcet, 'Charlie Hebdo, réseaux sociaux, religions… Sophia Aram s'engage à rire de tout', *Télérama*, 14 October 2015, http://www.telerama.fr/sortir/charlie-hebdo-reseaux-sociaux-religions-sophia-aram-s-engage-a-rire-de-tout,132776.php [accessed 27 July 2017].

48   See for example: Gilles Renault, 'Sophia Aram: "Je suis athée, donc pour moi, le délit de blasphème n'existe pas"', *Libération*, 9 January 2015, http://next.liberation.fr/culture/2015/01/09/je-suis-athee-donc-pour-moi-le-delit-de-blaspheme-n-existe-pas_1177307 [accessed 27 January 2017]; Stéphane Arteta and Sophie Grassin, 'Sophia Aram: "La liberté d'expression ne peut s'accompagner d'un "mais"', *Le Nouvel Observateur*, 19 February 2015, http://teleobs.nouvelobs.com/actualites/20150219.OBS2949/citoyenne-aram.html [accessed 27 July 2017].

and Christianity competing against each other on a television game show before closing by declaring 'il vaut mieux être athée que d'être de mauvaise foi' ['it is better to be atheist than of bad faith'].

In her third stand-up show *Le Fond de l'air effraie* [*There's a Chill in the air*], Aram also discussed religion although does so within a broader context. This show, which she performed from 2015 to 2018, focuses on the political climate in a France that has experienced several terrorist attacks in recent years. Aram mocked Muslim extremists as well as others – especially those on the right and reactionary intellectuals – who have sought to either exploit the attacks for their own benefit or made nonsensical comments about how to combat terrorism. Aram takes a nuanced approach to evoking Islam that focuses both on her belief that it is important to be able to mock the religion and also the need to avoid scapegoating French Muslims. She expresses strong opposition to the sociologist Emmanuel Todd's criticism of those who mock a minority religion, and declares towards the end of the show 'le blasphème c'est sacré' ['blasphemy is sacred'].[49] Aram also uses dark humour to deride those in France who have called for French Muslims to condemn the attacks against *Charlie Hebdo* by saying 'je pense que les mêmes demandent à Gaz de France de condamner le Shoah' ['I think the same ones are calling on Gaz de France (a French gas company) to condemn the Shoah']. In other words, Aram mocks both Muslim extremists and those who hold French Muslims as a whole responsible for the actions of extremists.

Despite the fact that mocking Islam is considered to be a risky endeavour by some (see start of this chapter), many of the threats made against Sophia Aram have emanated from non-Muslims. Since 2011, her acerbic comments in stand-up shows and her regular radio appearances on France Inter have resulted in her receiving menacing comments from supporters of the Front national (FN). Many of the party's members and supporters were angry to hear Aram describe

---

49   In an interview about her show *Le fond de l'air effraie*, Aram explained that her criticism of Todd was based on her belief that 'considérer que tous les musulmans seraient incapables de vivre dans un pays dans lequel la liberté d'expression prime sur le religieux' ['to consider that all Muslims were incapable of living in a country where freedom of expression took precedence over religion'] was 'une forme de racisme' ['a form of racism']. Laurent Nunez, 'Sophia Aram: "Le blasphème, c'est sacré!"', *Marianne*, 3 October 2015, https://www.marianne.net/culture/sophia-aram-le-blaspheme-cest-sacre [accessed 27 July 2017].

party followers who blame all of France's problems on immigrants as 'gros cons' ['stupid idiots'].[50] Indeed, the response to her comments about the far-right political party have led to her receiving police protection. When she was performing her stand-up show *Crise de foi*, Aram said that it was often people from Catholic rather than Muslim or Jewish groups who contacted her to express their anger at how she had portrayed their religion.[51] Furthermore, she said in 2015 that the show led to 'des menaces limitées en comparaison de celles consécutives à mes chroniques en radio sur le FN' ['few threats compared to what has happened after my comments on radio about the FN'].[52]

Despite the fact that she has at times received threats as a result of how she has tackled controversial issues onstage or during her radio appearances, Sophia Aram argued in a 2013 interview that laughter can help to reduce rather than inflame tensions. Furthermore, she suggested that this can provide a welcome antidote to the way that religious issues are often discussed.[53] Although she has acknowledged that she performed her show *Crise de foi* in a somewhat calmer climate than that which has existed since the January 2015 terrorist attacks,[54] she has continued to insist on the importance of defending the freedom of expression in a similar manner to that which *Charlie Hebdo* has done. She made this clear in an interview with *Le Nouvel Observateur* in February 2015 by stating the following:

> Je partage avec eux la nécessité de brocarder la religion et l'idée que la liberté d'expression ne peut s'accompagner d'un 'mais', à plus forte raison lorsqu'il s'agit de lui opposer des croyances. J'ai du mal à supporter les déclarations commençant par 'Je suis pour la liberté d'expression' et se terminant par 'mais faudrait voir à ne pas froisser les croyants'. Ces crétins n'ont toujours pas compris que la liberté d'expression des uns ne pouvait s'arrêter aux croyances des autres.[55]

50   Valérie Lehoux, 'Sophia Aram: "Contrairement aux apparences"'.
51   See: Valérie Lehoux, 'Sophia Aram, menacée mais pas intimidée', *Télérama*, 6 December 2011, http://www.telerama.fr/radio/sophia-aram-menacee-mais-pas-intimidee,75704.php [accessed 27 July 2017].
52   Renault, 'Sophie Aram'.
53   In: Valérie Lehoux, 'Sophia Aram: "Contrairement aux apparences"'.
54   See: Valérie Lehoux, 'Sophia Aram: "Contrairement aux apparences"'.
55   Stéphane Arteta and Sophie Grassin, 'Sophia Aram'.

[I share with them the belief in the necessity of mocking religion and the idea that the freedom of expression cannot be followed by a 'but', especially when it concerns religious beliefs. I find it hard to support declarations beginning with 'I am in favour of freedom of expression' that end with 'but it is essential to avoid offending the religious'. These idiots have still not understood that the freedom of expression of some cannot stop at the religious beliefs of others.]

In *Le Fond de l'air effraie*, Aram made several references to *Charlie Hebdo*'s defence of the freedom of expression and suggested that they were at times somewhat isolated in defending this principle. Her show provides a poignant tribute to the values defended by the *Charlie Hebdo* staff killed in January 2015, and the bagpipe rendition of *Amazing Grace* that is audible at the end of Aram's performance is a call-back to her earlier reference during the show to this piece of music featuring in the somewhat anarchic funeral of *Charlie Hebdo* editor Charb. The arguments presented by Aram in the quotation cited above could potentially be read as a sign that she is not in favour of restraint when it comes to criticizing religion, but she has in several interviews suggested that she does not seek to use her freedom of expression simply to provoke. In 2010, she told the magazine *Elle* that 'le but n'est pas de choquer, d'être corrosif' ['the aim isn't to shock or to be caustic'] but rather that she wanted to '[s]'amuse[r] simplement des religions' ['simply have fun with religions'].[56] This approach to exercising her freedom of expression is somewhat different to that evoked by Mustapha El Atrassi at the start of some of his recent stand-up shows. El Atrassi underlines his desire to relieve tension by telling provocative jokes that he feels one is not supposed to tell, whereas Aram is less explicitly provocative. Although it is perhaps not as frequent in her stand-up shows, Sophia Aram does on occasion also use dark humour to make a point about controversial issues (see discussion above about her comments in *Le fond de l'air effraie* about those who called on Muslims to condemn the January 2015 attack on *Charlie Hebdo*). It is also important to note that Aram and El Atrassi's recent shows suggest that they have differing attitudes to

---

56 Axelle Szczygiel, 'Sophia Aram: la "Crise de foi" d'une féministe convaincue', *Elle*, 22 September 2010. http://www.elle.fr/Loisirs/Sorties/Dossiers/Sophia-Aram-la-Crise-de-foi-d-une-feministe-convaincue-1354094 [accessed 27 July 2017].

Charlie Hebdo; Aram showed in *Le Fond de l'air effraie* that she identified with the publication whilst El Atrassi was critical of what he saw as the divisiveness of the 'je suis Charlie' spirit in his show *Troisième degré*.

As well as being a subject evoked by comedians who are Muslims or who grew up as Muslims, Islam has also been a topic that has featured in recent shows by non-Muslim comedians in France. One of the most prominent French comedians to tackle Islam – and indeed religion in general – in recent years has been Jérémy Ferrari. Ferrari, whose humour is often provocative, dark, and focused on contemporary issues considered taboo, performed a show entitled *Mes 7 péchés capitaux* [*My 7 Deadly Sins*] from 2008 to 2009 in which he mocked Christianity, Judaism, and Islam. He later re-worked this show in order to create *Hallelujah bordel!* [*Hallelujah Chaos!*], which he performed from 2011 to 2014 and released on DVD in 2013. In this show, Ferrari ridicules key tenets of the three religions and draws on having read the Bible, Torah, and Koran while preparing the show. He explains that he was inspired to write the show after a friend suggested he considered turning to religion while experiencing a difficult time in his life. Ferrari reads, and mocks, extracts of all three holy texts whilst energetically cavorting around the stage. He also recounts short news stories about extreme religious views and what various people around the world have done in the name of religion. He jokes that he feels that Islam is the best religion for him due to the way that he says men are allowed to treat women and reads out passages from the Koran that concern the subjugation of women, polygamy, and the use of violence against women suspected of having been unfaithful. Shortly afterwards, he comments that having read the Koran gives him an advantage over many Muslims. Ferrari is unafraid of making provocative statements and declares at one point 'les musulmans c'est dangereux pour ta vie, les juifs c'est dangereux pour ta carrière' ['Muslims are a danger to your life, Jews are a danger to your career']. He ends his show by encouraging his audience to 'fout[re] le bordel!' ['stir things up!']. Although the focus of *Hallelujah bordel!* is similar to *Crise de foi* by virtue of tackling Christianity, Judaism, and Islam, Ferrari focuses more on extremism and also seeks to engage more closely with religious texts than Aram. Ferrari described his show *Hallelujah bordel* as 'très dénonciateur, parfois absurde, parfois léger mais surtout provocateur et noir' ['very denunciatory, sometimes absurd, sometimes light but certainly provocative and dark'], adding that 'donc il faut venir avec pas mal de second degré' ['so it is important not to take it too literally'].[57] He added that he felt his brand of humour was suited to the context and aims of his show:

> Je pense que les gens sont prêts à entendre de l'humour noir quand c'est fait pour les bonnes raisons. En l'occurrence, mon but dans *Hallelujah bordel* n'est pas de me moquer des croyants mais de me moquer des extrémistes. C'est quand même plus un message de réunification qu'autre chose. Et puis surtout, le spectacle est basé sur le rire et avant tout, je monte sur scène pour faire rire les gens.[58]

> [I think that people are prepared to hear dark humour when it's used for good reasons. In the case of *Hallelujah bordel*, my goal was not to mock the religious but rather to mock extremists. It's actually about a message that brings people together rather than anything else. And in particular, the show is based on laughter and above all, I go on stage to make people laugh.]

This shows that Ferrari believes that provocative humour concerning religion is capable of creating unity rather than division. He is thus evoking a similar aspiration to that of *À part ça tout va bien* but employing a very different type of humour which is in many ways more akin to that of Mustapha El Atrassi. Like El Atrassi, Ferrari did not seek to position his show *Hallelujah bordel* as an initiative aimed at challenging stereotypes about religion and promoting *vivre ensemble* [social cohesion] in the way that the *À part ça tout va bien* website sought to present its sketches.

Conclusions

Just as it is important to avoid talking about French Muslims in a manner that ignores the diversity of beliefs and origins that exist within the community (or indeed communities in the plural), it is important to acknowledge the diversity that exists among comedians in France who

57   Olivier Eggermont, 'Entretien avec Jérémy Ferrari, prince de l'humour noir', *Le Vif*, 11 March 2014, http://focus.levif.be/culture/scenes/entretien-avec-jeremy-ferrari-prince-de-l-humour-noir/article-normal-13137.html   [accessed 28 July 2017].
58   Olivier Eggermont, 'Entretien avec Jérémy Ferrari'.

refer to Islam and Muslims in their performances. This chapter has shown that the ways French Muslims – and those who may define themselves as *de culture musulmane* [culturally Muslim] without being practicing Muslims – seek to use humour vary significantly and highlight the need to talk about forms of cultural expression in the plural. On one hand, the likes of *À part ça tout va bien* and also Nabil Zerrouki's *Muslim Comédie* provide examples of humour that deals with potentially sensitive topics in a gentle and cautious manner.[59] Indeed, one could argue that such humour exemplifies a traditional brand of Muslim humour identified by Ulrich Marzolph as being 'a moderate one, both in terms of frequency and intensity of jocular expression and practice'.[60] However, Mustapha El Atrassi and Sophia Aram show that a more provocative approach is favoured by other artists who have grown up in Muslim families in France. El Atrassi and Aram are also different from the likes of Zangro, Hassan Zahi, and Nabil Zerrouki as they have evoked Islam within their comedy shows after having already achieved a significant level of notoriety through their regular appearances on popular mainstream television and radio shows in France. Their trajectories thus need to be seen separately from those of artists who have participated in projects associating humour and Islam before having become as established on radio and television. Collectively, the performers analysed in this chapter illustrate a variety of ways that comedians are seeking to use humour in a way that challenges the perceived incompatibility between Islam and humour that was discussed at the start of this chapter. As we have seen, their attempts to use comedy to tackle stereotypes are in keeping with developments in many other countries. Giselinde Kuipers argues that 'joking back requires power, access and confidence',[61] and the use made of humour by French Muslims discussed in this chapter points towards their progress in exploiting modes of cultural expression that allow them to respond to ways in which their religion has been perceived by others. Here, it is important to remember that Muslims in France have traditionally lacked the same level of cultural and media visibility of other minority religions in France that they outnumber.[62]

59   Guidi, 'Rire et Islam', pp. 176–7.
60   Marzolph, 'The Muslim Sense of Humour', p. 177.
61   Kuipers, 'The Politics of Humour in the Public Sphere', p. 74.
62   Alec Hargreaves, *Multi-ethnic France: Immigration, Politics, Culture and Society*, 2nd edition, (Oxford: Routledge, 2007), pp. 103, 107.

The time and effort it took for Zangro and Hassan Zahi to develop a follow-up project after the success of *À part ça tout va bien* points towards the fact that establishing a cultural visibility that allows Muslims in France to utilize comedy to challenge the stigmatization and misunderstanding of their religion is an ongoing quest. This experience led the creators of the web series to suggest that France is a country where there has been a reluctance to embrace projects that have sought to take a humorous look at Islam and Muslims. The previous chapter about the *Jamel Comedy Club* has shown that, in some situations, France is prepared to embrace comedy that focuses on difference. The *Jamel Comedy Club* has sought to counter both the lack of cultural visibility of a minority group and allow members of the group to engage with discourses that have been used to stigmatize them. Given this state of affairs, it is worth asking why the same has not been as true of the humour used by French Muslims. As previously mentioned, the presence and influence of Jamel Debbouze as a leading figure in the *Jamel Comedy Club* was a major factor in it generating the publicity that allowed it to gain momentum. Furthermore, one must also take into account that French laws in the last two decades have increasingly sought to regulate and restrict the wearing of visible markers of Muslim identity in public spaces.

The way in which mainstream parties on the left as well as the right in France have sought to take an uncompromising approach to combating terrorism and radicalization risks adding to the stigmatization suffered by French Muslims that performers, and others, seek to challenge. Despite the impact that stigmatizing discourses have had on the image of France's *banlieues* and their inhabitants, it is nevertheless the case that these suburban areas have for several decades been associated with a form of cultural dynamism thanks in no small part to the development of hip-hop culture in France since the early 1980s. The association between French Muslims and cultural dynamism is less well established, although the forms of comedy discussed in this chapter have the potential to play a role in changing this. Indeed, Nilüfer Göfe argues that 'la création de nouvelles formes esthétiques peut [...] signaler une volonté de dépassement des antagonismes, de l'incommensurabilité entre normes, des divisions identitaires entre Européens et musulmans' ['the creation of new aesthetic forms can (...) signal a desire to go beyond antagonism, the incommensurability of norms, divisions of identity between Europeans and Muslims'].[63] However, *wanting* to get beyond clichéd representations of Muslims and *succeeding* in doing so are two different things. In a climate where the political opportunism of far-right groups is in part based on demonizing Islam, the uses made of *laïcité* [French secularism] by more mainstream parties have contributed to a situation whereby almost four out of five French people polled in a 2015 survey were critical of the wearing of the Muslim headscarf.[64] The historians Pascal Blanchard, Nicolas Bancel, and Dominic Thomas have argued that the way in which European countries such as France have introduced restrictions concerning issues such as the wearing of the headscarf, complete veil or burqa, and building of minarets has contributed to an '"invisibilisation de l'islam" dans l'espace public' ['the "rendering invisible of Islam" in the public sphere'].[65] This type of process – allied to a sense of fear that has stemmed from terror attacks in recent years[66] – does little to facilitate the emergence of further attempts to challenge stereotypes about Islam and Muslims via cultural forms such as comedy. Nevertheless, Rachid Benzine argues that the fact that Muslims account for almost a tenth of the French population means that 'un avenir de paix ne peut se penser qu'"avec les musulmans" et non "contre eux"' ['a peaceful future can only be conceived of "with Muslims" and not "against them"'].[67] This provides a further argument for exploring ways in which humour is used by Muslims as part of a process of identity negotiation rather than merely as a device exploited by others to depict Muslims.

63   Göle, *Musulmans au quotidien*, p. 288.
64   In the survey conducted by the *Commission nationale consultative des droits de l'homme* (CNCDH, National Consultative Commission on Human Rights), 79% of respondents were critical of the wearing of the Muslim headscarf, Bancel et al., p. 120.
65   Pascal Blanchard, Nicolas Bancel and Dominic Thomas, 'Introduction. Qui veut la guerre des identités?', in Blanchard, Bancel and Thomas, Dominic (eds.), *Vers la guerre des identités? De la fracture coloniale à la révolution ultranationale* (Paris: La Découverte, 2015), p. 41.
66   See: Rachid Benzine, 'La peur de l'islam, ferment d'un nouveau lien identitaire en France?', in Blanchard et al. (eds), *Vers la guerre des identités? De la fracture coloniale à la révolution ultranationale* (Paris: La Découverte, 2015), p. 107.
67   Benzine, 'La peur de l'islam', p. 109.

Conclusions

Although this book has sought to demonstrate that debates about *Charlie Hebdo* in recent decades are far from the only lens through which to view French humour, it is undeniable that the impact of the January 2015 attacks on the *Charlie Hebdo* offices have been far reaching. They have led to much reflection on the nature and limits of humour, as well as broader questions concerning the freedom of expression. Furthermore, such discussions have concerned much more than just cartoons and indeed several of the stand-up comedians whose work has been discussed in this book have commented on the impact of the attacks on either their own attitude to being a comedian or French society as a whole. In 2016, the comedian Stéphane Guillon commented that 'si on peut mourir pour un dessin, alors on peut mourir pour un sketch' ['if you can die for a drawing, then you can die for a sketch'].[1] Although the 2015 attacks have undoubtedly led some comedians to reconsider how they treat potentially sensitive issues – and indeed had an impact on some attempts by academics to organize events focused on the *Charlie Hebdo* attacks – they have also led to other performers steadfastly refusing to alter the way that they approach controversial topics. After exploring the general impact of the 2015 terrorist attacks on French humour and humourists, this conclusion will focus on the perennial question of 'peut-on rire de tout?' ['can one laugh about everything?'] in order to assess contemporary attitudes to humour in France. It will then broaden its focus to consider what humour can

---

1 Sandrine Blanchard, 'Continuer à rire de tout, plus que jamais', *Le Monde*, 6 January 2016, http://www.lemonde.fr/culture/article/2016/01/06/continuer-a-rire-de-tout-plus-que-jamais_4842605_3246.html [accessed 27 October 2017].

achieve before assessing what the four case studies examined here demonstrate about French humour and the ways in which it focuses on others and otherness.

The impact of the *Charlie Hebdo* attacks on humour in France

When discussing the impact of terrorist attacks in France on those who perform stand-up comedy, it is important to consider the impact of not just the January 2015 attacks on *Charlie Hebdo* but also the November 2015 attacks on sites in Paris such as the Bataclan. Although the event taking place at the Bataclan was a concert being performed by the American rock band Eagles of Death Metal rather than a comedy event, it was still an event that – like stand-up comedy – can be categorized as part of what is known in France as *le spectacle vivant* [live performance]. Furthermore, the Bataclan plays host to a wide range of different types of performances that on occasion includes comedy shows. The targeting of a concert attended by over a thousand people on the night of 13 November 2015, in addition to the France versus Germany football match at the Stade de France the same evening, appeared to be part of a deliberate attempt to create fear and panic within large groups of people. In the face of such hostility, there have been acts of defiance such as fans making their way home from the France against Germany match singing *La Marseillaise* in the métro as a sign of resistance and solidarity. Against this backdrop, several of the performers discussed in this book have ended their shows by praising audiences who have continued to attend live shows. Claudia Tagbo (a former member of the *Jamel Comedy Club*) was in 2017 still ending her shows by thanking audiences for continuing to support *le spectacle vivant* in a manner that did not explicitly mention the attacks of 2015 but could be read as being influenced by these events. Given that the attacks of 2015 have led to increased security measures at venues such as theatres and comedy clubs, Tagbo's declaration can be interpreted as an expression of gratitude that such reminders of what happened at the Bataclan on the night of 13 November 2015 have not prevented audiences from continuing to enjoy live performances. As mentioned in the chapter about Muslims and humour, Sophia Aram was in 2017 ending her stand-up shows by exhorting audiences to continue to support live performances in a manner that more explicitly focused on the idea of maintaining *l'esprit*

Charlie [the spirit of *Charlie Hebdo*] and remaining undeterred by those who seek to spread division and fear. However, it is also important to acknowledge that comedians such as Mustapha El Atrassi have suggested that the #JeSuisCharlie spirit is not as inclusive as is often assumed, and suggested that a comedian's ethnicity can have an impact on how audiences and critics respond to their attempts to perform material that deals with recent terrorist attacks.[2]

For audiences who continue to attend comedy events in France, and for that matter go to concerts, plays, and sporting events, reminders of the November 2015 attacks remain present in the form of restrictions put in place as part of the reinforced *plan Vigipirate* [National Security Alert System] which remained active as of autumn 2019. Websites of several venues make clear revised rules about sizes of bags that are permitted at events and some venues feature signs about the *plan Vigipirate* [National Security Alert System] to explain why certain entrances or exits to auditoriums are kept closed both before and during performances. This was the case at the Théâtre des Bouffes du Nord near the Gare du Nord when a roundtable discussion about humour was taking place on 24 September 2017. At the event, comedians Fabrice Éboué and Jérémy Ferrari evoked the importance of not allowing the attacks to influence the topics they joke about but the signs up at the venue itself showed that the attacks do have an impact on the venues in which such comedians perform. When discussing the security measures in place at performances by leading comedians in France, it is however important to remember that they are not all uniquely a consequence of terrorist attacks that took place in 2015. For example, Sophia Aram started to receive police protection several years before the *Charlie Hebdo* attacks following threats she received from supporters of the Front national.[3]

Peut-on rire de tout?

The question 'peut-on rire de tout?' is one that has been debated for a great many years, and has often led into discussions not just about whether one can laugh about anything and everything but also in what situations it is possible to do so. Pierre Desproges famously

2   See pp. 149-50 in this book
3   See pp. 155-6 of this book.

responded to this question by answering 'oui, mais pas avec tout le monde [...] mieux vaut rire d'Auschwitz avec un Juif que jouer au Scrabble avec Klaus Barbie' ['yes, but not with everyone (...) it is better to laugh about Auschwitz with a Jew than to play Scrabble with Klaus Barbie'].[4] Desproges's answer introduces an important nuance that focuses on how the act of sharing a joke, and with whom one shares a joke, can make a big difference when it comes to the nature of the laughter that may follow. Following the attacks on the *Charlie Hebdo* offices, it is worth asking to what extent comedians, and others, in France believe that it is possible to 'rire de tout', and to what extent they seek to qualify their responses in the way that Desproges did. Although the ethos of *Charlie Hebdo* has generally been that it is possible to 'rire de tout', and be unafraid of being provocative or causing offence when doing so, many comedians have, like Desproges, argued that it is possible to 'rire de tout', subject to certain conditions.

Before pursuing this analysis further, it is important to first observe that the question 'peut-on rire de tout?' can be understood in several different ways. One interpretation is to assume that it is tantamount to asking if it is morally acceptable to laugh at anything and everything. However, the quote from Stéphane Guillon at the start of this concluding chapter reveals another possible interpretation of what it can be taken to mean. Guillon's focus on the potential consequences for humourists who mock Islam is centred more on personal risk than the broader question of morality; in this situation 'peut-on rire de tout?' becomes more of a pragmatic question than an ethical one.

Although Freud's approach to humour has its critics and is increasingly seen as being somewhat dated,[5] the Freudian notion that one of the key functions of humour is to relieve tension is highly applicable to the way that it has been used by some performers and writers in France following terrorist attacks. As discussed in the chapter about *Charlie Hebdo*, the immediate aftermath of the attacks saw some humorous television programmes such as *Les Guignols* evoke the attacks in sketches that appeared within hours of the events that led to the deaths of twelve people at the offices of the satirical publication in Paris's 11th

4   Comte-Sponville, 'Peut-on rire de tout?'.
5   See discussion of criticisms of Freud in this in pp. 6-9 of this book's introduction.

arrondissement. Furthermore, Mustapha El Atrassi has begun some of his 2016 and 2017 stand-up shows by stating that the climate of tension in France since the attacks creates a real need to tell jokes, and especially to tell jokes about topics that some may see as taboo.[6] Nevertheless, it is also the case that recent years in France have seen several attempts to police or restrict humour that fail to take into account its potential to relieve tension. A prime example came in 2015 from the school teacher who ordered a pupil to write 'on ne rit pas de choses sérieuses' ['one does not laugh about serious things'].[7] This appears to be part of a wider trend that has seen people such as politicians make judgements about what is appropriate to consider amusing, and what is an appropriate subject for humour. Such judgements are often somewhat subjective, and indeed appear to be made by people without any evident expertise on humour and who do not seek to engage with experts on humour. Reactions to shows by Dieudonné in recent years show that the accusation that someone or something is simply not funny is at times used by politicians, and others, primarily as a means to express a form of moral (or political) disapproval that implicitly positions the speaker as someone who is qualified to make a judgement about controversial humour. Indeed, such judgements also often seem to be based on the idea that it is possible to objectively determine whether or not something (or someone) is funny. Some of Manuel Valls's comments about Dieudonné in late 2013 – especially his argument that 'Dieudonné ne fait plus rire personne depuis longtemps' ['It is quite some time since Dieudonné has made anyone laugh'][8] – sought to exploit a notion of supposedly shared disapproval in a somewhat misleading manner given that the performer in question has performed many shows to sell-out audiences in recent years. Furthermore, Valls' public criticism of Dieudonné was in some ways counterproductive as they helped to keep Dieudonné in the public eye at a time when he was rarely being invited to put his views across in mainstream television and radio shows. The ultimate failure of Valls to succeed in using legal mechanisms to prevent Dieudonné from performing also played into the hands of the controversial performer, providing Dieudonné with a victory to celebrate.

6   See p. 148 of this book.
7   See p. 51 of this book.
8   Di Stefano and Mirabeau, *Interdit de rire*, p. 32.

Although Dieudonné has provoked controversy due to the nature of material he has performed in his stand-up shows in recent years, and regularly faced allegations of anti-Semitism, it is important to note that the same period has seen several well-known French comedians perform shows about religion that have not led to as widespread criticism. As mentioned in the chapter about Muslims and humour, recent years have seen several other French comedians perform shows that have focused on religions and in particular mocked extreme elements that are present within the three main monotheistic religions (Christianity, Judaism, and Islam). Performers such as Jérémy Ferrari have emphasized that it is extreme followers of religion rather than the religious as a whole that they have set out to mock.[9] However, it is worth asking if this focus on the more fanatical elements of an individual religion can create a somewhat skewed picture of a religion as a whole, as can occur with some media coverage of Islam.[10] A comedian's decision to specifically mock the extreme fringes of a religion rather than the religion as a whole does not necessarily mean that those watching the comedian will interpret their material in this manner, especially if they feel that the material increases the focus on negative stereotypes that can contribute to the stigmatization of an entire religion. Nevertheless, deciding not to mock religious extremism could be seen as an approach that leads to dogmatic and fundamental beliefs going unchallenged and thus plays into the hands of those who subscribe to such principles. One can also argue that a reluctance to joke about religion in general could be seen as a form of self-censorship symbolizing tension and uncertainty. It would also constitute a very different approach to that of *Charlie Hebdo*'s cartoonist Cabu, who argued that 'il n'y a pas de limite à l'humour, qui est au service de la liberté d'expression, car là où l'humour s'arrête, bien souvent la place est laissée à la censure et l'autocensure' ['there is no limit to humour, which is at the service of freedom of expression, because precisely where humour stops is where censorship and self-censorship begins'].[11] This notion is similar to Christophe Alévêque's argument that 'une société bien portante devrait pouvoir rire de tout et éviter l'humour communautariste' ['a healthy society should be able to laugh

---

9   Eggermonth, 'Entretien avec Jérémy Ferrari'. See discussion on pp. 158-9 of Chapter 4 about Muslims and humour.

10   Kamal Salhi, 'Editorial', *Performing Islam*, 1.1 (2012), pp. 11-12.

11   Blanchard, 'Continuer à rire de tout, plus que jamais'.

about everything and avoid community-specific humour'].[12] However, Edwy Plenel has argued that fears of 'communautarisme' are at times false fears that are based on an attempt to exploit the principle of *laïcité* [French secularism] in a manner that betrays its original meaning; he has also argued that the mocking of minority groups in France has in fact been a symbol of an 'idéologie barbare des civilisations supérieures contre des peoples maudits qui rôde de nouveau parmi nous' ['the barbaric ideology of superior civilizations opposed to wretched peoples which once again rears its ugly head'].[13] Thus, one needs consider the values on which jokes are based and what they suggest about power relations within a society. If 'rire de tout' involves exercising freedom of speech to perpetate a majority population's stereotypical perspective on minority groups, it can hardly be said to be a progressive use of a supposed entitlement, or one that helps to uphold key French Republican principles such as *égalité* [equality] and *fraternité* [fraternity].

What can humour achieve?

As well as exploring the ethical and practical issues concerning whether one can 'rire de tout', it is also worth exploring the broader question of what humour can achieve. In the introduction to this book, I alluded to Michel Boujenah's somewhat simplistic argument that 'si on peut rire ensemble, on peut vivre ensemble' ['if we can laugh together, we can live together'].[14] However, Pierre Desproges's often-cited response to the question 'peut-on rire de tout?' shows that the true significance of laughing together can take on a different significance depending on who is laughing and the subject of their laughter. As the Dutch sociologist Giselinde Kuipers has argued, 'humor can bring people together, but it can also emphasize and augment differences in status'.[15] In fact, humour can potentially do both of the things that

---

12   Gaccio and Dieudonné, *Peut-on tout dire?* p. 73. See discussion of this notion in pp. 73–4 of Chapter 2 about Dieudonné.
13   Edwy Plenel, *Pour les Musulmans* (Paris: Éditions La Découverte, 2016), pp. 148, 155.
14   Bellenger, *Rire et faire rire*, p. 11; see pp. 2–3 of this book.
15   Giselinde Kuipers, *Good Humour, Bad Taste: a Sociology of the Joke* (Berlin/Boston: Walter De Gruyter, 2015), p. 8.

Kuipers identifies in the aforementioned quotation if the motivations of the joke teller – or the assumptions that underpin a joke – are far from innocent. In a book that sets out to explore what makes people laugh in different countries around the world, Peter McGraw and Joel Warner argue that 'good comedy is a conspiracy' and that it involves 'creat[ing] an in-group with those you want to get the joke'.[16] Although the process by which a comedian seeks to establish a rapport with an audience can be relatively innocent, this is not always the case. Indeed, critics of Dieudonné have sought to argue that there is something far from benign about the way that he seeks to connect with his audience at the same time as voicing views that have led to him being accused of inciting racial hatred, being anti-Semitic and/or seeking to perpetuate conspiracy theories.[17] In other words, the comedy of Dieudonné – and indeed other performers who set out to shock or push the boundaries of taste – cannot easily be framed within the context of McGraw's 'benign violation' theory that is discussed in the aforementioned work by McGraw and Warner.[18]

Controversies surrounding on- and offstage declarations by Dieudonné, and questions of perceived notions of taste and the limits of humour that have been provoked by *Charlie Hebdo*, have meant that comedy has received significant media coverage in France during the last two decades. However, it has also attracted media attention due to the presence of high-profile initiatives such as the *Jamel Comedy Club* and the ways that members of many different groups have sought to use it as part of a process of identity negotiation.[19] The status that has been afforded to some of the comedians from the initial *Jamel Comedy Club* cohort within highly popular television and radio shows has provided them not just with media exposure but also opportunities to mock or question those in positions of power. In a documentary about black comedians in France, Judith Sibony argued that 2007 was a year when 'des comédiens deviennent de vrais acteurs politiques'

---

16   Peter McGraw and Joel Warner, *The Humor Code*, p. 200.
17   See: Haziza, *Vol au-dessus d'un nid de fachos*, pp. 118-19; Briganti et al., *La Galaxie Dieudonné*, p. 7, 63-146; Gaccio and Dieudonné, *Peut-on tout dire?*, p. 39; Lichfield, 'Heard the One About the Racist Black Comedian?'.
18   See: McGraw and Warner, *The Humor Code*, pp. 8-10, 60.
19   See: Quemener, *Le Pouvoir de l'humour*, p. 87; Quemener, '"Mère black, père noir, je suis métisse!"', p. 17.

['comedians became true political players'].[20] These words preceded an extract from a 2007 edition of the Canal Plus topical entertainment show *Le Grand Journal* where Thomas Ngijol tells Nicolas Sarkozy that he is not a fully integrated member of French society as he does not drink alcohol, before asking the then presidential candidate if the reason for this is due to being Muslim. On one hand, the rise in profile of stand-up comedy in France has afforded comedians such as the aforementioned members of the *Jamel Comedy Club* an opportunity to hold figures such as politicians to account. On the other hand, it is important to differentiate between questions that are asked of politicians by comedians in a tongue-in-cheek manner and those that constitute a more far-reaching probing of a politician's acts and declarations. In 2017, for example, Jamel Debbouze combined mocking Nicolas Sarkozy's attempts at humour by making a political point about the former president's comparison between the arrival of migrants in Europe to a leaking pipe in a kitchen.[21] Over a decade previously, Debbouze had accused Sarkozy of being divisive and confrontational at the time of the autumn 2005 unrest in France's *banlieues*.[22]

In Sibony's documentary, Noom Diawara – another member of the initial *Jamel Comedy Club* cohort – suggests that it is easier to bring about change via humour than politics or sport, a comment which appears to stem from the level of profile that comedy and comedians in France have experienced in the last two decades. Rather than seeing the tongue-in-cheek nature of some comedians' comments on socio-political issues as a weakness, he argued in a 2017 interview that this quality actually constituted an asset:

> Dans l'humour il n'y a pas un côté moralisateur, il y a un côté en détente; on rigole et le message passe. Si on arrive avec des gros sabots, professeur d'école, on n'aime pas ça, que l'on fasse

---

20   *Chocolat: une histoire du rire.*
21   Fabien Morin, 'Jamel Debbouze veut recruter Nicolas Sarkozy dans sa bande de comiques', *Le Figaro*, 24 June 2015, http://tvmag.lefigaro.fr/le-scan-tele/people/2015/06/24/28008–20150624ARTFIG00206-jamel-debbouze-veut-recruter-nicolas-sarkozy-dans-son-emission.php [accessed 7 December 2017].
22   Florence Aubenas, 'Quartier maître', *Libération*, 7 August 2006, http://www.liberation.fr/portrait/2006/08/07/quartier-maitre_47886 [accessed 7 December 2017].

de la morale. Les gens n'aiment pas que l'on fasse de la morale. Mais si à travers une blague ils rigolent, ils prennent conscience. La subtilité est beaucoup plus simple, l'humour est plus facile.[23]

[In humour, there isn't a moralizing tone, there's a relaxed tone; one laughs and the message gets across. If one is heavy-handed, acts like a school teacher, and lectures, people don't like that. But if via joke they laugh, they become aware. Subtlety is a lot simpler, humour is easier.]

Here, it appears that Diawara is identifying what he sees as comedy's relationship with authority as a strength. Implicitly, he seems to be stating that comedians can more easily create a rapport with an audience by placing themselves on the same level and creating an antidote to the hierarchical tone that he associates with the way that people in authority present their views. However, one could argue that this conception of humour – which perhaps does not fully encapsulate the myriad ways in which humour can operate – explains why some people may be more willing to listen to a comedian rather than a politician without necessarily demonstrating that comedy can bring about change. Indeed, Christie Davies has argued that 'jokes can have no significant impact because there are so many other far more powerful material and ideological forces shaping the world'.[24] In follow-up questions during the interview cited above, Diawara suggested that humour has a role to play in making people aware of 'la bêtise de leur pensée' ['the stupidity of their thinking'] and that this can be achieved via a process whereby 'on part d'un stéréotype et des préjugés pour jouer avec ces préjugés ou pour les contrer' ['one starts with a stereotype and prejudices in order to counter them'].[25] This focus on how people can seek to make use of stereotypes within comedy is reminiscent of the work of Rappoport and Mintz that was discussed in the introduction to this book. Although Rappoport and Mintz have assessed the ways in which humour can be used by minority groups in different ways that depend on their position within a society, they stop short of suggesting that it is through using

---

23   Noom Diawara, interviewed by Jonathan Ervine (unpublished), 25 March 2017.
24   Davies, *Mirth of Nations*, p. 222.
25   Noom Diawara, interviewed by Jonathan Ervine (unpublished), 25 March 2017.

humour that minority groups can re-define their place within society. Rather, they argue that it can provide an indication as to the status and/ or cultural visibility of a minority group within a given society.

An important trend in recent decades, which is demonstrated by *À part ça tout va bien*, is that the internet as well as the stage is becoming an ever more important space in which comedians can present their work and their vision of their place within society.[26] Sites such as YouTube provide performers with the means of engaging fans via predominantly short videos that can be easily shared on social media, and be used to generate publicity in a manner that does not necessitate passing via mainstream media. For Hirzalla and his co-authors, there is insufficient evidence to prove that people who commented on the humorous videos discussed in their article changed their perspective on the issues evoked in the sketches.[27] Although this analysis could be seen as providing a pessimistic view of humour's potential to bring about changes in mentalities, it is important to acknowledge that Hirzalla et al. primarily evaluated comments and discussions within the vlogs they studied without seeking to assess the broader impact that the vlogs generated. Another method of assessing the impact of a vlog, or blog, is to examine the extent to which it attracts coverage from offline and online media. For example, the extent to which the *À part ça tout va bien* was successful could be gauged by the amount of newspaper articles and television reports it generated rather than simply the number of views its videos received online or the nature of the comments they generated. However, even this method may well fall short of providing a clear picture of the impact of humorous videos as there is a difference between measuring the level of media interest generated and assessing the effect of the media coverage.

One of the most significant trends within French comedy in recent decades is the opening up of an increasing number of spaces – both within comedy clubs and online – in which performers from a variety of different backgrounds can explore complex issues of identity. This can involve exploring the trials and tribulations of hybrid identities and being mixed race, topics that are evoked regularly by members of the *Jamel Comedy Club*.[28] In *Chocolat: une histoire du rire*, Judith Sibony's

26   See: Quemener, *Le Pouvoir de l'humour*, p. 9.
27   Hirzalla et al., 'How Funny Can Islam Controversies Be?', pp. 59-60.
28   See: Quemener, *Le Pouvoir de l'humour*, pp. 109–11.

documentary about black comedians in France, Shirley Souagnon describes simultaneously evoking her status as a black person, a woman, a Rastafarian, and a lesbian in her shows. This contrasts with the way that the earlier parts of the documentary focus on how French theatre and television previously treated black performers as exotic others who needed to play up to recognizable stereotypes in order to amuse predominantly white audiences.[29] The emergence of spaces within which complex notions of identity can be explored is significant as it provides an arena in which processes of simplification can be challenged. As Bancel, Blanchard, and Boubeker argue in their 2015 work *Le Grand Repli*, the French media has a tendency to overly homogenize minority groups:

> En France, il n'existe ni communauté maghrébine ou africaine ni communauté musulmane. Ce sont des chimères, des mythes bien utiles. Et c'est la force du préjugé et des clichés médiatiques qui construisent de toutes pièces une communauté de gueules d'Arabes ou de métèques. Malentendu public ou paradoxe républicain, les héritiers de l'immigration ne s'en retrouvent pas moins soumis à une double contrainte: l'assignation à une communauté d'origine par ceux-là mêmes qui leur demandent de s'en émanciper.[30]

> [In France, there is neither a Maghrebi or African community, nor a Muslim community. These are highly useful illusions. And the strength of prejudices and media clichés is that they construct from beginning to end a community of Arab or immigrant faces. Whether a public understanding or a Republican paradox, the descendants of immigration find themselves nevertheless subject to a double constraint: assigned to a community of origin by those who demanded that they freed themselves from it.]

The diversity of experiences presented by comedians who may share certain characteristics – be they elements connected to race, ethnicity, religion, or sexuality – may thus play a role in projecting a wider range of perspectives on minority groups in France. Indeed, the focus on hybrid identities within performances by comedians associated

29   *Chocolat: une histoire du rire.*
30   Bancel et al., *Le Grand Repli*, p. 88.

with the *Jamel Comedy Club* suggests that the French comedy scene is becoming a space where more nuanced explorations of identity are taking place.[31] To dismiss this sort of humour that frequently focuses on racial and ethnic identity as *humour communautaire* is a strategy that goes against Republican universality by treating experiences of minority populations as not being relevant to the French nation as a whole.

Comedy and otherness

The aforementioned optimism about the way in which French comedy is exploring questions of identity needs to be placed within the context of comedy's long history of using others and otherness as a source of humour.[32] Furthermore, Kuipers has argued that 'people who don't laugh when others do, or laugh when others are silent, expose themselves as others'.[33] Debates explored in the first two chapters of this book provided examples of the potentially divisive nature of humour. Terms such as 'others' and 'otherness' are relevant to discussions of depictions of minority groups such as Muslims within *Charlie Hebdo* and also the question of who did or did not identify with the #JeSuisCharlie sentiment following the January 2015 attacks. The career trajectory of Dieudonné exhibits an evolution in how the performer has engaged with concepts of otherness. In the 1990s, he primarily used his otherness – as a member of a visible minority from the *banlieues* of Paris – in a largely unthreatening manner in light-hearted sketches that he performed with Élie Semoun at a time when he was also an anti-racist activist who campaigned against the Front national. Since the turn of the millennium, Dieudonné has increasingly sought to challenge the 'othering' or demonization of controversial figures such as the Front national's founder Jean-Marie Le Pen as well as the Holocaust-denier Robert Faurisson. The ways in which he has done so both onstage and offstage has raised questions about where the boundaries lie between being a comedian, polemicist, and activist. The fact that Dieudonné has both evoked political issues onstage during his stand-up shows and sought to intervene in political debates offstage marks him out as

---

31 See: Quemener, *Le Pouvoir de l'humour*, pp. 109–11.
32 See: Carr and Greeves, *The Naked Jape*, p. 208.
33 Kuipers, *Good Humour, Bad Taste*, p. 1.

quite different from the famous French comedian Pierre Desproges. Although Desproges at times evoked political and/or controversial issues during his comedy performances, he sought to define himself as apolitical offstage and once declared 'la seule conscience politique que j'ai, c'est de tenir à ne pas en avoir' ['the only political awareness I have is that I am not political'].[34] Given his famous notion that 'on peut rire de tout mais pas avec tout le monde' ['one can laugh about everything but not with everyone'], his comments about lacking a political conscience should not be read as a justification for joking about anything, with anyone, in any situation. However, they do provide a clear example of a comedian seeking to establish a distinction between proffering views on socio-political issues onstage and making political interventions offstage. As the academic Anna Chamayou has observed, this is in stark contrast with the way that 'on peut relier les sketchs de Dieudonné à un discours posé, qu'il tient en dehors des spectacles' ['one can link Dieudonné's sketches to a thought-out vision that he expresses away from his shows'].[35] As mentioned in the second chapter of this book, it is precisely due to his political interventions offstage that certain critics class Dieudonné – somewhat inaccurately – as a former comedian.

The *Jamel Comedy Club*, and projects such as *À Part ça tout va bien* show that recent years have also seen significant ways in which comedy projects in France have sought to unite rather than divide. In fact, the way in which several of the *Jamel Comedy Club's* protagonists perform material about their *banlieue* and/or minority roots that is generally not extremely aggressive in its denunciation of French society is slightly reminiscent of the type of material that helped Dieudonné to become famous in the 1990s. The diverse routes of the comedians who have performed in the *Jamel Comedy Club* has led to it being held up as a symbol of France's cherished principles of *liberté, égalité, fraternité*.[36]

34   Cited in: Nathalie Simon, 'Dieudonné étrangle le rire', *Le Figaro*, 24 January 2014, http://www.lefigaro.fr/culture/2014/01/24/03004–20140124 ARTFIG00232-dieudonne-etrangle-le-rire.php [accessed 14 December 2017].
35   Cited in: Olivier Monod, 'Après Dieudonné, Bedos, qu'est-ce que l'humour?', *L'Express*, 24 January 2014, https://www.lexpress.fr/actualite/societe/apres-dieudonne-bedos-qu-est-ce-que-l-humour_1315725.html [accessed 14 December 2017].
36   See: Florence Broizat, 'Jamel Comedy Club', *Télérama*, no. 3023, 18 December 2007, www.telerama.fr/divers/23419-.php [accessed 19 July 2010].

However, the way in which many of the performers have focused on their race or ethnicity within their routines is in contrast with what several scholars have described as French Republicanism's tendency to obscure difference via its focus on the concept of a single and indivisible state in which citizens are not defined by criteria such as race or ethnicity.[37] As previously mentioned, this tendency illustrates one of the ways in which the *Jamel Comedy Club* largely adopts an approach to comedy that is more associated with the United States and the United Kingdom than France, and points towards evolving attitudes to the concept of multiculturalism in France.[38]

On occasion, performers in the *Jamel Comedy Club* have actually sought to present themselves in a way that seeks to simplify their roots in order to play up to a collection of more recognizable ethnic stereotypes. This is particularly true of two performers of East Asian descent. Much of Frédéric Chau's material focuses on French stereotypes about Chinese people despite the fact that he was born in Vietnam to Cambodian parents, and the same is true of Bun Hay Mean, a Bordeaux-born comedian who is also of Cambodian parentage and who has performed solo shows under the name 'le Chinois ['the Chinese funnyman']. Thus, some performers present themselves as simplified 'others' despite the fact that several of the humourists have discussed their hybrid identity in a nuanced manner. Consequently, we may well ask if such portrayals in fact raise the following question that Ania Loomba uses to summarize Gayatri Spivak's seminal work 'Can the subaltern speak: in what voices do the colonized speak – their own, or in accents borrowed from their masters?'.[39] Given that Frédéric Chau and Bun Hay Mean use a deliberately exaggerated Chinese accent in some of their performances, one could actually say that there are times when they are literally performing using an accent ascribed to them by their masters. Since the *Jamel Comedy Club* was launched at a time when there were calls for television channels to do more to ensure

---

37   See: Alana Lentin, *Racism and Anti-Racism in Europe* (London: Pluto Press, 2004), p. 116; Jeremy Jennings, 'Citizenship, Republicanism and Multiculturalism in Contemporary France', p. 589; Silverman, p. 119.

38   See discussion of this in Chapter 3.

39   Ania Loomba, *Colonialism / Postcolonialism: The New Critical Idiom* (London: Routledge, 1998), p. 231. See: Gayatri Spivak, 'Can the Subaltern Speak?', in Charles Lemert (ed.), *Social Theory: the Multicultural and Classic Readings* (Boulder, CO: Westview Press, 1993), pp. 609-14.

greater visibility of young people from ethnic minorities on screen, it is somewhat paradoxical that some aspects of the show risked perpetuating stereotypes surrounding members of minorities. As previously discussed, this was particularly true of comments made by several performers about Romanians and Pakistanis.[40]

As mentioned in this book's introduction, the transition from being a subject of jokes to becoming a teller of jokes is a significant one when it comes to the cultural visibility and confidence of minority groups.[41] The fact that the rising profile of Muslim comedians has been during a period that has seen considerable political sensitivity surrounding Islam in France, and relations between humour and Islam, makes this all the more significant. However, when discussing responses to the humour of people often seen as 'others' within society it is important to return to a key aspect of Spivak's discussion of the question 'can the subaltern speak?'. As Landry and MacLean state, 'when she claims that the subaltern "cannot speak", she means that the subaltern as such cannot be heard by the privileged of the First or Third Worlds'.[42]

One of the factors that has an impact on the extent to which someone is able to challenge stereotypes via comedy is the degree to which they are able to reach a wide audience. As was mentioned in Chapter 4, the protagonists of *À Part ça tout va bien* struggled to make the transition from creating a successful online series about young Muslims in France to managing to evoke similar issues in a project for French television. This suggests that there is still a reluctance in France to acknowledge ways in which humour can play a role in reducing tensions as opposed to inflaming them, and also an overriding fear of attempts to associate Islam and humour. This has had an impact on the extent to which such issues can be debated both in the media and in an academic context. At a round table event about the question 'l'humour devient-il plus politique?' hosted at the Théâtre des Bouffes du Nord in Paris on 24 September 2017, the comedian Jérémy Ferrari told of several television channels cancelling planned interviews with him following the *Charlie Hebdo* shootings of January 2015. He mentioned that the channels paradoxically decided to make more

---

40   See pp. 116-17 of Chapter 3 on the *Jamel Comedy Club*.
41   See pp. 3-4.
42   Donna Landry and Gerald MacLean (eds), *The Spivak Reader: Selected Works of Gayatri Chakravorty Spivak* (New York: Routledge, 1996), p. 5.

room for discussion about freedom of expression, but did not feel it was the right time to interview Ferrari about how he mocked war and terrorism in his stand-up show *Vends deux pièces à Bayrouth*. In 2015, some universities were reluctant to hold academic conferences about *Charlie Hebdo* due to security fears. Queen's University in Belfast initially cancelled a planned conference entitled 'Understanding Charlie: New Perspectives on Contemporary Citizenship after the *Charlie Hebdo* Attacks' for security reasons before relenting and allowing the event to take place in June 2015.[43] It is, nevertheless, worth pointing out that the fears of management at Queen's were not shared by certain other universities in the United Kingdom. Indeed, Manchester University – which is located in a city with a much larger Muslim population than Belfast – hosted an event on 30 January 2015 entitled 'Are We Charlie?'. The organizers invited speakers from a range of academic disciplines and the former *Charlie Hebdo* journalist Olivier Cyran, and the speeches and discussion were able to take place without a large-scale visible security presence. However, the same university's student union had earlier in the month prevented its own Free Speech Society from displaying copies of the 14 January 2015 edition of *Charlie Hebdo* featuring the Prophet Muhammad holding up a sign saying 'je suis Charlie' ['I am Charlie'] underneath the headline 'tout est pardonné' ['all is forgiven']. The Free Speech Society had been planning to display the publication on its stall at an event aimed at encouraging students to join academic societies but were told by their Student Union's general secretary that 'the open presence of the magazine was not in the interests of the event'.[44]

Fears that academic discussions of *Charlie Hebdo* would create potential security problems were also evident in France during 2015. The University of London Institute in Paris (ULIP) hosted the sixth annual International Graphic Novel and Comics Conference in Paris from 22–27 June 2015, and had planned to include two panels about *Charlie Hebdo*. However, the university management decided that the *Charlie Hebdo* panels could not go ahead due to security concerns. Part

---

43   For discussion of this issue, see: Isabel Hollis-Touré, 'Introduction: Risk Assessing *Charlie Hebdo*', *French Cultural Studies*, 27.3 (2016), pp. 219–22.

44   Laura FitzPatrick, 'SU censors ban Charlie Hebdo magazine from refreshers fair', *The Tab*, 2 February 2015, https://thetab.com/uk/manchester/2015/02/02/outrage-uni-ban-charlie-hebdo-refreshers-fair-8721 [accessed 21 August 2019].

of these concerns revolved around the fact that the university shared the building where the conference was taking place with the British Council, and that the British Council was worried that the event would expose its visitors – including children – to an unacceptable level of risk.[45] Nevertheless, the prolonged state of emergency in France did not prevent other debates about the way in which humour engages with potentially controversial topics from taking place. In addition to the previously mentioned September 2017 roundtable asking 'l'humour devient-il plus politique?' ['is humour becoming more political?'], the Théâtre des Bouffes du Nord hosted a similar event about 'humour et engagement' ['humour and political commitment'] in September 2016.

Such events demonstrate that the cultural importance of humour is being increasingly acknowledged in France, and the presence of several stand-up comedians on the panels at the two roundtables hosted at the Théâtre des Bouffes du Nord illustrated the growing cultural recognition for stand-up comedy in France. The concerns that sometimes arise when it comes to the consequences, or perceived appropriateness, of debating controversial humour point towards the way that exploring humour in contemporary France reveals tensions and contradictions within a nation that is currently feeling a great deal of unease about issues of social cohesion. It would be overly simplistic to say that putting aside such concerns by instead focusing on the ways in which humour can be used to challenge fears and stereotypes provides an easy means to improve the national mood in France during a challenging period. Indeed, it appears more reasonable to perceive of comedy as a potential bellwether of change rather than an instrument of change.

However, one should not understate the cultural, social, and political significance of the emergence in recent years of forms of comedy in France that bring a degree of novelty in both their form and subject matter. The first two chapters of this book showed how humour in France has in the last two decades has revealed tensions within the supposedly single and indivisible republic, and at times a degree of uncertainty, hypocrisy, and clumsiness from representatives of the state when it has come to defining and regulating what forms of humour are or are not acceptable. The relatively late emergence of a form of

45   David Huxley and Joan Omrod, 'Editorial', *Journal of Graphic Novels and Comics*, 6.4 (2015), p. 315.

stand-up comedy that involves performers discussing their sense of racial, ethnic, or national identity (or identities) onstage appears to owe much to French Republicanism's attempts to mask difference and division within a supposedly egalitarian society in which there exists a concept of citizenship that focuses on individuals rather than groups. Comedy may not change France on its own, but it certainly remains a significant cultural indicator of change in contemporary French society during a turbulent period.

Bibliography

Abdallah, Mogniss, '"L'Effet Zidane", ou le rêve éveillé de l'intégration par le sport', *Hommes et migrations*, 1226 (2000), pp. 5–14.

Abrams, Nathan, *The New Jew in Film: Exploring Jewishness and Judaism in Contemporary Cinema* (London: I.B. Tauris, 2011).

Amour sur place ou à emporter, dir. Amelle Chabi (LGM Productions, 2014).

Arrêt sur images, Daniel Schneiderman with Dieudonné M'Bala M'Bala, *Arte*, 7 December 2003 [television interview].

Arteta, Stéphane and Sophie Grassin, 'Sophia Aram: 'La liberté d'expression ne peut s'accompagner d'un "mais"', *Le Nouvel Observateur*, 19 February 2015, http://teleobs.nouvelobs.com/actualites/20150219.OBS2949/citoyenne-aram. html [accessed 27 July 2017].

Association du manifeste des libertés, 'Persévérance', *Charlie Hebdo*, no. 713, 22 February 2006, p. 2.

Aubenas, Florence, 'Quartier maître', *Libération*, 7 August 2006, http://www. liberation.fr/portrait/2006/08/07/quartier-maitre_47886 [accessed 7 December 2017].

Bancel, Nicolas, Pascal Blanchard and Ahmed Boubeker, *Le Grand Repli* (Paris: La Découverte, 2015).

Beauvallet, JD, 'Farces à Trappes', *Les Inrockuptibles*, 17–23 March 1999, p. 25.

Bellenger, Michel, *Rire et faire rire: pourquoi l'humour change la vie* (Paris: ESF Éditeurs, 2008).

Benzine, Rachid, 'La peur de l'islam, ferment d'un nouveau lien identitaire en France?', in Pascal Blanchard, Nicolas Bancel and Dominic Thomas (eds), *Vers la guerre des identités? De la fracture coloniale à la révolution ultranationale* (Paris: La Découverte, 2015), pp. 101–9.

Bergson, Henri, *Le Rire* (Paris: Presses Universitaires de France, 1940).

Béru, Laurent, 'Un humour ethnoculturel et socio-générationnel: L'exemple du programme télévisuel Jamel Comedy Club', *French Cultural Studies*, 22.2 (2011), pp. 163–72.

Billig, Michael, *Laughter and Ridicule: Towards a Social Critique of Humour* (London: Sage, 2005).

— 'Violent Racist Jokes', in Sharon Lockyer and Michael Pickering (eds), *Beyond a Joke: The Limits of Humour* (Basingstoke: Palgrave Macmillan, 2009), pp. 27–46.

Blanchard, Pascal, Nicolas Bancel and Dominic Thomas, 'Introduction. Qui veut la guerre des identités?', in Blanchard, Bancel and Thomas, Dominic (eds), *Vers la guerre des identités? De la fracture coloniale à la révolution ultranationale* (Paris: La Découverte, 2015), pp. 7–45.

Blanchard, Sandrine, 'Continuer à rire de tout, plus que jamais', *Le Monde*, 6 January 2016, http://www.lemonde.fr/culture/article/2016/01/06/continuer-a-rire-de-tout-plus-que-jamais_4842605_3246.html [accessed 27 October 2017].

Boespflug, François, *Caricaturer Dieu? Pouvoirs et dangers de l'image* (Paris: Bayard, 2012).

Bontinck, Maurice, 'Les bus de Dieudonné en gare d'Angoulême', *Charente Libre*, 21 March 2010, http://www.charentelibre.fr/article/article-5-le-bus-de-dieudonne-en-gare-d-angouleme,316086.php [accessed 1 May 2012].

Boucher, Sandrine, 'Dieudonné persiste et signe', *Le Journal du dimanche*, 8 February 2004, p. 27.

Bourcet, Michel, 'Charlie Hebdo, réseaux sociaux, religions... Sophia Aram s'engage à rire de tout', *Télérama*, 14 October 2015, http://www.telerama.fr/sortir/charlie-hebdo-reseaux-sociaux-religions-sophia-aram-s-engage-a-rire-de-tout,132776.php [accessed 27 July 2017].

Briganti, Michel, André Déchot and Jean-Paul Gautier, *La Galaxie Dieudonné: pour en finir avec les impostures* (Paris: Syllepse, 2011).

Broizat, Florence, 'Jamel Comedy Club', Télérama, no. 3023, 18 December 2007, www.telerama.fr/divers/23419-.php [accessed 19 July 2010].

— 'La Griffe Jamel', *Télérama*, 13–19 January 2007, p. 22.

Camus, Jean-Yves, 'Cathos et musulmans intégristes main dans la main', *Charlie Hebdo*, no. 1011, 2 November 2011.

'Caricatures: choc des images ou des civilisations?', *Ripostes*, France 5, 12 February 2006.

Carr, Jimmy and Lucy Greeves, *The Naked Jape: Uncovering the Hidden World of Jokes* (London: Penguin, 2007).

Cervulle, Maxime, Sébastien M. Barat, Julien Mustin and Nelly Quemener, 'Du rire aux armes', *Poli: politique de l'image*, 2 (March 2010), pp. 7–12.

C'est dur d'être aimé par des cons, dir. by Daniel Leconte (Films en Stock, 2008).

Chabal, Emile, *The Divided Republic: Nation, State And Citizenship in Contemporary France* (Cambridge: Cambridge University Press, 2015).

Chambers, Simone, 'Free Speech and Civility in Pluralist Societies', in Edward M. Iacobucci and Stephen J. Toope (eds), *After the Paris Attacks* (Toronto/ Buffalo/London: University of Toronto Press, 2015), pp. 13–20.

Chapuis, Clothilde, 'Quenelle de Dieudonné: pourquoi ce geste antisémite est moralement condamnable', *Le Nouvel Observateur*, 8 April 2014, http://leplus.nouvelobs.com/contribution/1185077-quenelle-de-dieudonne-pourquoi-ce-geste-antisemite-est-moralement-condamnable.html [accessed 28 September 2017].

Charb, 'Même pas mal', *Charlie Hebdo*, no. 1012, 9 November 2011.

Charb and Zineb, *La Vie de Mahomet* (Paris: Les Échappés, 2013).

Chau, Frédéric, *Je viens de si loin* (Paris: Philippe Rey, 2015).

Chocolat: une histoire du rire, dir. Judith Sibony (Balina Films, 2016).

Chrisafis, Angélique, 'French Magazine Offices Petrol-Bombed After It Prints Muhammad Cartoon', *The Guardian*, 2 November 2011, https://www.theguardian.com/world/2011/nov/02/french-magazine-bomb-muhammad-cartoon [accessed 27 March 2017].

Cohen, Ted, *Jokes: Philosophical Thoughts on Joking Matters* (Chicago: Chicago University Press, 1999).

Comte-Sponville, André, 'Peut-on rire de tout?', *Psychologies Magazine*, February 2001, http://www.psychologies.com/Planete/Societe/Articles-et-Dossiers/Peut-on-rire-de-tout [accessed 30 April 2012].

Critchley, Simon, *On Humour* (Abingdon: Routledge, 2002).

D., Oman and K2C, 'Moment, Dieudonné', *Blackmap*, 22 October 2002 http://web.archive.org/web/20021022134311/www.blackmap.com/contenus/art_culture/moment_dieudo.htm [accessed 26 April 2012].

Davies, Christie, *The Mirth of Nations* (New Brunswick and London: Transaction Publishers, 2011).

De Cabarrus, Thierry, 'Jérémy Ferrari répond à Dieudonné sur Youtube: comment il démonte la "machine à fric"', *Le Nouvel Observateur*, 18 April 2014, http://leplus.nouvelobs.com/contribution/1191845-jeremy-ferrari-repond-a-dieudonne-sur-youtube-comment-il-demonte-la-machine-a-fric.html [accessed 28 September 2017.

Dédo, interviewed by Jonathan Ervine (unpublished), 24 March 2017.

De Stefano, David and Sanjay Mirabeau, *Interdit de rire: l'affaire Dieudonné par ses avocats* (Sion: Éditions Xenia, 2014).

Diawara, Noom, interviewed by Jonathan Ervine (unpublished), 25 March 2017.

'Dieudonné condamné en appel pour un spectacle avec le négationniste Faurisson', *L'Express*, 17 March 2011, http://www.lexpress.fr/actualites/1/styles/dieudonne-condamne-en-appel-pour-un-spectacle-avec-le-nega-tionniste-faurisson_973427.html [accessed 27 April 2012].

'Dieudonné, star de la semaine judiciaire', *Le Figaro*, 26 June 2008, http://www.lefigaro.fr/actualite-france/2008/06/26/01016-20080626ARTFIG00373-dieudonne-star-de-la-semaine-judiciaire.php accessed 30 April 2012.

Duvivier, Michel, *Je suis Charlie…?* (Paris: CreateSpace, 2015).

Eggermont, Olivier, 'Entretien avec Jérémy Ferrari, prince de l'humour noir', *Le Vif*, 11 March 2014, http://focus.levif.be/culture/scenes/entretien-avec-jeremy-ferrari-prince-de-l-humour-noir/article-normal-13137.html [accessed 28 July 2017].

El Rhazoui, Zineb, 'Le Guide Routard de la Charia', *Charlie Hebdo*, 1011 (2 November 2011).

'En savoir plus', *À part ça tout va bien* [n.d.], http://comediemuslim.apartcatout-vabien.com/en-savoir-plus-sur-a-part-ca-tout-va-bien.php [accessed 20 July 2017].

Ervine, Jonathan, 'L'Islam et l'humour: du rire libérateur au rire communautaire', *Temps des Médias*, 28 (2017), pp. 144–57.

— 'Nicolas Anelka and the Quenelle Gesture: a Study of the Complexities of Protest in Contemporary Football', *The International Journal of the History of Sport*, 24.3–4 (2017), pp. 236–50.

— '(Re-)presenting Islam: a Comparative Study of Comedians in the United States of America and France', *Performing Islam*, 2.1 (2013), pp. 89–104.

Etchegoin, Marie-France, 'Antisémite, "national-socialiste": comment devient-on Alain Soral?', *Le Nouvel observateur*, 26 January 2014, http://tempsreel.nouvelobs.com/l-enquete-de-l-obs/20140124.OBS3766/antisemite-national-socialiste-comment-devient-on-alain-soral.html [accessed 4 May 2017].

Etchegoin, Marie-France, Marie-Amélie Lombard-Latune, Dorothée Moisan and Thierry Lévêque, *Et soudain ils ne riaent plus* (Paris: Éditions des Arènes, 2016).

Favret-Saada, Jeanne, *Comment produire une crise mondiale avec douze petits dessins* (Paris: Les Prairies ordinaires, 2007).

— 'On y croit toujours plus qu'on ne croit: sur le manuel vaudou d'un président', *L'Homme*, 190 (2009), pp. 7-25.

Ferenczi, Aurélien, 'Jamel Debbouze: l'entretien', *Télérama*, 19 January 2011, p. 18.

FitzPatrick, Laura, 'SU censors ban Charlie Hebdo magazine from refreshers fair', *The Tab*, 2 February 2015, https://thetab.com/uk/manchester/2015/02/02/outrage-uni-ban-charlie-hebdo-refreshers-fair-8721 [accessed 21 August 2019].

Fourest, Caroline, 'Les confusions de l'antiracisme', *Charlie Hebdo*, no. 713, 15 February 2006, p. 7.

— 'Tout ce fouin pour douze dessins!', *Charlie Hebdo*, no. 712, 8 February 2006, p. 4.

Freud, Sigmund, *The Joke and Its Relation to the Unconscious*, tr. Joyce Crick with introduction by John Carey (London: Penguin Classics, 2002).

Gaccio, Bruno and Dieudonné, *Peut-on tout dire?* (Paris: Éditions Mordicus, 2010).

Geisser, Vincent, *La Nouvelle islamophobie* (Paris: La Découverte).

Génération éclectique, le magazine des cultures urbaines, Chakib Lahssaini with Thomas Ngijol, Fabrice Éboué and Patson (France Culture, 28 July 2006) [radio interview].

Geybels, Hans, 'The Redemptive Power of Humour in Religion', in *Humour and Religion: Challenges and Ambiguities*, eds. Hans Geybels and Walter Van Herck (London and New York: Bloomsbury, 2012).

Girbig, Pascal, 'Communautarisme: peut-on rire de tous?', *Atlantico.fr*, 14 July 2011, http://www.atlantico.fr/decryptage/humour-laique-communautaire-stand-jamel-correzien-128888.html [accessed 18 April 2012].

Goffman, Erving, *Stigma: Notes on the Management of Spoiled Identity* (London and New York: Penguin, 1968).

Göle, Nilüfer, *Musulmans au quotidien: une enquête sur les controverses autour de l'islam* (Paris: La Découverte, 2015).

Gresh, Alain,'D'étranges défenseurs de la liberté de la presse à la manifestation pour "Charlie Hebdo"', *Le Monde Diplomatie*, 12 January 2015, http://blog.mondediplo.net/2015-01-12-D-etranges-defenseurs-de-la-liberte-de-la-presse [accessed 29 March 2017].

Guidi, Diletta, 'Rire et Islam', in Dorra Mameri-Chaambi (ed.), *L'Islam et la France: chroniques d'une histoire commune* (Paris: Chronique Éditions, 2012), pp. 174–5.

Hargreaves, Alec, *Multi-ethnic France: Immigration, Politics, Culture and Society*, 2nd edition (Oxford: Routledge, 2007).

— 'The Contribution of North and Sub-Saharan African Immigrant Minorities to the Redefinition of Contemporary French Culture', in C. Forsdick and D. Murphy (eds), *Postcolonial Studies: a Critical Introduction* (London: Arnold, 2003), p. 154.

Haziza, Frédéric, *Vol au-dessus d'un nid de fachos: Dieudonné, Soral, Ayoub et les autres* (Paris: Fayard, 2014).

Hirzalla, Fadi, Liesbet Van Zoonen, and Floris Müller, 'How Funny Can Islam Controversies Be? Comedians Defending Their Faiths on YouTube', *Television and New Media*, 14.1 (2013), pp. 46-61.

Hollis-Touré, Isabel, 'Introduction: Risk Assessing *Charlie Hebdo*', *French Cultural Studies*, 27.3 (2016), pp. 219–22.

Huxley, David and Joan Omrod, 'Editorial', *Journal of Graphic Novels and Comics*, 6.4 (2015), pp. 315–18.

Iacobucci, Edward M. and Stephen J. Toope (eds), *After the Paris Attacks: Responses in Canada, Europe and Around the Globe* (Toronto/Buffalo/London: University of Toronto Press, 2015).

Icher, Bruno, 'Jamelting potes', *Libération*, 9 February 2007, http://www.liberation.fr/culture/010193469-jamelting-potes [accessed 23 January 2012].

Jeanjean, Jérôme, 'Un Show rêvé', *Les Inrockuptibles*, 17–23 mars 1999, p. 21.

Jennings, Jeremy 'Citizenship, Republicanism and Multiculturalism in Contemporary France', *British Journal of Political Science*, 30.4 (2000), pp. 575–98.

Jocher, Marie and Alain Kéramoal, *Jamel Debbouze: la vérité* (Paris: Seuil, 2008).

Jouan, Anne, 'Dieudonné, du rire à la nausée', *L'Express*, 8 September 2018, https://www.lexpress.fr/actualite/societe/dieudonne-du-rire-a-la-nausee_2033680.html [accessed 21 January 2019].

Karmitz, Elisha, 'La Comédie des banlieues', *L'Express*, 21 July 2006, http://www.lexpress.fr/culture/scene/la-comedie-des-banlieues_459349.html [accessed 1 June 2017].

Kishtainy, Khalid, *Arab Political Humour* (London: Quarter Books, 1985).

Klausen, Jytte, *The Cartoons That Shook the World* (New Haven and London: Yale University Press, 2009).

Kuipers, Gisèle, *Good Humour, Bad Taste: a Sociology of the Joke* (Berlin/Boston: Walter De Gruyter, 2015).

— 'The Politics of Humour in the Public Sphere: Cartoons, Power and Modernity in the First Transnational Humour Scandal', *European Journal of Cultural Studies*, 14.1 (2011), pp. 63–80.

Landry, Donna and Gerald MacLean (eds), *The Spivak Reader: Selected Works of Gayatri Chakravorty Spivak* (New York: Routledge, 1996).

Landzelius, Kyra, *Native on the Net: Indigenous and Diasporic Peoples in the Virtual Age* (Oxford: Routledge, 2006).

Le Bars, Stéphanie, 'Caricatures: les organisations musulmanes hésitent à lancer des poursuites systématiques', *Le Monde*, 7 February 2007, http://abonnes.lemonde.fr/societe/article/2007/02/07/caricatures-les-organisations-musulmanes-hesitent-a-lancer-des-poursuites-systematiques_864552_3224.html?h=15 [accessed 16 March 2017].

Lefébure, Pierre, 'Rire malgré tout: comment les humoristes d'actualité font face au choc', in Pierre Lefébrure and Claire Sécail (eds), *Le Défi Charlie: les médias à l'épreuve des attentats* (Paris: Lemieux Éditeur, 2016), pp. 49–77.

Le Gros, Julien, 'Fabrice Éboué: "parlons d'une nouvelle génération qui a la couleur d'aujourd'hui"', *Africultures*, 25 November 2011, http://www.africultures.com/php/index.php?nav=article&no=10498 [accessed 18 April 2012].

Lehoux, Valérie, 'Sophia Aram: "Contrairement aux apparences, je ne suis pas une petite chose fragile"', *Télérama*, 5 January 2013, http://www.telerama.fr/radio/sophia-aram-contrairement-aux-apparences-je-ne-suis-pas-une-petite-chose-fragile,91447.php [accessed 25 July 2017].

— 'Sophia Aram, menacée mais pas intimidée', *Télérama*, 6 December 2011, http://www.telerama.fr/radio/sophia-aram-menacee-mais-pas-intimidee,75704.php [accessed 27 July 2017].

Lentin, Alana, *Racism and Anti-Racism in Europe* (London: Pluto Press, 2004).

Lichfield, John, 'Heard the One About the Racist Black Comedian?', *The Belfast Telegraph*, 22 March 2006, https://www.belfasttelegraph.co.uk/incoming/heard-the-one-about-the-racist-black-comedian-28107315.html [accessed 30 April 2012].

Lipovetsky, Gilles, *L'Ère du vide* (Paris: Folio, 1989).

Lizé, Hubert, 'L'Olympia annule le show de Dieudonné', *Le Parisien*, 19 February 2004, http://www.leparisien.fr/culture-loisirs/l-olympia-annule-le-show-de-dieudonne-19-02-2004-2004768834.php [accessed 21 August 2019].

'L'Olympia annule le show de Dieudonné', *Libération*, 19 February 2004, https://www.liberation.fr/societe/2004/02/19/l-olympia-annule-le-show-de-dieudonne_469482 [accessed 21 August 2019].

Loomba, Ania, *Colonialism / Postcolonialism: The New Critical Idiom* (London: Routledge, 1998).

Lozès, Patrick, *Nous, les Noirs de France* (Paris: Éditions Danger Public, 2007).

Lundi investigations, Émile Raffoul and Paul Moreira (Canal Plus, 17 May 2005) [television programme].

Luz, 'Soyons syncrétiquement corrects', *Charlie Hebdo*, no. 712, 8 February 2006, pp. 8–9.

Macé, Eric, 'Rions ensemble des stéréotypes: Anti-stéréotypes humoristiques d'Arabes et de musulmans dans les médiacultures', *Poli: politique de l'image*, 2 (March 2010), pp. 17–35.

Manzoor, Sarfraz, 'Funny Old World', *The Guardian*, 6 April 2007, https://www.theguardian.com/stage/2007/apr/06/comedy.religion [accessed 20 July 2017].

Marzolph, Ulrich, 'The Muslim Sense of Humour', in Hans Geybels and Walter Van Herck (eds), *Humour and Religion: Challenges and Ambiguities* (London and New York: Bloomsbury).

McGraw, Peter and Joel Warner, *The Humor Code: a Global Search for What Makes Things Funny* (New York: Simon and Schuster, 2014).

Mercier, Anne-Sophie, *Dieudonné démasqué* (Paris: Seuil, 2009).

— *La Vérité sur Dieudonné* (Paris: Plon, 2005).

Miles, Tim, 'Halal? Ha! LOL: An Examination of Muslim Online Comedy As Counter-Narrative', *Comedy Studies*, 6.2 (2015), pp. 167–78.

Minuit Dix, Laurent Goumarre with Fabrice Éboué, Thomas Ngijol and Patson (France Culture, 27 September 2006) [radio interview].

Mongin, Olivier, *De quoi rions-nous? Notre société et ses comiques* (Paris: Plon, 2006).

Monod, Olivier, 'Après Dieudonné, Bedos, qu'est-ce que l'humour?', *L'Express*, 24 January 2014, https://www.lexpress.fr/actualite/societe/apres-dieudonne-bedos-qu-est-ce-que-l-humour_1315725.html [accessed 14 December 2017].

Morin, Fabien, 'Jamel Debbouze veut recruter Nicolas Sarkozy dans sa bande de comiques', *Le Figaro*, 24 June 2015, http://tvmag.lefigaro.fr/le-scan-tele/people/2015/06/24/28008-20150624ARTFIG00206-jamel-debbouze-veut-recruter-nicolas-sarkozy-dans-son-emission.php [accessed 7 December 2017].

Morris, Steven, 'Paul Gascoigne Admits Racially Abusing Black Bodyguard', *The Guardian*, 19 September 2016, https://www.theguardian.com/uk-news/2016/sep/19/paul-gascoigne-pleads-guilty-to-racially-aggravated-offence [accessed 25 July 2017].

Moura, Jean-Marc, *Le sens littéraire de l'humour* (Paris: Presses universitaires de France, 2010).

Mukuna, Olivier, *Dieudonné: entretien à coeur ouvert* (Antwerp: EPO, 2005).

— *Égalité zéro: enquête sur le procès médiatique de Dieudonné* (Paris: Editions Blanche, 2005).

Nascimbeni, François, 'Dieudonné condamné pour des propos antisémites sur la mémoire de la Shoah', *La Dépêche du Midi*, 11 September 2007, http://www.ladepeche.fr/article/2007/09/11/11212-dieudonne-condamne-pour-des-propos-antisemites-sur-la-memoire-de-la-shoah.html [accessed 30 April 2012].

Noiriel, Gérard, *Chocolat, clown nègre: l'histoire oubliée du premier artiste noir de la scène française* (Paris: Bayard, 2012).

Nunez, Laurent, 'Sophia Aram: "Le blasphème, c'est sacré!"', *Marianne*, 3 October 2015, https://www.marianne.net/culture/sophia-aram-le-blaspheme-cest-sacre [accessed 27 July 2017].

On ne peut pas plaire à tout le monde, Marc-Olivier Fogiel and Ariane Massenet (France 3, 5 December 2003) [television programme].

Ory, Pascal, *Ce que dit Charlie: treize leçons d'histoire* (Paris: Gallimard, 2016).

Palmer, Jerry, *Taking Humour Seriously* (London: Routledge, 1994).

Pascaud, Fabien, 'Ouvrir la brèche pour les autres, c'est le kif du kif', *Télérama*, 19 July 2006, p. 15.

Pelloux, Patrick, 'En route vers le moyen âge!', *Charlie Hebdo*, no. 1011, 2 November 2011.

Person, Pauline, 'Interview Jamel Debbouze', *Télé 2 semaines*, http://www.tele-2-semaines.fr/contenu_editorial/pages/echos-tv/7651-jamel-debbouze-je-serai-heureux-quand-on-pourra-caricaturer-tout-le-monde   [accessed 22 Feburary 2011].

'Peut-on rire de tout?', *Question d'actu*, LCI, 6 February 2006.

Plenel, Edwy, *Pour les Musulmans* (Paris: Éditions La Découverte, 2016).

P.M., 'Olivier Mukuna: "Ce film s'est réalisé dans des conditions semi-clandestines"', *AgoraVox*, 25 November 2009, http://www.agoravox.fr/tribune-libre/article/olivier-mukuna-ce-film-s-est-65555 [accessed 27 April 2012].

'"Pornographie mémorielle": Dieudonné condamné', *Le Nouvel Observateur*, 11 September 2007, http://tempsreel.nouvelobs.com/societe/20070911.OBS4352/pornographie-memorielle-dieudonne-condamne.html   [accessed 30 April 2012].

Quemener, Nelly, *Le Pouvoir de l'humour* (Paris: Armand Colin/INA, 2014).

Qu'est-ce que l'on a fait au bon dieu?, dir. Philippe de Chauveron (Les Films du 24/UGC Images, 2014).

Rappoport, Michel, *Punchlines: The Case for Racial, Gender and Ethnic Humor* (Westport, CT: Praeger, 2005).

Rassoul Allah, Mohamed, 'L'Édito de Mahomet', *Charlie Hebdo*, no. 1011, 2 November 2011, p. 3.

Reiss, Tom, 'Laugh Riots: the French Star Who Became a Demagogue', *The New Yorker*, 19 November 2007, http://www.newyorker.com/reporting/2007/11/19/071119fa_fact_reiss [accessed 26 April 2012].

Renault, Coline, 'Comment Dieudonné parvient à contourner l'interdiction de ses spectacles', Le Figaro, 18 June 2018, http://www.lefigaro.fr/actualite-france/2018/06/18/01016-20180618ARTFIG00329-comment-dieudonne-parvient-a-contourner-l-interdiction-de-ses-spectacles.php [accessed 10 January 2019].

Renault, Gilles, 'Sophia Aram: "Je suis athée, donc pour moi, le délit de blasphème n'existe pas"', *Libération*, 9 January 2015, http://next.liberation.fr/culture/2015/01/09/je-suis-athee-donc-pour-moi-le-delit-de-blaspheme-n-existe-pas_1177307 [accessed 27 January 2017].

Reynaert, François, 'La France multiculturire', *Le Nouvel Observateur*, 5 November 2009, p. 94.

Rio, Knut, 'The *Barbariat* and Democratic Tolerance', in Alessandro Zagato (ed.), *The Event of Charlie Hebdo: Imaginaries of Freedom and Control* (New York/Oxford: Berghahn, 2015), pp. 12–24.

Ripostes, Serge Moati (France 5, 22 February 2004) [television programme].

Robertson, Ritchie, 'Historicizing Weininger: The Nineteenth-Century German Image of the Feminized Jew' in B. Cheyette and L. Marcus (eds), *Modernity, Culture and the Jew* (Cambridge: Polity Press, 1998), pp. 23–39.

Robin, Jean, *Soral et Dieudonné: la tentation antisémite* (Paris: Éditions Tatamis, 2014).

Rosello, Mireille, *Declining the Stereotype: Ethnicity and Representation in French Cultures* (Hanover, NH: University Press of New England, 1998).

Roussel, Frédérique and Isabelle Hanne, '"Charlie", satire dans tous les sens', *Libération*, 7 January 2015, http://www.liberation.fr/ecrans/2015/01/07/charlie-satire-dans-tous-les-sens_1175870 [accessed 14 March 2017].

Salhi, Kamal, 'Editorial', *Performing Islam*, 1.1 (2012), pp. 11–12.

Salza, Luca, 'La République mise à nue par sa satire, même', in Collectif (eds), *Je suis Charlie. Ainsi suit-il…* (Paris: L'Harmattan, 2015).

Schmidt, Jean-Jacques, *Le Livre de l'humour arabe* (Paris: Actes Sud, 2005).

Séry, Macha, 'Jamel assure sa relève', *Le Monde*, 9 July 2006, https://www.lemonde.fr/vous/article/2006/07/07/jamel-assure-sa-releve_793032_3238.html [accessed 24 February 2012].

Siankowski, Pierre, 'Jamel, un homme intègre', *Les Inrockuptibles*, 30 March 2011, p. 32.

— 'La Force d'en rire', *Les Inrockuptibles*, 31 July–6 August 2002, p. 27.

Siddiqui, Haroon, *Being Muslim* (London: A&C Black, 2010).

Silverman, Max, *Deconstructing the Nation: Immigration, Racism and Citizenship in Modern France* (London: Taylor and Francis, 1992).

Sifaoui, Mohamed, *L'Affaire des caricatures: dessins et manipulations* (Paris: Éditions Privé, 2006).

Simon, Nathalie, 'Dieudonné étrangle le rire', *Le Figaro*, 24 January 2014, http://www.lefigaro.fr/culture/2014/01/24/03004-20140124ARTFIG00232-dieudonne-etrangle-le-rire.php [accessed 14 December 2017].

Sloan, Delphine, *Jamel Debbouze: d'un monde à l'autre* (Saint-Victor-d'Épine: City Editions, 2004).

Soir 3 Journal, Michel Vial and Melissa Monteiro (France 3, 19 February 2004) [television news report], http://www.ina.fr/art-et-culture/arts-du-spectacle/video/2505466001006/annulation-en-refere-du-spectacle-dieudonne-a-l-olympia.fr.html [accessed 30 April 2012].

Spivak, Gayatri, 'Can the Subaltern Speak?', in Charles Lemert (ed.), *Social Theory: The Multicultural and Classic Readings* (Boulder, CO: Westview Press, 1993), pp. 609–14.

Steel, Mark, *What's Going On? The Meanderings of a Comic Mind in Confusion* (London: Simon and Schuster, 2008).

Stora, Benjamin, *La Guerre des mémoires: la France face à son passé colonial* (Paris: Éditions de l'Aube, 2011).

Stott, Andrew, *Comedy: The New Critical Idiom* (London: Routledge, 2005).

Szczygiel, Axelle, 'Sophia Aram: la "Crise de foi" d'une féministe convaincue', *Elle*, 22 September 2010, http://www.elle.fr/Loisirs/Sorties/Dossiers/Sophia-Aram-la-Crise-de-foi-d-une-feministe-convaincue-1354094 [accessed 27 July 2017].

Titley, Gavan 'Becoming Symbolic: from Charlie Hebdo to "Charlie Hebdo"', in Gavan Titley, Des Freedman, Gholam Khiabany and Aurélien Mondon (eds), *After Charlie Hebdo: Terror, Racism and Free Speech* (London: Zed Books, 2017), p. 2.

Todd, Emmanuel, *Sociologie d'une crise religieuse: Qui est Charlie?* (Paris: Points, 2016).

Uleski, Serge, *Dieudonné: chroniques d'un succès inespéré* (London: Amazon, 2014).

'Un nouveau dérapage antisémite de Dieudonné', *20 minutes*, 18 July 2008, https://www.20minutes.fr/debats/242288-20080718-nouveau-derapage-antisemite-dieudonne [accessed 27 April 2012].

Val, Philippe, 'Le Choix de Chirac', *Charlie Hebdo*, no. 715, 8 March 2006, p. 2.

— 'Les preuves de la manipulation', *Charlie Hebdo*, no. 713, 15 February 2006, p. 2.

— 'Provocation', *Charlie Hebdo*, no. 713, 15 February 2006, p. 3.

— 'Petit glossaire d'une semaine caricaturale', *Charlie Hebdo*, no. 712, 8 February 2006, p. 3.

Vanderschelden, Isabelle, 'Jamel Debbouze: a New Popular French Star?', *Studies in French Cinema*, 5.1 (2005), pp. 61–72.

Violet, Bernard, *Jamel Debbouze: l'as de coeur* (Paris: Fayard, 2008).

Weston, Jane, '*Bête et méchant*: Politics, Editorial Cartoons and *Bande dessinée* in the French Satirical Newspaper *Charlie hebdo*', *European Comic Art* 2.1 (2009), pp. 109–29.

Weston Vauclair, Jane and David Vauclair, *De Charlie Hebdo à #Charlie: enjeux, histoire, perspectives* (Paris: Eyrolles, 2016).

Wieviorka, Michel, *L'Antisémitisme est-il de retour?* (Paris: Larousse, 2008).

Wilde, Oscar, *The Picture of Dorian Gray* (Leipzig: Bernard Tauchnitz, 1908).

Zagato Alessandro (ed.), *The Event of Charlie Hebdo: Imaginaries of Freedom and Control* (New York/Oxford: Berghahn, 2015).

Zahi, Hassan, interviewed by Jonathan Ervine (unpublished), 23 March 2017.

Zone de libre échange, Xavier de la Porte et al. with Kader Aoun and Jean-Michel Ribes (*France Culture*, 6 December 2008) [radio interview].

Index